Conceiving the Christian College

Conceiving the Christian College

Duane Litfin

WILLIAM B. EERDMANS PUBLISHING COMPANY
GRAND RAPIDS, MICHIGAN / CAMBRIDGE, U.K.

Wm. B. Eerdmans Publishing Co.
255 Jefferson Ave. S.E., Grand Rapids, Michigan 49503 /
P.O. Box 163, Cambridge CB3 9PU U.K.

Printed in the United States of America

10 09 08 07 06 05   8 7 6 5 4 3 2

Library of Congress Cataloging-in-Publication Data

Litfin, A. Duane.
   Conceiving the Christian college / Duane Litfin.
      p.   cm.
   Includes bibliographical references and index.
   ISBN 0-8028-2783-7 (pbk.: alk. paper)
      1. Church and College. 2. Church and college — United States.
   3. Education — Aims and objectives. I. Title.

   LC383.L58 2004
   378'.071 — dc22

                          2004050607

www.eerdmans.com

Contents

1   Introduction

This book might have been titled *The Ideas of a Christian College.* Conjuring up John Henry Newman's classic, *The Idea of a University,* and a century and a quarter later, Arthur Holmes's widely used *The Idea of a Christian College,* such a title might have suggested these chapters are about how we are to understand the task of this unique type of educational institution, the Christian college. And that would have been a good thing, for it is indeed what this book is about.

In other ways, however, such a title would not do. First, it would be presumptuous to associate this book so closely with two such important and influential works. Second, the title skirts too close to Holmes's own to be fair to that estimable text, which after twenty-five years is still in print. Third, the distinction between *Idea* in these older titles, and the plural *Ideas* in my own, would be so small as likely to be lost. Yet it's an important difference. Newman and Holmes attempt to flesh out the overall concept of their respective subjects; my focus is more selective. Fourth, and in consequence, the definite article suggests too much. The book you hold in your hands is not about *the* requisite ideas of a Christian college, as if to suggest I will deal with them all. As I say, my goal is more modest.

I am after only a handful of salient ideas that currently need some special attention. Despite their critical importance to Christian higher education, some of these ideas are so overworked as to be, paradoxically, under-appreciated, under-developed, or even misunderstood. In other instances they are simply neglected. In a few cases, somewhat mysteriously, they are ideas one hardly finds discussed at all in the literature on Christian higher education.

What these ideas hold in common, however, is that each in its own way is important, even crucial, to the task of Christian higher education. Hence each deserves our clearest and most careful thinking. Those who are engaged in Christian higher education — teachers, administrators, board members, students, parents, supporters, and even those who are simply interested bystanders — are alike in their need to grapple with these ideas with skill and sophistication.

Furthermore, if the concepts we will discuss in this book are important to the world of Christian higher education, some of them are also painfully out of step with the intellectual climate of our times. Yet if we ignore these ideas, or take them for granted, or downplay them because of their being out of step, they will not merely atrophy and die away; they will be swept away by those who oppose them, and Christian higher education will go with them. What we require, anew for every generation, are clarion calls designed to remind us of what it is we do and why. I hope it is not too audacius to claim that the goal of this book is to offer a few such calls. Whether it succeeds or not, the reader will decide. But that is my intent. As Oscar Wilde once quipped, "On an occasion of this kind it becomes more than a moral duty to speak one's mind. It becomes a pleasure."

This book therefore focuses not simply on the ideas of a Christian college, but on the clarity with which we understand these ideas and the strength with which we hold them. There are, I believe, a number of fresh insights in the following chapters — or at least insights I cannot find much discussed elsewhere, despite their importance — but in many ways these chapters do not attempt to say much that is novel. Quite the contrary, they are exercises, as Plato's Thamus might have put it, "not of memory, but of reminding." They are efforts to state again what must be stated again — and again, and again. They constitute an attempt to think through some age-old responses to our contemporary challenges, to wrestle anew with questions such as: What is unique about us? How are we to conceive of ourselves against the backdrop of other types of institutions, even other religious institutions? How do we maintain our bearings in the tumultuous intellectual seas of the twenty-first century? What, after all, *are* those bearings? How do we keep moving forward amidst the inevitable buffetings of our secularized academic environment? What is required to sustain our institutions — that is, to ensure that we will deliver them to future generations in recognizable form? What is our unique contribution to the marketplace of ideas? How does Christian higher education fit within the broader academic culture, and to what ends should we be working there?

I hold no illusion that this treatment will exhaust the list of challenges facing the contemporary Christian college. There are many daunting problems I will leave untouched. Consider for example this very different set of questions: How can Christian colleges attract and retain an excellent student body? How do we recruit and then facilitate the work of a first-rate faculty? How do we keep pace with the ever-quickening demands of technological change, much less harness these changes to enhance our students' learning? How do we keep our costs low enough, and our student aid high enough, to remain accessible to a wide variety of students, all the while funding strong academic programs? How are we to diversify our campus communities, drawing in more of those minority populations who have not traditionally been attracted to Christian colleges? How can we resist the inexorable pressures toward the vocationalizing of our curriculum? How do we globalize our curriculum?

These and other practical issues weigh daily upon Christian colleges, demanding our best efforts. But I will not attempt to address them here. As important as these issues are, our present concerns cut deeper, to matters of the core. Our focus in what follows has less to do with means than with ends, less with these pressing practical dilemmas than with key conceptual challenges relating to our core mission as Christian scholars and educators.

Even with regard to this missional core, however, we must acknowledge some limitations. For instance, while we will touch upon it here and there, contemporary writers such as George Marsden, James Burtchaell, Robert Benne, Philip Gleason, and Douglas Sloan[1] give far more atten-

---

1. George M. Marsden, *The Soul of the American University: From Protestant Establishment to Established Nonbelief* (New York: Oxford University Press, 1994); James T. Burtchaell, *The Dying of the Light: The Disengagement of Colleges and Universities from Their Christian Churches* (Grand Rapids: Eerdmans, 1998); Robert Benne, *Quality with Soul* (Grand Rapids: Eerdmans, 2001); Philip Gleason, *Contending with Modernity: Catholic Higher Education in the Twentieth Century* (New York: Oxford University Press, 1995);

tion than I do to the challenges of the so-called slippery slope on which modern religious institutions reside. In a sense, my purpose is not so much to explore that slope as to render it less slippery, or at least to point us again to our strong footholds. Or, taking a different tack, writers such as Mark Noll, Richard Hughes, Cornelius Plantinga, Cliff Williams, and (again) George Marsden have focused on the larger challenges and opportunities of the Christian's intellectual task.[2] I will crisscross their tracks in what follows, but without trying to walk in their footsteps.

Most pertinent of all to what follows is the work of Arthur Holmes. No one has done more over the last forty years to help the members of Christian college communities think through what they are, what they are doing, and why. I have already alluded to his book *The Idea of a Christian College*. To this must be added other influential titles such as *All Truth Is God's Truth, The Making of a Christian Mind,* and *Building the Christian Academy*. These along with many other offerings from Holmes have made an immeasurable contribution to Christian higher education. Holmes has helped build the overarching conception of the Christian college we all live beneath; under that canopy I wish to target some specific contemporary problems.

A Presidential Caveat

I must acknowledge at the outset the personal dimensions of what follows. The issues I will explore are inevitably those most pressing to me; they are the matters I believe need discussion, concerns about which I have become exercised, blind spots I think need to be highlighted, challenges I have discerned and which I believe require a response. I recognize the inevitable personal character of the very selection of this subject matter.

Douglas Sloan, *Faith and Knowledge: Mainline Protestantism and American Higher Education* (Louisville: Westminster John Knox Press, 1994).

2. Mark A. Noll, *The Scandal of the Evangelical Mind* (Grand Rapids: Eerdmans, 1994); Richard T. Hughes, *How Christian Faith Can Sustain the Life of the Mind* (Grand Rapids: Eerdmans, 2001); Cornelius Plantinga, Jr., *Engaging God's World: A Christian Vision of Faith, Learning, and Living* (Grand Rapids: Eerdmans, 2002); Clifford Williams, *The Life of the Mind: A Christian Perspective* (Grand Rapids: Baker, 2002); George M. Marsden, *The Outrageous Idea of Christian Scholarship* (New York: Oxford University Press, 1997).

What's more, I know the answers I provide are also, in a sense, my own. Much of what follows was written specifically for this book. Other sections were adapted from other things I've written — books, articles, papers, even correspondence. Still other sections are based on notes from the countless talks I've given over the years. With only a few exceptions, I will not attempt to identify prior uses of this material, mainly because it scarcely matters. For our purposes it is enough to say that, for good or ill, I am responsible for the whole. The ensuing discussion must in its entirety be preceded by the phrase, "It seems to me." In these pages the reader will inevitably be hearing the voice of this author.

This is an important acknowledgment, not least because I do not offer this work as an official document of Wheaton College. It's tricky business for a sitting president to write this kind of book without appearing to obligate his institution to every word. Presidents are inevitably their school's chief spokespersons; in fact, their role is sometimes frighteningly described as that of a "living logo" for the school. Thus their personal pronouncements can easily be mistaken for official documents of the college itself, as if the institution were no more than the lengthened shadow of its president.

In their treatment of *Myths and Realities of Academic Administration*, Patricia Plante and Robert Caret describe the care with which a president's words are often dissected. Plante and Caret's focus is the initial phase of a new president's tenure, but in a sense, the phenomenon they describe is one a president never fully escapes: "Every word, every memo, every act, every smile or frown is interpreted and reinterpreted as an exercise in forecasting. Everyone from the president of the faculty senate to the president of the chamber of commerce becomes temporarily engaged in textual analysis. Even the knowledge that such close readings often distort perspective and may be as profitable as divining by examining the shoulder blades of sacrificial sheep deters only a few from becoming instant deconstructionists. . . . Representatives of every constituency within and without the academy are . . . above all explicators of text."[3]

I know this phenomenon well and I understand why it exists. A president's words are closely examined because of the power and influ-

3. Patricia Plante and Robert Caret, *Myths and Realities of Academic Administration* (New York: The American Council on Education, Macmillan, 1990), pp. 1-2.

ence he or she typically wields within the institution. As its chief administrator, the president is the one at whose desk the institutional buck stops, the one who must give an account to the governing board and beyond for most everything that takes place within the institution. Because severing authority from responsibility, or responsibility from authority, in any organizational structure is disastrous, carrying the final responsibility means the president must also have a good deal of institutional clout. It cannot and should not be otherwise.[4]

Yet this very concentration of institutional power — combined with the dramatic enlargement of administrative and fundraising duties over the past century — has in our day contributed to the demise of the president's role as intellectual leader. If it was not always so, during the last century many college presidents came to be viewed more as managers than leaders, as administrators and facilitators rather than important participants in the intellectual life of the campus. Today's president may be asked to open the campus's academic conferences with a ceremonial welcome and "appropriate remarks," but seldom does a president wind up delivering one of its academic papers. That task falls to others.

I cite this phenomenon not as a complaint so much as an observation. I know only too well how difficult it is for a president to retain, much less to enhance, whatever hard-won academic expertise he or she may once have enjoyed. It is the unusual college president these days who can both run an institution and remain a productive scholar. I understand this, and thus I am unsurprised that in the minds of many today, the role of the college president is best likened to that of the captain of a large cruise ship, whose task it is to keep the passengers happy, the decks clean, and the fuel tanks full. He is to show up for ceremonial occasions and sit at the captain's table looking official. But he should not suppose that it is his responsibility, much less his prerogative, actually to steer the course of the ship.

Given their undeniable administrative power, presidents who do

---

4. For example, Henry Rosovsky on why academic institutions are not democracies: "What would be the effect of majority rule? One man, one vote would give those with the shortest time horizon the greatest influence. Influence would not be sufficiently weighted by the degree to which one has to live with the consequences of decisions and actions, and that is a bad idea." Rosovsky, *The University: An Owner's Manual* (New York: W. W. Norton, 1990), pp. 268-69.

aspire to keeping their hand, however lightly, on the intellectual tiller of their institution can actually become worrisome creatures. Presidents with ideas, particularly certain kinds of ideas, may be considered dangerous. This point is captured well in the sometimes-heard witticism about appropriate and inappropriate roles within the academy: The job of the president, says this bit of humor, is to speak for the institution; the job of the faculty is to think for the institution; while the job of the dean is to keep the faculty from speaking for the institution and keep the president from thinking for the institution. Buried in this witticism are several barbs, but the one we're after is this: a president who aspires to think for the institution can become an awkward problem indeed.

In his book on *How Academic Leadership Works,* Robert Birnbaum thankfully assures us that the situation is not quite so one-sided. Presidents need not be merely mindless bureaucrats, Birnbaum says; in fact, they must not be if their leadership is to be successful: "When they are perceived by their constituents as competent, legitimate, value-driven, of complex mind, and open to influence, presidents can be a vital source of leadership and a force for institutional renewal."[5] Birnbaum's observation embodies a good deal of wisdom. What it does not do is answer the question of how many ideas, and of what sort, a college president shall be permitted. On that question the jury remains permanently out.

All of which is why I say that writing a book like this, a book full of strong ideas, is tricky business for a sitting president. I wish to make it clear that this book is not an official document of the institution I serve. It is a book about some ideas that I, speaking as an individual, believe need exploration and reiteration. I use Wheaton in a few places as an illustration of this point or that because it is the institution I know best. But in most instances I do not have Wheaton particularly in mind. The topics I choose to handle and my particular way of handling them are the products of decades of academic training and experience, both as a teacher and administrator. They reflect much reading and listening, not to mention countless conversations with colleagues of every stripe from many different institutions. So despite my role as its sitting president, the topic of this book is not Wheaton College.

---

5. Robert Birnbaum, *How Academic Leadership Works: Understanding Success and Failure in the College Presidency* (San Francisco: Jossey-Bass, 1992), p. 151.

A Proactive Agenda

Having belabored this point, I do not wish, on the other side of the ledger, to overstate the personal dimension of this book, as if to leave the impression that what follows is, without residue, nothing more than my particular point of view. As the reader will come to see, I do not believe Christians either need or should allow themselves to be mired in a radical perspectivist epistemology that renders it impossible ever to rise above stating one's own viewpoint. What I am after in this book are ideas that run deeper and stronger than our own time and place, and certainly deeper and stronger than this one author. To dampen the purely personal dimension of the discussion and compensate for whatever weaknesses it may introduce, I have made an effort to avoid the idiosyncratic. Moreover, I have gone out of my way to draw upon and include a wide variety of voices besides my own. These citations are cumulatively designed to say to the reader: *This is not just one person talking.* My goal is to articulate some ideas around which a wide range of Christian thinkers can and do rally. I want to direct our attention to something larger than myself, larger than ourselves combined. I am after some strong ideas from our past, ideas we must keep strong in the present so that they will remain strong for the future.

Exploring these ideas will sometimes force us into confrontation with their competitors, but we must not shy away on that account. As philosopher Alvin Plantinga argues, we Christians are called to be about the business of what he terms "consciousness raising, or Christian cultural criticism." According to Plantinga, Christians must appreciate that our culture is involved in a "contest for basic human allegiance and that this conflict penetrates deeply into intellectual culture." It will not do, he insists, to take this matter lightly:

> We must really understand that there is a battle here, and we must know who and what the main contestants are and how this contest pervades the various scholarly disciplines. These perspectives are seductive; they are widespread; they are the majority views in the universities and in the intellectual culture generally in the West. We live in a world dominated by them; we imbibe them with our mother's milk; it is easy to embrace them and their projects in a sort of unthoughtful, un-self-conscious way, just because they do

dominate our intellectual culture. But these perspectives are also deeply inimical to Christianity; these ways of thinking distort our view of ourselves and the world. To the degree that we are not aware of them and do not understand their allegiances, they make for confusion and for lack of intellectual and spiritual wholeness and integrity among us Christians.[6]

Christian scholars, and the world of Christian higher education in general, must work hard to avoid a posture of defensiveness, much less that of bearing a chip on our collective shoulder. Christians have every reason to treat other ideas and those who hold them with charity and respect. But neither can we afford to be oblivious to the intellectual challenges of our day. The stakes are too high. Rather than rolling over and playing dead, our strategy should be an intentional and proactive one. As George Marsden says, "Our agenda ought to be directed toward building for our community as solid a place in the pluralistic intellectual life of our civilization as is consistent with our principles. Helping to establish the intellectual viability of our worldview and pointing out the shortcomings of alternatives can be an important service to our community and an important dimension of our witness to the world."[7] We must acquit ourselves in this task, to be sure, as Christians; that is, in ways that honor and do not dishonor the One we claim to serve. This requires at all times, as Marsden says, "a delicate combination of modesty and assertiveness. Our intellectual life must display the Christian qualities of self-criticism and generosity to others."[8] But such qualities need not, in fact must not, preclude intentional efforts on our part to set forth the intellectual viability of our own ideas and to expose the defects of their alternatives.

The pursuit of any such strategy, however, first requires a strong grasp of our own ideas. We need to understand these ideas and appreciate why they are important. To help us do so is the purpose of this book. There surely are sections of this book designed to defend the via-

6. Alvin Plantinga, "On Christian Scholarship," in *The Challenge and Promise of a Catholic University,* ed. Theodore Hesburgh (Notre Dame: University of Notre Dame Press, 1994), p. 291.

7. George Marsden, "The State of Evangelical Christian Scholarship," *Christian Scholar's Review* 17, no. 4 (1988): 356.

8. Marsden, "The State of Evangelical Christian Scholarship," p. 356.

bility of Christian ideas and critique their alternatives. But in the end this book is about, not defending or attacking, but alerting, explicating, and reminding. The ideas we will be examining are too many and too large for much beyond that. But the more important point has to do with my purpose: the goal of this book is not to prove these ideas to the unconvinced, but to strengthen the grip of those who already hold them.

What follows, then, are some exercises in clarity as we attempt to respond to the conceptual challenges facing the contemporary Christian college.

2 Two Academic Models

CHALLENGE *To Understand More Clearly Our Own Identity*

E arly in the 1990s two scholars from Pepperdine University set out on an ambitious quest to assess the practice of Christian higher education in America. To render their task more manageable, they began by setting some boundaries. Richard Hughes and William Adrian, with funding from the Lilly Endowment, identified educational institutions related to seven different Christian traditions. They then recruited scholars from each institution to describe the salient features of their faith tradition — that is, those features that most shaped that tradition's understanding of the academic task — and to tell the story of how these features work themselves out, for good or ill, in the chosen institutions. This process culminated in a book of stimulating essays entitled *Models for Christian Higher Education.*[1] It also generated six regional conferences where representatives of each institution and faith tradition gave presentations to an invited audience.

The seven faith traditions Hughes and Adrian chose were Roman Catholic, Lutheran, Wesleyan/Holiness, Baptistic/Restorationist, Evangelical/Interdenominational, Reformed, and Mennonite. Wheaton College was one of the institutions chosen to represent the Evangelical tradition, so when one of the conferences was scheduled in our area I attended with interest.

I was struck during this conference by how different these tradi-

1. Richard Hughes and William Adrian, eds., *Models for Christian Higher Education: Strategies for Success in the Twenty-First Century* (Grand Rapids: Eerdmans, 1997).

tions can be and how differently they tend to construe the Christian's intellectual task. But for that same reason I was also struck by how much we have to learn from one another. I came away from each presentation, as I did from each of the chapters in the subsequent book, with a deeper understanding of what I as a Christian educator should be about. A fully Christian approach to higher education has something to learn from each of these traditions.

But I also came away from this conference with several frustrations, one of which is pertinent to our present discussion. It was the category error of setting up these several schools as parallel to one another without acknowledging, much less exploring, the fact that the schools represent two very different approaches to education. I do not refer here to the theological or ecclesiastical differences that mark these institutions, nor to the fact that two are universities while the remaining three are colleges, though both issues may be related to my concern. What I have in mind is another kind of difference: these five institutions are designed along the lines of two quite different models. Notre Dame and Valparaiso follow one archetype; Goshen, Calvin and Wheaton another. Whether their respective choice of models is related somehow to substantive theological or philosophical differences among the five institutions is an open question. I suspect it may be,[2] but the two models were never acknowledged, nor were they treated in the later book.

I think it is crucial that we acknowledge these two models and distinguish between them. Otherwise we quite literally may not know what we're doing, or why. If we do not understand the contrasts between our own model and its alternative, we may be oblivious to the differences and therefore unable to appreciate their relative strengths or weaknesses. Or we may find ourselves unwittingly using the language of the first to describe the second, or criticizing the second on the criteria of the first. It's a prescription for confusion.

Let us briefly sketch these two models. They represent institutional archetypes, of course, and as such are subject to permutation.

2. For example, Ernest L. Simmons in *Lutheran Higher Education: An Introduction* (Minneapolis: Augsburg Fortress, 1998) argues that Lutheran institutions follow essentially what I refer to below as an Umbrella model due to Lutheran theological distinctives.

But for our purposes the archetypes will do. For lack of better terms, we will call them the *Umbrella model* and the *Systemic model.*

The Two Models

To an outsider, all church-related institutions may seem alike. But they're not. Whatever their origins, many formerly religious schools are just that, formerly religious; their religiosity is merely historical or nominal. Such schools do not fit either of our models. The schools to which our two models apply are something more. They remain, to use David O'Connell's term, "religious colleges."

> The expression "religious colleges" refers to those institutions of higher learning where the religion of the *founding* or *sponsoring* religious group has some *direct* influence upon the institution itself. By "direct" I mean real, observable, clear, and effective, with an active connection between a particular religion and a particular academic institution. It is not a "religious college" simply because its origins were religious, or its founders were clergymen or other religious women or men, or because the campus is peppered with religious symbols and works of art, or because there is a chapel. The direct influence to which I refer can be seen in terms of institutional identity, mission, governance, administration, criteria for faculty hiring, curricula, student life, campus ministries, policies, operations and procedures, and so forth.[3]

The schools to which our two models apply are those that have retained the direct influence of which O'Connell speaks. But even within this group there have developed over the years a number of variations, making for a complex landscape various authors have attempted to describe. Most notably, the 1966 Report of the Danforth Commission, *Church-Sponsored Higher Education in the United States,* suggested four categories for "institutions of higher education associated with religious bodies in the United States." They were (1) the *defender of the faith college,*

---

3. David O'Connell, "Staying the Course: Imperative and Influence Within the Religious College," in *The Future of Religious Colleges,* ed. Paul J. Dovre (Grand Rapids: Eerdmans, 2002), pp. 63-64.

(2) the *non-affirming college,* (3) the *free Christian college,* and (4) the *church-related university.*[4] The report went on to point out that these categories "do not exhaust the possibilities, and many institutions combine features of two or more of the patterns described."[5] That this was so was indicated by the fact that a number of evangelical colleges quickly proposed a fifth category that they believed more adequately captured their essence, that of *affirming colleges.*[6] Our Systemic model comes closest to this *affirming college* category, while the Umbrella model might take the form of any of the Danforth categories except *defender of the faith.*

More recently, Robert Benne, in his book *Quality with Soul,* has suggested a different fourfold typology of religiously affiliated institutions. Benne's last two types, *intentionally pluralist* and *accidentally pluralist,* fall outside the boundaries of our discussion because, as Benne says, there "the religious paradigm has been dethroned from its defining role. . . . It is no longer 'established' or normative; some other conception of the educational enterprise has taken its place."[7] Benne's first two categories, however, *critical-mass* and *orthodox,* correspond roughly to what we are calling the Umbrella and Systemic models.

The Umbrella Model

Umbrella institutions seek to provide a Christian "umbrella" or canopy under which a variety of voices can thrive. Typically a certain "critical mass" represents the voice of a sponsoring Christian tradition, so that sponsoring voice remains a privileged one. But the institution will nonetheless demonstrate genuine diversity. Some campus voices may be unhesitatingly secular, others open but searching, while still others may represent competing religious perspectives. Yet all are welcome under the umbrella so long as they can at least support the broad educa-

4. Manning M. Pattillo, Jr., and Donald M. Mackenzie, eds., *Church-Sponsored Higher Education in the United States* (Washington: American Council on Education, 1966), pp. 191-97.

5. Pattillo and Mackenzie, eds., *Church-Sponsored Higher Education,* p. 197.

6. "The Affirming College," *Christianity Today,* September 10, 1965, pp. 25-26.

7. Robert Benne, *Quality with Soul: How Six Premier Colleges and Universities Keep Faith with Their Religious Traditions* (Grand Rapids: Eerdmans, 2001), p. 51.

tional mission of the school. The institution has made room for them; they are asked only to make room for the institution.

In such institutions the sponsoring perspective will typically be kept more or less discernable. It may show itself in such things as the school's architecture, traditions, curriculum, and extracurricular activities, as well as in the makeup of its governing board, faculty, and student body. Yet many non-Christian voices, groups, and activities can also be found, and the institution makes a genuine effort to keep the campus hospitable to them. The result is a relatively non-sectarian environment that can encourage rigorous Christian thinking even while serving as a venue where that thinking can engage other ideas in full.

Religious colleges and universities from various traditions have designed themselves after some variant of this Umbrella model. For example, in an article in *America*, a Jesuit publication which bills itself as "a magazine for thinking Catholics and those who want to know what Catholics are thinking," David Carlin described what a Roman Catholic version of the Umbrella model might look like.[8] Carlin addresses the concerns of those who worry that Catholic institutions are becoming so nonsectarian that they cease to be Catholic. How can such institutions maintain their Umbrella character without sacrificing the sponsoring voice of the Catholic Church?

First, Carlin says, make sure that the campus retains a critical mass of committed Catholics, or as he puts it, "persons with high CQs (Catholic Quotient)." When it comes to personnel decisions, "hire as many Catholic priests, nuns and brothers as possible; where these are not available, hire committed Catholic laypersons; and where these are not available, hire non-Catholics (preferably committed Protestants) who have a genuine respect for the Catholic mission of the college." In addition to hiring practices, keep high CQs "in key power positions: on the board of trustees, in the higher administration, especially the presidency, in the deanships."

What about the student body? "Recruit a student body among which Catholics have a very decided predominance," and then make available to them on campus "a variety of extracurricular activities hav-

8. David Carlin, "What Future for Catholic Higher Education?" *America*, February 24, 1996, pp. 15-17.

ing a Catholic or at least a generalized Christian flavor about them." Such things as "concerts of Christian sacred music (defining 'sacred music' broadly)" should be frequent, all served up in a decidedly Catholic physical environment: "There should always be a church building, handsome inside and out, and the campus should be well stocked with religious statues, paintings and crucifixes."

On the academic side Carlin considers the most important issue to be the curriculum. Says he, "Design a curriculum that, while not skimping on secular subjects, has a distinctively Catholic character to it. Some of the 'Catholic courses' will be required for all students, but a generous offering of others should be available on an elective basis." More broadly, "invite the larger Catholic world onto the campus for lectures by prominent Catholic intellectuals, novelists, politicians, bishops and the like." Create special academic centers, "unique repositories for the study of subjects distinctively Catholic." And where feasible, "publish books and periodicals, both academic and popular, that treat subjects having special Catholic interest."

"In short," Carlin says, "an institution will be Catholic if it is run and taught by high-CQ people, is attended mainly by Catholic students, deals with a variety of Catholic topics on both a curricular and extra-curricular basis and in general forms a focal point at which people can come into contact with Catholic ideas and experiences."

Not all Roman Catholic educators would agree with Carlin's vision for Catholic schools. Some would find it too sectarian; others might find it insufficiently so. But that debate is not for us. However one decides the question of how "Catholic" Catholic institutions must be to be considered truly Catholic, the debate largely revolves around a core Umbrella model.[9]

Yet the Umbrella model is by no means limited to Roman Catholic institutions. Mark Schwehn, Dean of the Honors College at Valparaiso University and author of the widely-read *Exiles from Eden,* offers a similar vision, one generic enough to be implemented in many

---

9. See, for example, *Ex Corde Ecclesiae: The Application to the United States,* United States Conference of Bishops; or Joseph Herlihy's analysis in "Reflections on *Ex Corde Ecclesiae,*" in *The Future of Religious Colleges,* pp. 283-303; *The Challenge and Promise of a Catholic University,* ed. Theodore M. Hesburgh (Notre Dame: University of Notre Dame Press, 1994); George Dennis O'Brien, *The Idea of a Catholic University* (Chicago: University of Chicago Press, 2002).

different faith traditions. According to Schwehn, the minimal constitutional requirements of a Christian university are as follows:

> It must have a board of trustees composed of a substantial majority of Christian men and women, clergy and lay, whose primary task is to attend to the Christian character of the institution. They will do this primarily but not exclusively by appointing to the major leadership positions of the school persons who are actively committed to the ideal of a Christian university. These leaders will in turn see to it that all of the following things are present within the life of the institution: A department of theology that offers courses required of all students in both biblical studies and the Christian intellectual tradition; an active chapel ministry that offers worship services in the tradition of the faith community that supports the school but that also makes provision for worship by those of other faiths; a critical mass of faculty members who in addition to being excellent teacher-scholars carry in and among themselves the DNA of the school, are for the perpetuation of its mission as a Christian community of inquiry; and a curriculum that includes a large number of courses, required of all students, that are compellingly construed as parts of a larger whole that taken together constitute a liberal education.[10]

In short, despite the fact that such a model "privileges and seeks to transmit, through its theology department, its official rhetoric, the corporate worship it sponsors, and in myriad other ways, a particular tradition of thought, feeling and practice," the voices of this tradition on campus are joined by others as well.

The Umbrella model, then, seeks to house a variety of perspectives without sacrificing its sponsoring perspective. Unlike many secular settings that strike a neutral pose but are in fact hostile to genuine Christian thought, Umbrella institutions create an environment congenial to Christian thinking, but without expecting it of everyone.

---

10. Mark Schwehn, "A Christian University," *First Things*, May 1999, pp. 26-27.

The Systemic Model

Systemic institutions reach for more, but in another sense settle for less. As the name suggests, they seek to make Christian thinking systemic throughout the institution, root, branch, and leaf. Their curriculum is typically all-encompassing. Their goal is to engage any and all ideas from every perspective, but they attempt to do so from a particular intellectual location, that of the sponsoring Christian tradition. Thus they draw their faculty exclusively from those who know what it means to live and work from that tradition — indeed, from those who embody it. What is true of the critical mass in the Umbrella model is to be true of all of the scholars in the Systemic model. They seek to live and work *as Christians*.

At purely secular institutions these days, Christian ideas are often quarantined to the realm of the personal. If they show up at all in the public forum, it's more than likely in their being discredited. Christian truth may be refuted in the classrooms of such institutions, but not propounded. By contrast, with the Umbrella model Christian ideas are not only allowed on campus, they are encouraged; they may even enjoy a privileged position. But with the Systemic model, these ideas are the institution's *raison d'etre*.

Systemic institutions may range from the generic to the sectarian. The common faith tradition at their core may be defined as broadly as, say, the Apostles' Creed, or as narrowly as a denomination's full panoply of theological and ecclesiastical markers. But what marks off Systemic institutions from their Umbrella counterparts is that all of their faculty are drawn from those who embody the institution's sponsoring faith tradition, however broadly or narrowly it may be defined. In this way that sponsoring faith tradition permeates the institution. Anthony Diekema, former president of Calvin College, describes such institutions as follows: Christian colleges, he says, must "give constant attention to institutional mission and its extensive articulation. And then by logical extension that mission must permeate everything we do, giving internal consistency to teaching, scholarship, student life, administration, community relations . . . everything. We need to daily strive toward that end. I am persuaded that a truly Christian college is distinguished by a mission statement that articulates a Christian worldview and implements it throughout the curriculum, and by a faculty whose scholarship is anchored in that same worldview."[11]

The variety of Systemic institutions may be gauged by examining the membership of the Council for Christian Colleges and Universities (CCCU). Of the approximately 4200 degree-granting institutions of higher learning in the United States, about 1600 are private. Of these private institutions, approximately 900 define themselves as "religiously affiliated." And of these religiously affiliated institutions, a little over 100 belong to the CCCU.[12] These CCCU schools represent a wide variety of denominations and faith traditions. Some define themselves generically, others more specifically. But all share the criteria for CCCU membership, which include these two standards:

> *A Christ-centered mission:* A public mission based upon the centrality of Jesus Christ and evidence of how faith is integrated with the institution's academic and student life programs.
>
> *An employment policy:* A current hiring policy that requires of each full-time faculty member and administrator a personal faith in Jesus Christ.

Each of the CCCU institutions is thus designed along the lines of the Systemic model. All of their professors are to be scholars who embody the Christian commitments of the institution, with the expected result that genuinely Christian thinking will permeate the school's "academic and student life programs." This is what renders these institutions "systemically" Christian.

With these two models in mind, we can clarify our terminology. I will employ the term "Christian higher education" in this book

11. Anthony Diekema, *Academic Freedom and Christian Scholarship* (Grand Rapids: Eerdmans, 2000), p. 57.

12. It is worth noting that this sector of the educational market is growing dramatically. According to the National Center for Education Statistics, from 1990-99, the composite of all U.S. educational institutions grew by 7.04 percent, the public sector grew by 4.28 percent, the private sector grew by 17.08 percent, and religiously affiliated schools grew by 16.78 percent, but CCCU institutions grew by 41.89 percent. When the CCCU figures are updated to 2002, the numbers show that during the period 1990-2002, CCCU institutions grew by 60 percent ("The State of Christian Higher Education: Thriving," November 2003, published by the CCCU).

broadly enough to encompass, at least potentially, both Umbrella and Systemic institutions. In other words, the term will not be used to stipulate automatically one model or the other. So also for the term "Christian university." But I will use the term "Christian college" differently. Unless otherwise indicated, I will use this term to imply the Systemic model.

A Framework for Evaluation

What should we make of these two models? Is one of them, Umbrella or Systemic, superior to the other, and therefore preferable? Thinking about how one might answer this question requires a context; we must establish a framework for analysis and identify some criteria. For that we may turn to a helpful if somewhat unlikely source.

In 1963 Clark Kerr, then President of the University of California, delivered the Godkin Lectures at Harvard. These lectures were subsequently published under the title *The Uses of the University*.[13] Kerr sought in these lectures to examine what American universities had become, and to explore the future toward which they seemed to be headed. In doing so he introduced into common parlance the term "multiversity."

Kerr spent his first lecture exploring "The Idea of a Multiversity." This title was a takeoff on the work we have already mentioned, John Henry Newman's *The Idea of a University*. It was in fact Newman's older vision of the university, as well as Abraham Flexner's 1930 portrayal of "The Idea of the Modern University,"[14] against which Kerr set out to define his own portrait.

According to Kerr, "The beautiful world [envisioned by Newman] was being shattered forever even as it was being so beautifully portrayed." In the same way, "the 'Modern University' was as nearly dead in 1930 when Flexner wrote about it as the old Oxford was in 1852 when Newman idealized it. History moves faster than the observer's pen. Neither the ancient classics and theology nor the German philosophers

---

13. Clark Kerr, *The Uses of the University*, 3rd ed. (Cambridge: Harvard University Press, 1982).

14. Abraham Flexner, *Universities: American, English, German* (New York: Oxford University Press, 1930), pp. 3-36.

and scientists could set the tone for the really modern university — the multiversity."

The contrast between Kerr's multiversity and the earlier versions of Newman and Flexner occupied much of Kerr's attention in *The Uses of the University*. In fact, that contrast would be drawn all the more clearly a decade later in a postscript to his 1972 edition.[15] There Kerr drew upon William James's *A Pluralistic Universe*,[16] a book he had come across in the intervening years. Said Kerr, "I wish I had then read William James on the 'multiverse.' It would have given me a good footnote to employ . . . and helped me to clarify my ideas."

What was it that Kerr found so useful in James? It was the contrast between what James calls "pluralism" and "monism":

> The monistic approach . . . is to find a single "Absolute." Such absolutes might be (although [James] did not use them as illustrations) the word of God, or the class struggle of Marx, or the survival of the fittest of Darwin, or the infantile sex of Freud; some absolute that determined everything else, that lent a unity to thought, that posited a community where all the parts were internally related, where there was an organic unity with no independent parts, and that yielded an inherent consistency. James noted that such an absolute was effective in conferring mental peace, a degree of certainty. The absolute (and James was against all absolutes) sought to define what was right and what was wrong in the present, to explain the past, to describe the future. It sought to provide sure standards for making decisions and a clear vision of both past and future events.
>
> The pluralistic approach, by contrast, as James noted, sees several forces at work in more or less eternal conflict, sees everything in "flux," sees a state of indeterminism. There is said to be more free will for the individual, and more dysfunction within and between organizations. Parts of the whole, James said, "may be externally related" rather than only internally related. . . . Thus there was a "strung-along type" of unity or a "contiguity" rather than one central absolute to which every part was tied directly. "Nothing includes everything, or dominates over everything."

15. The following quotations are from Kerr, *The Uses of the University*, pp. 135-41.
16. William James, *A Pluralistic Universe* (New York: Longmans, Green and Co., 1909).

While James was primarily addressing the world of philosophy, Kerr found his categories useful in describing different types of institutions. Newman's classical concept of the university, and even Flexner's early twentieth century version, tended toward the monistic pole, while the "multiversity" Kerr was attempting to describe tended toward the pluralistic. Thus he speaks of the multiversity's "strung-along type of unity," marked by a "lack of devotion to any single faith and its lack of concentration on any single function, with a condition of cohesion at best or coexistence at next best or contiguity at least." Kerr originally used "multiversity" as a purely descriptive phrase, but he acknowledges it was easily misunderstood. It subsequently became, he says, "on the lips of some, a term of opprobrium."

Little more than a year after delivering his Harvard lectures to considerable acclaim, Kerr became in the eyes of many the bungler of what would become epoch-defining student protests on Sproul Plaza at the Berkeley campus.[17] The 1960s proved to be difficult for Clark Kerr, and by the time he wrote the preface to the 1972 edition of his book he was eager to demonstrate that he was a champion of the contemporary university, not its adversary. Hence he valorizes the multiversity over its classical counterparts: "To the extent that universities are a generating force for new ideas and for critical commentary on the status quo, they are more likely to fulfill this role where Absolute confronts Absolute, where thesis meets antithesis, where one culture contests another; just as biological generation most often occurs where one ecological environment shades into another, where the sea meets the land." Kerr asks, "Should the model of the university be based more on productive conflict or on doctrinal unity, on the interaction of disparate entities or on the integration of fully compatible parts?" The multiversity, he says,

> is based more on conflict and on interaction; the monistic university more on unity and integration. Monistic universities are more like Plato's hierarchical Republic, and multiversities more nearly correspond to Aristotle's search for the Golden Mean. That ancient controversy, over the closed versus the open society, over rigidity of

17. Garry Wills, *Certain Trumpets: The Nature of Leadership* (New York: Simon and Schuster, 1994), p. 84. For a rather different account of these events, see Clark Kerr, *The Gold and the Blue: A Personal Memoir of the University of California, 1949-1967*, vol. 2: *Political Turmoil* (Berkeley: University of California Press, 2003).

purpose and hierarchy as against constant adaptation and adjustment, has been going on for a long time in many guises, and so will
the controversy between the bitter principled enemies and the re-
luctant pragmatic supporters of the multiversity.

Kerr was not oblivious to the shortcomings of his subject. He
notes its fragmentation and over-specialization and cites those critics
who scorn it as little more than an "inter-section of freeways" — the
"Los Angeles of the intellect," said one critic in the *New York Review of
Books*. In such institutions, "loyalty is not so readily given, conflicts are
not so easily settled in terms of absolute principles, borders to confine
the extension of efforts are harder to define." But Kerr was nonetheless
a believer in the multiversity. He cites the relative strengths of a monistic model, but by the time he finishes doing so it is clear these are only
weaknesses in disguise. "Monistic universities," he says, "based on the
Bible, or the Koran, or the Communist Manifesto, or the Great Books
can test loyalty more precisely, can settle disputes more on principle,
can limit their functions more readily. But they also tend to be more
static in a dynamic world, more intolerant in a world crying for understanding and accommodation to diversity, more closed to the unorthodox person and idea, more limited in their comprehension of total reality." Kerr wanted it to be clear where his sympathies lay: he was a citizen
in good standing in the new world, the multiversity.

> The older term . . . carried with it the older visions of a unified
> "community of masters and students" with a single "soul" or pur-
> pose. There was, however, a new reality and it seemed that it would
> be helpful to have a new word to carry the image of this new reality;
> to make the point that Alma Mater was less an integrated and eter-
> nal spirit, and more a split and variable personality; to call atten-
> tion to the fact that what had once been a community was now
> more like an environment — more like a city, a "city of infinite vari-
> ety." Thus the word — "multiversity."

Kerr was not the first to coin the term "multiversity": "The word
. . . was in the air," he says, "and had several more or less simultaneous
authors." But he was the one who added it permanently to the vocabulary of higher education, and it was his usage that has stuck. "What I
meant by the word," he says, "was that the modern university was a

'pluralistic' institution — pluralistic in several senses: in having several purposes, not one; in having several centers of power, not one; in serving several clienteles, not one. It worshiped no single God; it constituted no single, unified community; it had no discretely defined set of customers. It was marked by many visions of the Good, the True, and the Beautiful, and by many roads to achieve these visions; by power conflicts; by service to many markets and concern for many publics. . . . What I wanted to do was to mark the contrast with a more nearly single-purpose institution having a more monistic spirit, a more monolithic leadership, and a single clientele."

Weighing the Models

Kerr's analysis, and that of William James before him, may best be seen, it seems to me, in terms of a continuum. The sprawling multiversity lies at one end, but neither Newman's idea of a university nor Flexner's lie at the other. In fact, it is not clear that any ideal or actual institution lies there, or could. Many American academic institutions today epitomize the multiversity Kerr had in mind; none I can think of epitomize the monistic model he describes. Once we move away from the genuine multiversities of our day, most schools, like the idealized models both Newman and Flexner describe, fall somewhere along the continuum between the extremes.

Yet this continuum does provide a useful framework for reflecting on the relative merits or weaknesses of our two types of Christian institutions, the Umbrella and Systemic. If neither lies at the extremes of the continuum, it is certainly the case that, as Christian institutions, both tend toward the monistic pole, with the Systemic model further along than the Umbrella, and their differences can usefully be analyzed according to their respective locations on the continuum.

We can see this more clearly by distilling Kerr's description of the two extremes. His language is skewed in favor of the model he (and James) certainly preferred, but it can still serve our purposes. According to Kerr, the multiversity

- knows no transcendent unifying point, but rather views multiple forces at work in more or less eternal conflict;

- considers all to be in flux, in a state of indeterminism;
- demonstrates a split and variable personality;
- stresses infinite variety, constant adaptation and adjustment;
- enables more free will for the individual;
- endures more dysfunction within and between segments;
- demonstrates no devotion to any single faith, worships no single God;
- experiences cohesion at best, or coexistence at next best, or contiguity at least;
- views its parts as externally related rather than internally related;
- knows only a "strung-along type" of unity or a "contiguity" rather than a core unity;
- lacks concentration on any single function;
- is an "environment" rather than a community;
- is more likely to fulfill its role as a generating force for new ideas and for critical commentary on the status quo because it is a place where Absolute confronts Absolute, where thesis meets antithesis, where one culture contests another;
- is a place of power conflicts, where loyalty is not so readily given, conflicts are not so easily settled in terms of absolute principles, and borders to confine the extension of efforts are harder to define; is based on a model of productive conflict, on the interaction of disparate entities;
- embraces many visions of the Good, the True, and the Beautiful, and many roads to achieve these visions.

By contrast, monistic institutions are

- centered around some transcendent reference point that is allowed to determine all else;
- more of a unified community of masters and students with a single soul or purpose;
- more likely to stress unity and integration;
- more likely to aspire to a unity of thought, where all the parts are organically related;
- more likely to experience mental peace and a degree of certainty;
- more likely to possess sure standards for making decisions and a clear vision of both past and future events;

- more able to define what is right and wrong in the present, past, and future;
- more closed, with a rigidity of purpose and hierarchy;
- more monolithic in leadership, with a single clientele;
- more able to test loyalty precisely, settle disputes on principle, and limit their functions more readily;
- more static in a dynamic world;
- more intolerant in a world crying for understanding and accommodation to diversity;
- more closed to the unorthodox person or idea;
- more limited in their comprehension of total reality.

These descriptions represent the two ends of Kerr's continuum. As such, they describe neither our Umbrella nor Systemic models. Yet the two extremes do represent the relative tendencies of our two models. In neither instance do the descriptions apply fully, but in both cases they highlight the potential strengths and weaknesses of the two types of institutions.

If neither model can be found at the ends of Kerr's continuum, the Umbrella model certainly falls further along the continuum toward the pluralistic end, while the Systemic model falls toward the monistic end. How far apart they may be will vary with the institutions being compared, but it is largely their different locations on this continuum that distinguish the two. The Systemic model allows for more pluralism than the above monistic description would suggest, while the Umbrella model looks more monistic than the true multiversity. The two are thus thrown together toward the middle on the continuum. But their differences remain.

Both Umbrella and Systemic institutions stress in their own ways a strong engagement with a full range of viewpoints. Yet both in their own ways also manage to do so while privileging a particular viewpoint. For an Umbrella institution, it's an intramural engagement between and among a pluralism of voices on campus, with the sponsoring voice always retaining a more or less privileged status. For Systemic institutions the engagement occurs as students are exposed both on and off campus to that same full range of voices. But in the Systemic model this engagement takes place, with great intentionality, *within each course* as professors seek to help students think Christianly about each and every subject. Students are introduced to competing voices at every turn, though typically with a view, in the end, to developing them into effective Christian thinkers.[18]

More so than the Umbrella model, then, the Systemic model is an explicit exercise (to borrow a phrase from the title of Stanley Hauerwas and John Westerhoff's book)[19] in "schooling Christians." If the pluralism of Umbrella institutions sometimes lends a liveliness to their campus dialogue, moving them closer to the multiversity, by the same token the focus, intentionality, and synergy of the Systemic model generate for these institutions the strengths of the monistic end of the continuum, lending them a peculiar liveliness and power of their own.

The answer to the question of which model is better, then, will likely depend on who is offering the answer. Which features of Kerr's continuum do we consider strengths, and which weaknesses? And what relative weight should we apply to each strength and each weakness? The secularist will likely be more amenable to the Umbrella model, since it is closer to what secularists have come to expect of an academic institution, and many Christian thinkers prefer its breadth and variety as well. On the other hand, not a few Christians are drawn to the intentionality, synergy, and focus of the Systemic model. They worry when they hear someone like Carlin speak of ensuring the availability within the curriculum of an appropriate number of "Catholic courses" amidst all the "secular subjects." Their understanding of the Christian's intellectual task calls into question any such divide. As Arthur Holmes argues in his rationale for the Christian college, the broader model "does not envision bringing the creative contribution of Christian perspectives to bear in all disciplines and all campus activities. The elaboration of a coherent worldview and the development of college life as a Christian academic community would simply not be possible under such an arrangement."[20]

---

18. Our focus here is on Christian thought. The matters of spiritual formation and service are important issues in both types of institutions, but they require treatments of their own and will not be discussed here.

19. *Schooling Christians: "Holy Experiments" in American Education,* ed. Stanley Hauerwas and John H. Westerhoff (Grand Rapids: Eerdmans, 1992).

20. Arthur Holmes, *The Idea of a Christian College,* rev. ed. (Grand Rapids: Eerdmans, 1975), p. 73. But on this point we should note the "systemic" nature of Executive Director of the Association of Catholic Colleges and Universities Monika Hellwig's vi-

Yet we should qualify Holmes's observation by defining somewhat more carefully what we mean by "a Christian academic community." In his book *Exiles from Eden,* Mark Schwehn is at pains to explain that sense of Christian community that can be found in either an Umbrella or Systemic institution. In making his case he appears to valorize the Umbrella model because he considers Systemic institutions today to be no more than "a potentially saving remnant." They are places, he says, that "should be supported as wholeheartedly as possible," but there are too few of them "to constitute by themselves a national strategy." And in this judgment, at least relative to the larger academic picture, Schwehn is surely right: "Very few colleges in this country have the self-assurance, the endowment strength, and the depths of spiritual conviction to resist the external constraints placed upon them by accrediting agencies, professional schools, and the modern research university."[21]

Yet if this is true, would it not seem to leave the field to the broader, more pluralistic Christian universities as our only hope for creating viable Christian academic communities? Schwehn will have none of that. Citing David Riesman and Christopher Jenks, two champions of pluralism in the academic world, Schwehn insists that the question is not whether Christian institutions can compete with "Harvard and Berkeley on the latter's terms," but whether they can provide a Christian alternative to "the Harvard-Berkeley model of excellence." Says Schwehn, "We need very much to remember this insight as it applies to all religiously affiliated colleges and universities, for it points

---

sion of the Catholic college: "The third characteristic that contributes to the Catholic identity is fidelity to the Christian message as it comes to us through the Church. This affects all aspects of the life of the campus. Certainly it applies to the teaching of theology and ethics, but it also has implications for the choice and conduct of every kind of research and for the teaching of such subjects as biology, history, sociology, economics, and political theory. It has implications for the approach taken in every field. . . . Fidelity to the Christian message has to be evident in the life of the campus in all aspects. Thus, the training and functioning of student-services professionals is critical. It is not only a question of specific moral teachings (in relation to sexual behavior, for instance), but also of the positive values and expectations for just, charitable, and mutually respectful behavior, concern for the needs of others, compassion for the less fortunate, and a habit of concern for the common good." Monika K. Hellwig, "What Makes Our Colleges Catholic?" *Current Issues in Catholic Higher Education* 23, no. 2 (Summer 2003): 29.

21. Mark Schwehn, *Exiles from Eden: Religion and the Academic Vocation in America* (New York: Oxford University Press, 1993), p. 80.

to the kind of pluralism that is most healthy for the world of higher learning, an institutional pluralism that is based upon alternative models of human excellence."

But, Schwehn asks, do not such communities, whether Umbrella or Systemic, by their distinctively Christian focus "finally stultify inquiry, which is often linked to disagreement and conflict rather than to consensus and harmony?" Because he is sympathetic to such a concern, Schwehn acknowledges the potential for such stifling in Christian schools, where a "cult of niceness" often presides. Such places can experience an "intellectual oppression that takes the form of an overt pretense of community combined with a covert persecution of those regarded as deviants. In the name of community, public conflict is repressed; superficial charity becomes a kiss of intellectual betrayal." But, says Schwehn, "this situation is . . . the antithesis of community as I understand it." Academic communities are to be places where "human beings are drawn together through the practice of such spiritual virtues as humility and charity," which in turn "enables, even promotes, productive conflict. Covert competition, not overt conflict, is the main enemy of this form of community."[22]

Schwehn is right both to acknowledge this problem but also to resist the notion that it is somehow inherent in Christian academic communities, even within the more "monistic" Systemic institutions. On core issues such institutions consist of the like-minded, but beyond the core these communities are often highly diverse. What's more, the very things they share in common often provide a sturdy foundation for tolerating their often impassioned and wide-ranging differences. The healthiest give and take often occurs in the most cohesive groups, such as large, committed, garrulous families. Where there is an underlying climate of trust we typically find *more* open disagreement, not less. High levels of cohesion tend to strengthen rather than inhibit the completeness or openness of communication. The group's underlying ties make the strongest disagreements both possible and manageable, disagreements that more fragile communities could not bear without spinning apart. Members of such communities are enabled and often encouraged to explore their differences openly and fully, and when these differences wind up unresolved, to "agree to disagree, agreeably."

22. Schwehn, *Exiles from Eden*, p. 82.

Thus the very cohesiveness of Umbrella or Systemic institutions can actually foster the airing of differing points of view. That such cohesiveness can and sometimes does hunker down into forms of intellectual oppression, however well intended, does not mean it must do so. Umbrella and Systemic institutions are both capable of providing vibrant, engaging intellectual environments where all voices are heard and all ideas weighed. Both models display relative advantages, and both carry relative disadvantages; thus it seems to me the two may best be viewed as augmenting one another. They serve complementary purposes, and we can be grateful for them both.

Need for Clear Thinking

It does seem important, however, that we at least try to keep our thinking about these two models clear; or more pointedly, that each institution remain clear about which type of institution it aspires to be. Clarity here can help in a number of ways.

It is not uncommon, for example, to hear an institution of one type measured by the criteria of the other. Predictably the institution fails to measure up, but is such criticism fair? Perhaps an Umbrella institution will be criticized because it tolerates non-Christians on its faculty, people who write and teach non-Christian, even anti-Christian things. How can it call itself Christian? asks the critic from the Systemic school. At the same time, Systemic institutions may be chided for having *only* Christians on their faculty. Insular and defensive, says the critic from the Umbrella school. How can they consider themselves "academic" institutions at all? Never mind that first-rate Christian scholarship and teaching may be taking place in both institutions, helped along in both cases by the relative merits of their respective models. Employing the wrong criteria will always cast an institution in a bad light.

Sometimes the criticisms come from within. A faculty member who teaches in an Umbrella school would perhaps prefer the more focused environment of a Systemic institution. But instead of moving there she settles for undermining her own school by complaining to all who will listen about the decline of its Christian identity. Or conversely, perhaps a professor at a Systemic institution would prefer the breadth of an Umbrella institution, but instead of joining one settles for undermining his own institution by pining publicly for the idealized features of the Umbrella model.

Such criticisms stem from a failure to appreciate each model for what it is, and to appreciate the different institutions for what they are. It seems perfectly appropriate to prefer one model to the other, but neither should simply dismiss, much less work against, the other. In emphasizing their own strengths, advocates for one particular model have no business making points at the expense of its counterpart. The two types of institutions should see themselves as complementary and work to support one another.

A Working Example

Unfortunately, this does not always happen. As president of a well known Systemic institution I sometimes run across those who value what we do but who are quite unwilling to credit Umbrella institutions as being "Christian" at all. There may well be Christians doing their work there as Christians, they will acknowledge, but in what sense can these institutions themselves be considered Christian? Such criticisms challenge the legitimacy of not merely the particular institutions, but of the Umbrella model itself.

But that shoe can also be found on the other foot, sometimes in a much more public way. On occasion one will hear advocates for Umbrella institutions make points in public on the backs of their Systemic colleagues. I recall, for example, a newspaper editorial written by a high-profile leader of an Umbrella institution that valorized Umbrella institutions at the expense of their Systemic counterparts. I've run across similar examples of the same approach in connection with other Umbrella institutions as well. The goal of such efforts appears to be not merely a comparison of the two models for the sake of clarity, but a vaunting of the one over the other.

This sort of disparagement is disappointing enough. More damaging still is the stance of some Umbrella institutions on the subject of academic freedom. Since 1940 the combined AAUP/AAC *Statement on Academic Freedom and Tenure* has defined the concept of academic freedom for American higher education. Yet from the beginning that *State-*

ment also made room, in its famous "limitations clause," for not only the religious features of Umbrella schools, but also the more demanding Christian expectations of Systemic schools.[23] Umbrella institutions do not require all of their faculty to embody the sponsoring faith tradition, but Systemic institutions do. The *Statement* implicitly acknowledges this distinction and grants Systemic institutions legitimacy, provided they make their expectations public in advance. As Michael McConnell puts it, "In practice, the limitations clause was taken to mean that religious colleges and universities were free to adopt their own principles of academic freedom without interference or censure by the academic community, so long as those principles were clearly announced in advance."[24] This demand for explicitness most Systemic institutions are more than ready to fulfill, because they know it is in their best interests to do so, quite apart from the *Statement.*[25] Thus Systemic institutions have always viewed the *Statement,* with its implied acknowledgment of their contribution to the academy, as a friend.

Yet from the beginning some have insisted on eliminating from the *Statement* any "limitations clause." Such a change would have little impact on Umbrella institutions, but it would threaten Systemic institutions with a complete loss of academic legitimacy.[26] The views of those who have long held that Systemic institutions have no place in the academy would now become established doctrine. That would be a tragic day for an entire category of colleges and universities that have long made useful contributions to the academy.

One of the arguments offered by those who seek to eliminate the *Statement's* "limitations clause" is this: Religious institutions say they do not require such a clause; so, because it apparently serves no func-

23. The clause reads as follows: "Limitations of academic freedom because of religious or other aims of the institution should be clearly stated in writing at the time of the appointment."

24. "Academic Freedom in Religious Colleges and Universities," in *Freedom and Tenure in the Academy,* ed. William W. Van Alstyne (Durham: Duke University Press, 1993), pp. 307-8. But see also the effort to refute this reading of the limitations clause by Judith Jarvis Thompson and Matthew W. Finkin ("Academic Freedom and Church-related Higher Education: A Reply to Professor McConnell," in *Freedom and Tenure in the Academy,* pp. 419-29).

25. On this point, see Chapter 10.

26. Cf. Committee A, "The Limitations Clause in the 1940 Statement of Principles," *Academe,* September-October 1988, pp. 53-54.

tion, let us do away with it.[27] But of course this argument is misleading. Perhaps these critics have heard from some Umbrella institutions that the clause is not necessary. But they certainly would not receive such a response from any Systemic institution.

This argument appears to be an attempt to drive a wedge between the two types of religious institutions; it is a strategy whose effect would be to split off the Umbrella institutions and leave the Systemic schools isolated. These critics would apparently like to see Systemic institutions disappear, or at least to undermine their legitimacy as institutions of higher learning. I will address their criticisms in a later chapter, but for now let us settle for pointing out the challenge. Umbrella and Systemic institutions must not allow the critics to divide them. Each must stand in support of the other.

27. "The Limitations Clause in the 1940 Statement of Principles," pp. 52-56. The actual wording of the 1970 Interpretive Comment to the 1940 statement reads as follows: "Most church-related institutions no longer need or desire the departure from the principle of academic freedom implied in the 1940 Statement, and we do not now endorse such a departure."

3 The Centerpiece

Advertisers know a good slogan when they see it. Along with being catchy and memorable, it must also convey something important about the product it represents. *Advertising Age* ranked these the top ten slogans of the twentieth century:

1. Diamonds are forever
2. Just do it
3. The pause that refreshes
4. Tastes great, less filling
5. We try harder
6. Good to the last drop
7. Breakfast of champions
8. Does she . . . or doesn't she?
9. When it rains it pours
10. Where's the beef?

After years of having them drummed into our ears, who could fail to connect these famous phrases with DeBeers, Nike, Coke, Avis, Maxwell House, or Wendy's? And more importantly, who of us has not been subliminally influenced by the messages they advance? To one extent or another we have all come to think in a certain way about each of these products through the force of their oft-repeated slogans.

Yet it is also striking to observe how many of these phrases are no longer used. Coke is no longer the pause that refreshes; Clairol answered its own question (she does); Wendy's has moved on to grilled chicken. Only a few of these top catchphrases can still be heard. Why would companies and their advertising agencies abandon such successful slogans?

The answer is that even the best slogans enjoy only a limited shelf life. When first used they strike the hearer as fresh; they communicate something attractive about the product. But with time and repetition their effect begins to wear off. Eventually the phrase becomes so familiar it no longer conjures up anything for the hearer. The mind pays it no attention. The ability of the slogan to serve its purpose has come to an end. The slogan has died.

Perhaps the clearest examples of how this works are our national motto "In God We Trust," and the phrase "one nation, under God" in our Pledge of Allegiance. Many Christians seem grateful that, as of this writing, the courts have seen fit to uphold the constitutionality of these phrases, deciding that they do not constitute a governmental endorsement of religion. But any relief Christians experience on this point should be tempered by observing how the courts manage this conclusion. If such theologically-charged phrases are not to be "understood as conveying government approval of particular religious beliefs,"[1] it is only because they have been judicially determined to have "an essentially secular meaning." How could such explicit God-language be deemed purely secular? According to Justice Brennan, these phrases "have lost through rote repetition any significant religious content."[2] They have become dead platitudes, no longer meaning what their words say. According to the court, these slogans now serve no more than a secular civic function.

It's not clear to me that this development represents any great boon to theism in American culture. In fact, it appears to represent the opposite. As John Henry Newman once commented, "Nothing is easier than to use the word, and mean nothing by it." But more to our purposes here, this situation also carries sobering implications for several of the most cherished bywords of Christian higher education.

Consider, for example, the slogan "Christ-centered education." It's one we hear often on the campuses of Christian colleges. In fact, a

---

1. Justice O'Connor, in concurrence *Lynch v. Donnelly,* 465 U.S. 668 (1984), at 693.
2. Justice O'Connor, in dissent *Lynch v. Donnelly,* 465 U.S. 668 (1984), at 716-17.

"Christ-centered mission" is said to be one of the essential hallmarks of the one hundred or so member institutions of the Council for Christian Colleges and Universities (CCCU). Because the slogan seems to summarize what we're about it rolls easily off our tongues. Perhaps too easily. I worry about that.

"Christ-centered education," we say. We like the weight, the heft of the words; they have a strong, reassuring ring of faithfulness to them. But I confess to wondering whether this venerable slogan has died on us, whether it any longer conjures up the crucial ideas it was designed to communicate. When we say that the education we offer is *centered* upon the person of Jesus Christ, do we mean what we say?

The sheer ease and readiness with which we affirm that we do may indicate that we have forgotten how dangerous and out of step this affirmation is. As an educational principle the phrase "Christ-centered education" has all the explosive possibilities of a pin-pulled grenade. Yet we toss it about as if it were benign as an apple. Is it possible we have domesticated the idea to render it more manageable, more acceptable, dumbing it down in the process to little more than an unctuous platitude?

Trinitarian Education

Consider the dual nature of the phrase. It posits an education that is not only Christ-*centered,* a claim we will take up in the following chapter, but also one which is, to shift the emphasis, *Christ*-centered. This is the side of the phrase I wish to address here.

When we speak of an education that is *Christ*-centered, do we really mean that we intend that education to center upon the Second Person of the Trinity? Our language here is very specific. Christians are Trinitarians; we believe the one God subsists in three co-equal Persons: Father, Son, and Holy Spirit. Yet our slogan specifies a *Christ*-centered education. It claims, not the Father, not the Spirit, but the Son as the center of our enterprise. Do we say *Christ*-centered but really mean only the more generic *God*-centered? Or is there some profound sense in which a Christian liberal arts education really is specifically *Son*-centered? And if so, what does this mean? Why would this not constitute a slighting of the Father and the Spirit, one that might border on heresy? In other words, do we really mean it when we affirm that the education we offer is genuinely *Christocentric,* not merely *theocentric?*

It is perhaps shocking to some to learn that the phrase "Christ-centered education" really does mean what it affirms. It speaks of an education that is specifically *Christ*-centered. It posits the Son, the Second Person of the Godhead, as the unifying key to all that humans can know or understand, such that in the end nothing can be adequately grasped apart from him. This is an astonishing claim, one that seems too much even for some Christian educators to swallow.

Perhaps we can sympathize with their reservations. After all, one might object, were we talking about issues of soteriology ("salvation"), or of the Christian life, or of the sort of training for ministry or evangelism one finds in a Bible college or seminary, it might make sense to think of the curriculum being "Christocentric." But if we are about the business of a liberal arts education we cannot thus limit our focus. Our task is not merely training for ministry; we want to expose our students to all the disciplines, to the full range of human experience and learning. We want to build within them an appreciation for God's entire created order, and for the best of what humans have discovered and said about it. We want to expose students to the finest of what humans themselves have created through the centuries. Jesus' death on the cross is certainly indispensable to our salvation, but even to understand the biblical theme of redemption requires that we place it in the broader context of God's purposes in creation, humanity's rebellion and fall, and the restoration that awaits the race and the universe. For that kind of education, surely the limitations of a Christocentric focus will not do.

All of this, I say, one *might* object, but only if one were to fall victim to a sadly truncated Christology. Fifty years ago, J. B. Phillips wrote a little book that warned of too limited a vision of God, entitled *Your God Is Too Small.* In the same way, is it possible that our *Christology* may be too small?

For some, it seems, their understanding of the person and work of Christ scarcely extends beyond the affirmation "Jesus died for me on the cross." They willingly celebrate Jesus as their sin-bearer but without ever comprehending who he really is, or the colossal scope of what he has done, or even what took place on that cross. But for the purposes of Christian higher education, such a stunted Christology will not do. We require a fuller vision, the vision of *Jesus Christ as Lord.*

The Lordship of Christ

From a biblical standpoint, human language can scarcely craft a more profound declaration than this one: *Jesus Christ is Lord.* In fact, this affirmation is so heavily freighted with spiritual and intellectual weight that, according to the Apostle Paul, no one can even utter it sincerely "except by the Holy Spirit" (1 Cor. 12:3). In our own time this declaration thus remains the essential confession of the Christian alone (Rom. 10:9; cf. John 20:28). But the Bible teaches that history is marching toward a very different day. On that day the acknowledgment that "Jesus Christ is Lord" will escape the lips of every created being. On that day, says the Apostle Paul, "at the name of Jesus every knee will bow, in heaven and on earth and under the earth, and every tongue will confess that Jesus Christ is Lord, to the glory of God the Father" (Phil. 2:9-11).

What do we mean by the Lordship of Christ? To speak of his Lordship is for some to speak at once of personal matters: *Jesus is Lord of my life.* This is understandable, because this surely is the ultimate issue every human being must face. But if we are to think biblically, we must remember that the question of one's personal allegiance to Christ is just that: the final issue. It is not where we must begin. The place to begin is with the person of Jesus himself; that is, we must come to grips with who this One is who makes such all-encompassing claims upon our allegiance.

In his famous sermon on the Day of Pentecost, Peter summarized his central point this way: "Let all the house of Israel . . . know assuredly that God has made him both Lord and Christ, this Jesus whom you crucified" (Acts 2:36). Later, in one of the most elevated passages in all of Scripture, a passage Martin Marty called "a fundamental charter for church-related higher education,"[3] the Apostle Paul elaborates upon this same affirmation. Jesus Christ, he says, is "the image of the invisible God, the first-born of all creation; for in him all things were created, in heaven and on earth, visible and invisible, whether thrones or dominions or principalities or authorities — all things were created through him and for him. He is before all things, and in him all things hold together" (Col. 1:15-17).

3. "The Church and Christian Higher Education in the New Millennium," in *Faithful Learning and the Christian Scholarly Vocation,* ed. Douglas V. Henry and Bob R. Agee (Grand Rapids: Eerdmans, 2003), p. 51.

Creator of All Things

It is quite impossible to overstate the significance of these affirmations. According to the Bible, as God's Son, the Second Person of the Godhead whom we know as Jesus Christ is, first, the creator of all things. The created order is specifically his handiwork.

But wait; has Christ's Church not always affirmed that God the Father is "maker of heaven and earth"? We do, and in this we merely echo the heavenly chorus: "Worthy are you, our Lord and our God, to receive glory and honor and power; for you created all things, and because of your will they existed and were created" (Rev. 4:11). But notice that it was specifically the Second Person of the Godhead *through whom* the Father effected his creating activities. Thus the writer to the Hebrews is able to say that "in these last days [the Father] has spoken to us in his Son, . . . through whom also he made the world" (Heb. 1:2). "In [Christ] all things were created, in heaven and on earth, visible and invisible, whether thrones or dominions or principalities or authorities — all things were created through him" (Col. 1:16). In fact, insists the Gospel of John, this was without exception: "All things were made through him, and without him was not anything made that was made" (John 1:3, 10).

Sustainer of All Things

As the world's creator the Son is not only "before all things," but "in him all things hold together." The one who created the world is also the one who sustains it. It is the Son who "upholds all things by the word of his power" (Heb. 1:3). Apart from the presence of sin and its effects, the universe is the way it is because the Son has said it shall be so. By the will of the Father the Son is the world's composer, and it is the Son's infinite word and will that holds it the way it is. The entire created order is contingent upon him at every point and in every moment. We may delight to exercise our God-given curiosity in discovering how the world works, and we honor him when we do so. But even when we have done our best and have probed deeply into the workings of the universe, we are forever left with the perplexing question such probing can never answer: *Why?* This is the way things work, but *why* do they work this way? The Bible's answer sends us back to the Son. The universe works the way it does because, in the end, the Son has ordained that it shall be so.

Goal of All Things

This same Son is also the *goal* of all things. Not only were all things created *"by* him"; they were also created *"for* him" (Col. 1:16). The nuances of Paul's language here are striking. We might say, "This gift is for Mrs. Smith" and mean by it only that Mrs. Smith is to be the recipient. What Paul is saying includes this but is also stronger. It has almost a sense of motion to it: The universe is "for Christ" in the sense of being "unto him, toward him." From the beginning it was the Father's purpose that the Son should be appointed "heir of all things" (Heb. 1:2). This ultimate purpose — this "summing up of all things in Christ, things in the heavens and things on the earth" (Eph. 1:9-10) — literally *delighted* the Father; it was his "good pleasure" *(eudokia),* says Paul. Somehow, in ways we can scarcely imagine, the universe is groaning toward the Son, leaning into its eschatological fulfillment in him. He is at once its destination and its destiny, its goal and its blessed hope.

Redeemer of All Things

And to all of this, of course, must be added the Son's role as redeemer. "When the fullness of the time came, God sent forth his Son" (Gal. 4:4). The Creation could be salvaged from its sin and brokenness only by God himself becoming part of it, and this task was assigned by the Father to the Second Person of the Godhead. It was the Father's intent, we are told, "to reconcile all things to himself" through the work of his Son, "whether things on earth or things in heaven" (Col. 1:20). Where before there was brokenness and alienation between God and a cosmos defiled by human sin, the Son introduced the possibility of peace "through the blood of his cross." The agent of the old creation was to become the agent of the new. This required the Son to leave the courts of heaven and take upon himself human flesh. The famous "emptying" *(kenosis)* passage in Philippians 2 describes the journey: "Though he was in the form of God, [the Son] did not count equality with God a thing to be grasped, but emptied himself, taking the form of a servant, being born in the likeness of men. And being found in human form he humbled himself and became obedient unto death, even death on a cross."

This is the incomparable story of Christmas, the account of the Son's incarnation. "Behold, the virgin shall be with child, and bear a Son, and they shall call his name *Immanuel,* which is translated, 'God with us'" (Matt. 1:23). And thus shall the Son ever be known: as the God-man. "The Word became flesh and dwelt among us, and we beheld his glory, the glory as of the only begotten of the Father, full of grace and truth" (John 1:14). Charles Wesley's lovely Christmas hymn, "Hark! the Herald Angels Sing," captures it perfectly: "Veiled in flesh the God-head see;/Hail the incarnate Deity."

Judge of All Things

Recall what follows immediately in the above *kenosis* passage, for it drives us on to another dimension of the Son: having recounted Christ's costly journey from the glories of heaven to a humiliating and excruciating death on a cross, the Apostle continues: "*Therefore* God has highly exalted him and bestowed on him the name which is above every name, that at the name of Jesus every knee should bow, in heaven and on earth and under the earth, and every tongue confess that Jesus Christ is Lord, to the glory of God the Father."

Because the Son had left nothing undone of his assignment, the Father was able to say Yes to one of the Son's last earthly requests. In the Upper Room Jesus prayed, "I glorified you on the earth, having accomplished the work you gave me to do; now, Father, will you glorify me together with yourself by re-clothing me with the glory I had with you before the world began?" (John 17:4-5). Because the Son had in fact fulfilled all the Father assigned him, the "emptying" was reversed; the Son was given back the full panoply of glory he'd enjoyed with the Father throughout eternity. He will remain forever the God-man, but to-day he sits clothed, not in the humble garments of a Galilean peasant but with the inexpressible splendors of heaven. "From thence," the great creeds of the Church tell us, "he shall come to judge the living and the dead."

"Truly, truly, I say to you." It was Jesus' standard way of seizing our attention, of impressing upon us the need to listen: "An hour is coming and now is, when the dead will hear the voice of the Son of God. . . . I can do nothing on my own initiative. As I hear, I judge; and my judgment is just, because I do not seek my own will, but the will of him who sent me" (John 5:24-30). "Behold," says John, "he is coming with clouds, and every eye will see him, even they who pierced him. And all the tribes of the earth will mourn because of him" (Rev. 1:7). On that day history will have reached its denouement. The redeeming work of the Son will be completed. The heavens and the earth will be refashioned and the Son will present to the Father a people for his name and a creation made new (1 Cor. 15:24).

Centrality of the Son

These are just some of the claims the Bible makes for this One we know as Jesus Christ. We have not even touched on his roles as prophet, priest, or "Head of the body, the Church" (Col. 1:18; Eph. 1:22). To Christians Jesus is "the firstborn from the dead," the One who "loved us and washed us from our sins in his own blood, and has made us kings and priests to his God and Father" (Rev. 1:5-6); he is the suffering servant, teacher, and reconciler who serves as the believer's pattern and guide. But our focus for the moment has been broader, on Christ's relationship to the created order. And what an astounding picture it is.

The Bible's claims for the person of Jesus Christ are breathtaking. "He is the radiance of [the Father's] glory and the exact representation of his nature" (Heb. 1:3). "In him all the fullness of deity dwells bodily" (Col. 2:9). "He is the image of the invisible God, the firstborn of all creation" (Col. 1:15). It is the Father's will that "in all things [the Son] may have the preeminence" (Col. 1:18). Indeed, here are the Father's own words to his beloved Son: "To the Son he says: 'Your throne, O God, is forever and ever. . . . In the beginning you laid the foundation of the earth and the heavens are the work of your hands. They will perish, but you remain. They will all grow old like a garment; like a cloak you will fold them up and they will be changed. But you are the same and your years will not fail'" (Heb. 1:8-12).

The mind reels: Jesus Christ, the divine *Logos,* the central principle and principal of the universe; the Word who "became flesh and dwelt among us, and we beheld his glory, the glory as of the only begotten of the Father, full of grace and truth" (John 1:14). Jesus is "the ruler over the kings of the earth" (Rev. 1:5), the centerpiece of human history. We are in over our heads.

"All authority has been given to me in heaven and on earth" (Matt. 28:18), said Jesus. He could make this claim only because it was true. "The Father loves the Son, and has given all things into his hands" (John 3:35). The Father constituted him "head over all rule and authority" in the universe (Col. 2:10). All life and light, whatever their proximate sources, flow ultimately from him: "In him was life, and the life was the light of men. . . . He is the true Light which, coming into the world, enlightens every man" (John 1:4, 9). All understanding has its source in him in whom "are hidden all the treasures of wisdom and knowledge" (Col. 2:3). He is the Way, the Truth, the Life, such that no one can come to the Father except through him (John 14:6). Could such language be more far-reaching? John Stott says, "The highest of all missionary motives is neither obedience to the Great Commission . . . nor love for sinners . . . , but rather zeal — burning and passionate zeal — for the glory of Jesus Christ. . . . Only one imperialism is Christian . . . and that is concern for His Imperial Majesty Jesus Christ, and for the glory of his empire or kingdom."[4]

All authority, all life, all light, all wisdom, all things — all summed up in the person of Jesus Christ. John Stackhouse, Jr., observes, "The person and work of Christ do not merely crown God's work of revelation and redemption as a sort of splendid ornament or even as the best example of God's activity in the world. The person and work of Christ constitute the defining chapter of the whole narrative, the hinge of history, the basis upon which everything else in creation makes sense."[5] Jesus Christ stands at the center of all humans can know or experience, and from that exalted center he proclaims, "I am the Alpha and the Omega, the first and the last, the beginning and the end" (Rev. 22:13).

---

4. *Romans: God's Good News for the World* (Downers Grove: InterVarsity, 1994), p. 53; cf. John Stott, *Basic Christian Leadership* (Downers Grove: InterVarsity Press, 2002), p. 37.

5. *Evangelical Landscapes: Facing Critical Issues of the Day* (Grand Rapids: Baker, 2002), p. 166.

The disciples asked, "Who then is this that even wind and sea obey him?" The Bible's answer: Jesus Christ is Lord!

What becomes clear from even this cursory review of what revelation teaches about Jesus, and what his church has always believed and proclaimed, is that the Son is the primary designated agent of the Father for virtually everything concerning the created order. The Apostle Paul expresses it this way: The Father is the One "*from* whom are all things and *for* whom we exist," while the Son, the Lord Jesus Christ, is the One "*through* whom are all things and *through* whom we exist" (1 Cor. 8:6). The Son called the universe into existence and he sustains it by his word. At the behest of his Father he ultimately and permanently joined that creation in order to redeem it. One day he will return to judge it and to restore it to all that it was intended to be. When John says, "No one has ever seen God; the only-begotten Son, who is in the bosom of the Father, he has made him known" (John 1:18), he is speaking of Jesus and his point is that it is the Son, the Second Person of the Godhead, who preeminently manifests the Father to the world: "No one knows the Father except the Son and those to whom the Son chooses to reveal him" (Matt. 11:27). He is the unique interface, the central point where the universe and the Godhead meet. He is the Father's appointed mediator for dealing with the world: its formation, its sustenance, its redemption, and its restoration.

All of this is what Paul has in mind when he informs us that the central affirmation of the Christian is "Jesus is Lord" (1 Cor. 12:3). It is an outrageous claim — unless it is true. But if it is true, as Christians do affirm, then it means that the person of Jesus is utterly central to all that humans can know or experience.[6] There is nothing imaginable that is irrelevant to him or to which he is irrelevant. There is no quarter of human learning in which he is not the central figure. Without him humans will never make full sense of either their world or themselves. That's why Paul says that in Jesus Christ are to be found "all the treasures of wisdom and knowledge" (Col. 2:3). In the end he is the key to all we can know (Luke 11:52) and nothing can be fully grasped without reference to him.

6. Hence the title of James Orr's classic work, *The Christian View of God and the World, as Centering in the Incarnation* (Grand Rapids: Eerdmans, 1947). "No one will dispute that, if Jesus Christ is what the creeds declare Him to be — an Incarnation of the Divine — His Person is necessarily central in His own religion, nay, in the universe" (p. 39).

A Potential Objection

One response to all of this might be to suspect that such a Christ-centered focus poses a theological problem. There are those who hold a modalistic "Jesus only" theology that constitutes a denial of the Trinity. But the Bible teaches no such thing, and the Church long ago branded such an idea heretical. Since the earliest Church Councils every major branch of Christendom has held that the Trinity consists of three eternal, co-equal Persons, one in substance but distinct in subsistence.

But if the three Persons of the Trinity are co-equal, does not a "Christ-centered" focus constitute an imbalanced emphasis and thus an insult to the Father and Spirit?

Surely not. It was precisely the Father's design that the Son should play this central role in the created order. Again, it is the Father's *delight*, his "good pleasure," that his Son should have preeminence in everything (Col. 1:18). Nothing gladdens the Father more than to see his Son receive this kind of prominence. To confess the magnificent Lordship of Jesus Christ is not to slight the Father; it is to glorify him (Phil. 2:11).

The notion of the Father being slighted by our focus on the Son represents a grotesque misunderstanding of the relationships among the members of the Godhead. It foists upon the triune God a sinful, human pattern by presuming there could exist a breach of envy or jealousy within the Trinity. But such a rupture is impossible. The Father and Son are one (John 10:30). This was Jesus' point to the disciples when, despite the years they'd spent with him, they still pressed him to "show us the Father." For this Jesus rebuked them: "Have I been so long with you and yet you do not know me?" asked Jesus. "He who has seen me has seen the Father" (John 14:9). To honor the Son is to honor the Father; to believe in the Jesus of the Bible is to believe in God. As Jesus said, "He who believes in me, believes not in me but in him who sent me. And he who sees me sees him who sent me" (John 12:44-45). The Apostle Peter sums it up this way: "Through [Jesus Christ] you believe in God, who raised him from the dead and glorified him, and so your faith and hope are in God" (1 Peter 1:21).

The Apostolic witness is clear: "Whoever acknowledges the Son has the Father also" (1 John 2:23). Conversely, as Jesus also said, "He who rejects me, rejects the One who sent me" (Luke 10:16). The Father allows no possibility of a stance that accepts him but rejects the Son. On the contrary, "He who does not honor the Son does not honor the Father who sent him" (John 5:23). To repudiate the Son is by definition to repudiate the Father (cf. 1 John 5:1, 10-12).

But what of the Holy Spirit? Does a Christocentric focus slight the Third Person of the Trinity? In a similar way we may be sure that it does not. The Spirit's assignment in the world is multi-faceted — regenerating, indwelling, sanctifying, revealing, empowering, comforting, even creating (Gen. 1:2, Ps. 104:30) — and is worthy of fuller understanding in its own right. But there can be no rupture here either. Whatever else the Father assigned to the Spirit, his role in the world is explicitly Christ-centered, as Jesus himself points out: "When the Counselor comes, whom I shall send to you from the Father, even the Spirit of truth, who proceeds from the Father, he will bear witness to me. . . . He will glorify me, for he will take what is mine and declare it to you. All that the Father has is mine; therefore I said that he will take what is mine and declare it to you" (John 15:26–16:15). As Stackhouse says, "The Holy Spirit remains — despite some impressive expositions by evangelicals of late — a relatively minor, shadowy figure in the New Testament compared with the center stage, fully lit person of Jesus."[7] But that is by design. The central aim of the Spirit is not to draw attention; it is to show us the Son, to "glorify" him. Stackhouse's reference to the "fully lit person of Jesus" suggests the image of perhaps a floodlight shining on a church steeple at night. The floodlight is not designed to draw attention to itself, but to display the steeple. So also the Father-assigned role of the Spirit is not to garner attention but to reveal and glorify the Son. The Spirit is scarcely slighted when we look to the Son; it is the Spirit's essential purpose in the world to help us do precisely that.

For Christians, it can be a serious theological mistake to try to replace the centrality of Jesus Christ with the centrality of the Holy Spirit. In fact, *Dominus Iesus,* a declaration of the Roman Catholic Congregation for the Doctrine of the Faith (August 6, 2000), strongly challenges those who, embarrassed by the exclusivity inherent in such strong Christocentric claims, have argued for an "economy of the Holy

7. Stackhouse, *Evangelical Landscapes,* pp. 168-69.

46

Spirit with a more universal breadth than that of the Incarnate Word" (II.12). In such a scheme Jesus Christ is subsumed under the Holy Spirit and taken to be merely one of the many ways the Holy Spirit is active in the world. Such a move displaces the Son from the center and renders the work of the Holy Spirit central. *Dominus Iesus* rightly repudiates this idea, insisting instead upon the historically orthodox Christ-centered focus that, when understood in its biblical fullness, shows itself to be fully trinitarian.

This Son-centered focus represents the historic stance of all three branches of the Christian Church. It has marked the Church's worship from the most ancient times. All the great councils and creeds give it testimony. Here is not the place to attempt an historical survey, but by way of simple illustration consider just the two most ancient and widely used creeds of the Church, the Nicene and the Apostles' Creeds. The Nicene Creed is twice as long as the Apostles' Creed, but the proportion both statements allocate to the Persons of the Trinity remains relatively uniform. By word count the Father receives 5 percent and 12 percent of the attention respectively, and the Spirit 16 percent and 6 percent. But the Son receives 59 percent and 64 percent. This is not because these creeds, or historic Christianity for that matter, ever considered the Son more important than the Father or the Spirit. All Christians worship one God who subsists in three co-equal Persons. It is due rather to the biblical emphasis we have cited above. The Son does not *eclipse* the Father and the Spirit; he *reveals* them, "for in him all the fullness of the Godhead *(theotes)* dwells in bodily form" (Col. 2:9; cf. 1:19). It was the Father's design that not just the Christian faith, but the entire cosmos he created, be profoundly Son-centered. This is the message of the Scriptures, a truth the Church has recognized from the beginning.

Christ-Centered Education

When we speak of a *"Christ*-centered education," therefore, it is crucial that we ask ourselves: Is this the Person we have in mind? Or is our Christology truncated and partial, a diminished thing too slight to fulfill its all-encompassing and organizing role?

The hypothetical conversation I described above is unfortunately not so hypothetical. It's modeled on conversations I've actually had. "If we were a Bible college or a seminary," I have heard on more than one occasion, "intent upon training people for missions, evangelism or church ministry, such an emphasis on Christology might make sense. But we're a liberal arts institution. We want to expose our students to the full range of human learning and experience, to all the disciplines, to God's vast created order. For us such a narrow focus would not be sufficient."

Perhaps I have misunderstood this argument. Maybe it's designed to make a point I've missed. But I suspect not. More likely it reveals a truncated Christology, a Christology which appears to entail little more than "Jesus died for me on the cross." It views Jesus as simply the world's divine sin-bearer. Such a focus would therefore be appropriate for training students for "evangelism" perhaps, but it would be insufficient for the expansiveness of a Christian liberal arts curriculum.

At one level, I have sympathy for this response. The cross of Jesus Christ is properly *crucial* — the very *crux* (from the Latin *cruces,* or "cross,") — to all we can know or be as Christians, and I have not the slightest interest in seeing it dislodged from that privileged position. Indeed, I will insist as loudly as any upon its centrality. But what seems to me lacking in this analysis is the full weight and sweep of what the biblical revelation tells us about *who it was* who was hung on that Roman cross. But without that fuller picture, can we truly understand the cross? Can we even begin to identify with the astonishment of the Apostle John when he informs us that the Second Person of the Godhead "was in the world, and the world was made by him — *yet the world did not know him*" (John 1:10). Or the outrage of Peter, and the dumbfounded grief of his Pentecostal listeners, when he proclaimed to them the shocking news that "God has made him both Lord and Christ, *this Jesus whom you crucified*" (Acts 2:36)? "Do you have any idea," Peter in effect asks, "who you executed on that cross? You have *killed* the Lord of Glory!"

One way to assess our own understanding of these issues is by thinking about how we picture Jesus. On those occasions when we conjure up an image of Jesus, what does he look like? Most of us probably picture him along the lines of the countless drawings, paintings, and Sunday School images we've seen. It's been estimated that Walter Sallman's well-known painting of the "Head of Jesus" is the most duplicated work in the history of art. This and every other artist's conception has left us with a common image: a man with dark, longish hair, a full beard, dressed in the garments of a Galilean peasant, perhaps teaching others or standing with children gathered about him.

Yet every one of these renderings is merely the product of someone's imagination. We do not know what Jesus looked like. It is perhaps startling to realize that, while we have four Gospels targeted on the person of Jesus Christ, each one designed to tell us what we need to know about him, not one of them provides a physical description of his appearance. We know he wore a beard — they plucked it out at his crucifixion. Or that he wore sandals — John said he was not worthy to untie them. But beyond these incidental glimpses we have no idea how the man we know as Jesus looked. Was he tall or short? Was he barrel-chested, or thin and frail? Did he have dark skin, or light? The truth is, we don't know. In fact, to my knowledge there was not even an early-church tradition about Jesus' appearance. There existed an early tradition about the appearance of the Apostle Paul — short, bald, crooked-legged, strong body, hooked nose (*Acts of Paul and Thecla* 3) — but we have no corresponding tradition about the physical appearance of Jesus.

But if the Gospels leave no physical portrait of the earthly Jesus, that is not to say we are left with no depiction at all. The Apostle John provides a vivid description:

> I was in the Spirit on the Lord's day, and I heard behind me a loud voice like a trumpet. . . . Then I turned to see the voice that was speaking to me, and on turning I saw seven golden lampstands, and in the midst of the lampstands one like a son of man, clothed with a long robe and with a golden girdle round his breast; his head and his hair were white as white wool, white as snow; his eyes were like a flame of fire, his feet were like burnished bronze, refined as in a furnace, and his voice was like the sound of many waters; in his right hand he held seven stars, from his mouth issued a sharp two-edged sword, and his face was like the sun shining in full strength. When I saw him, I fell at his feet as though dead. But he laid his right hand upon me, saying, "Fear not, I am the first and the last, and the living one; I died, and behold I am alive forevermore, and I have the keys of Death and Hades. (Rev. 1:10-18)

Few of us are likely to picture Jesus as John (or Paul, for that matter; cf. Acts 9:3; 22:6; 26:12) saw him. We usually imagine him as he is portrayed in the Gospels, a humble Galilean peasant. And rightly so. The Jesus of the Gospels is for us, and we will never outgrow our need for him. He is the one who left us an example that we might follow in his footsteps (1 Pet. 2:21). We are to study him and imitate him; we are to think like him, speak like him, act like him, live like him. But it is also important to observe that Jesus does not appear today the way he did in the Gospels. A theological watershed was crossed when the Father answered Jesus' Upper Room prayer (John 17:1-5) by returning him to the glory he had with the Father before the world began. Within hours of praying this private prayer Jesus publicly announced, *"From now on the Son of Man will be seated at the right hand of the power of God"* (Luke 22:69). Thus the only Jesus we know, the only Jesus we have ever talked to, the Jesus we serve, is the Jesus after this prayer, not the Jesus before this prayer, the Jesus who is seated at the right hand of the Father. It is the same Jesus, to be sure, but the acknowledgment of this watershed theological event, this "from now on," is nonetheless an important one for our own understanding of who it is we serve.

It may be no accident that the only fulsome description of Jesus we have in the Bible is that of the exalted Jesus of heaven. The impression begins to form that if anything, *this* is the way the Father wishes us to picture him — Creator, Sustainer, Incarnate Redeemer, the Goal of All Things, the Glorious Lamb of God who sits upon the Throne. The exalted Son of God is the One who took upon himself flesh and "humbled himself by becoming obedient to the point of death, even death on a cross," leaving us the ultimate paradigm for our own lives. What's more, this is the One who promised to stay at our side always, even unto the end of the age (Matthew 28:20). He is the majestic Jesus of heaven, and his glory is such today that if we were suddenly to see him as he is, as did John, his closest earthly friend, we, like John, would fall at his feet as though dead, utterly overwhelmed. All of this — the earthly Christ of the Gospels, but also the heavenly Jesus of today — is the One we affirm when we express the most profound claim a human being can utter: *Jesus Christ is Lord!* And all of this is what we mean, or at least should mean, when we speak of a *Christ*-centered education.

Christ and Scholarship

This Christ-centered focus carries with it critical implications for Christian thinkers. For instance, there exists a tendency within Christian scholarship in some circles to approach Christian thinking by abstracting from the Bible some of its grand theological motifs — creation, fall, incarnation, redemption, restoration — and then reflecting on how these themes shape our thinking about everything else. While on its face this would seem unobjectionable, such an approach is potentially problematic, on two counts. First, in focusing on these grand biblical themes, such an approach sometimes falls into the trap of leaving the actual text of the Bible behind, which is a mistake in its own right. But second, and more germane to our present concern, this approach also sometimes appears to obscure the fulsome role of the Son. In such a scheme we may find ourselves studying these themes as if they can be understood apart from Jesus. We allow ourselves to speak generically of God's creation, the effects of sin, and of the final restoration of all things. Christ takes center stage only when we arrive at the Incarnation and our focus turns to the cross. Otherwise the Second Person of the Godhead appears to play relatively little role.

A striking example of this can be found in a work we have already twice mentioned — a book Jaroslav Pelikan called "the most important treatise on the idea of the university ever written in any language"[8] — John Henry Newman's classic, *The Idea of a University*. As David Livingstone reminds us, "While Newman's later educational interpreters have tended to focus on his conception of a liberal education, . . . of no less significance to Newman was his defense of the place of theology in the curriculum."[9] This explains Newman's two long discourses on the "Bearing of Theology on Other Branches of Knowledge" and the "Bearing of Other Branches of Knowledge on Theology." God stands at the very center of all we can know, says Newman, so how could we leave him out?

> I lay it down that all knowledge forms one whole, because its subject matter is one; for the universe in its length and breadth is so inti-

8. Jaroslav Pelikan, *The Idea of the University: A Reexamination* (New Haven & London: Yale University Press, 1992), p. 9.
9. David N. Livingstone, "The Idea of a University: Interventions from Ireland," *Christian Scholar's Review* 30, no. 2 (Winter 2000): 190.

mately knit together, that we cannot separate off portion from portion, and operation from operation, except by a mental abstraction; and then again, as to its Creator, though He of course in His own Being is infinitely separate from it, and Theology has its departments towards which human knowledge has no relations, yet He has so implicated Himself with it, and taken it into His very bosom, by His presence in it, His providence over it, His impressions upon it, and His influences through it, that we cannot truly or fully contemplate it without in some main aspects contemplating Him.[10]

Newman believed the study of theology could scarcely be excluded from a balanced curriculum. What does he mean by theology? He offers a very "modern" definition to his very "modern" audience: "I simply mean the Science of God, or the truths we know about God put into a system."[11] Then there follows a long, multi-page section spelling out the details. It's a powerful theological disquisition, and far too long to quote, but here are a few samples:

I mean, for this is the main point, that, as in the human frame there is a living principle, acting upon it and through it by means of volition, so, behind the veil of the visible universe, there is an invisible, intelligent Being, acting on and through it, as and when He will. Further, I mean that this invisible Agent is in no sense a soul of the world, after the analogy of human nature, but, on the contrary, is absolutely distinct from the world, as being its Creator, Upholder, Governor, and Sovereign Lord. . . . I mean then by the Supreme Being, one who is simply self-dependent, and the only Being who is such; moreover, that He is without beginning or Eternal, and the only Eternal; that in consequence He has lived a whole eternity by Himself; and hence that He is all-sufficient, sufficient for His own blessedness, and all-blessed, and ever-blessed. Further, I mean a Being, who, having these prerogatives, has the Supreme Good, or rather is the Supreme Good, or has all the attributes of Good in infinite intenseness; all wisdom, all truth, all justice, all love, all holiness, all beautifulness; who is omnipotent, omniscient,

10. *The Idea of a University*, ed. Martin J. Svaglic (Notre Dame: University of Notre Dame Press, 1982), p. 38.

11. Newman, *The Idea of a University*, p. 46.

omnipresent; ineffably one, absolutely perfect; and such, that what we do not know and cannot even imagine of Him, is far more wonderful than what we do and can. I mean One who is sovereign over His own will and actions, though always according to the eternal Rule of right and wrong, which is Himself. I mean, moreover, that He created all things out of nothing, and preserves them every moment, and could destroy them as easily as He made them. . . . And further, He has stamped upon all things, in the hour of their creation, their respective natures, and has given them their work and mission and their length of appointed place. I mean, too, that He is ever present with His works, one by one, and confronts everything He has made by His particular and most loving Providence, and manifests Himself to each according to its needs; and has on rational beings imprinted the moral law, and given them power to obey it, imposing on them the duty of worship and service, searching and scanning them through and through with His omniscient eye, and putting before them a present trial and a judgment to come.

Such is what Theology teaches about God, a doctrine, as the very idea of its subject-matter presupposes, so mysterious as in its fullness to lie beyond any system, and in particular aspects to be simply external to nature, and to seem in parts even to be irreconcilable with itself, the imagination being unable to embrace what the reason determines. It teaches of a Being infinite, yet personal; all-blessed, yet ever operative; absolutely separate from the creature, yet in every part of the creation at every moment; above all things, yet under every thing. It teaches of a Being who, though the highest, yet in the work of creation, conservation, government, retribution, makes Himself, as it were, the minister and servant of all; who, though inhabiting eternity, allows Himself to take an interest, and to have a sympathy, in the matters of space and time.[12]

Now the Second Person of the Godhead appears nowhere in this picture, nor in the unquoted remainder. But this was by design. At the end Newman says, "I have been insisting simply on Natural Theology, and that, because I wished to carry along with me those who were not Catholics, and, again, as being confident, that no one can really set himself to master and to teach the doctrine of an intelligent Creator in

12. Newman, *The Idea of a University,* pp. 46-48.

its fullness, without going on a great deal farther than he at present dreams."[13] Newman intentionally avoided speaking in a distinctively Christian way, both because of his diverse audience and because he was confident that anyone willing to contemplate the God he put forward would likely be drawn further into this truth than intended. But the question to be raised here is, Did Newman, or for that matter do we, have any business bracketing Christ out in this way?

The answer is, if our thinking is to be *distinctively* Christian, no. Newman was aware that he was not lining out a specifically Christian stance. Distinctively Christian thinking takes place at the level of the Trinity, where the person of Jesus Christ stands at the Father-ordained center. How could we bracket him out without losing our uniquely Christian focus? Or to reverse the thought, "How else does something qualify as Christian if it does not bear some direct relationship to the Word incarnate, who is only revealed in the word inscripturated?"[14] Consider, for example, how such abstract themes as the origin and governance of the universe, God's immanence, his personhood, his love as "minister and servant of all" take on life and are given a face when fleshed out in the light of a fully biblical Christology. Think of how much richer and more concrete Newman's points become when followed through to their Christocentric core. This kind of follow-through is the mark of *distinctively* Christian thinking. As we will observe below, such bracketing out may sometimes be justified in our communication with non-Christians — as, for example, by Newman — but it must never be bracketed from our thinking.

I do not propose that we de-emphasize the immense theological themes of the Bible, much less displace them. They are indeed the grand motifs of the Christian faith and we can scarcely overstate their importance. But if our thinking is to be distinctively *Christian,* a more biblical approach requires that we insist upon retaining the profound Christ-centeredness of each of these themes; indeed, that we view each of them through the prism of Christology. The theme of Creation? Certainly, but who was the agent through whom all things were made, such that nothing which exists came into being apart from him? The

13. Newman, *The Idea of a University,* p. 52.
14. D. G. Hart, "When Disrespect Is Respectful," *Books and Culture,* January/February 2003, p. 6.

fall and the redemption it necessitated? By all means, but who was it who was sent to join the created order as the sinless Second Adam, and to give himself on its behalf so as to redeem it? The final judgment and restoration of all things? Absolutely, but who is the One who will drive history to its denouement, stand in judgment over the nations, preside over the remaking of the heavens and the earth and finally "deliver the kingdom to God the Father" (1 Cor. 15:24)? The answer in each case is the divine Son of God, Jesus Christ.

In studying Christ and his work we are inevitably drawn into the grand themes of the Bible. Such a Christological focus will not exhaust these themes, for if we are to do justice to the Trinity the Father and the Spirit must be present in our thinking as well. But in the end it is vital to remember that by the Father's design, Jesus Christ stands at the *center* of each of these great biblical motifs. We will not understand them aright apart from giving due emphasis to the Son. To consider these themes without carrying them through to their Christ-centered fullness leaves our thinking short. And if this be so, still less satisfying will be lesser schemes such as Mark Schwehn's, wherein the "constitutive beliefs" of Christian education — that is, those beliefs which "constitute" or make our education identifiably Christian — are identified as little more than abstract concepts such as "unity," "universality," "integrity," and "vocation."[15]

Intrinsic Motives

Many thinkers aspire to Christian scholarship from a sincere desire to fulfill, at least in part, the so-called "creation mandate." They desire to transform the world for Christ. Their goal is nothing less than the Christianization of culture and society and the thinking of the academy — not by force, mind you, but by the sheer depth, integrity and winsomeness of our intellectual or artistic work. Arthur Holmes sounds this note when he says, "To capture for Christ the modern mind, its attitudes and ideas concerning science, the arts and society, is both integral to the biblical mandate and crucial to future his-

15. "The Christian University: Defining the Difference," *Current Issues in Catholic Higher Education* 20, no. 2 (Spring 2000): 11-26.

tory."[16] Charles Malik put the challenge even more succinctly: "If you win the whole world and lose the mind of the world, you will soon discover you have not won the world."[17]

I heartily embrace this magnificent aspiration. Christians are to be salt and light in their culture. We are to make every difference for Christ we are able, not merely by spreading the good news of the Gospel, which is crucial, but also by exerting a Christian influence in the arts, in politics, in the media, in the academy. Like the Resistance in Vichy France, we are to be about the business of reclaiming for its rightful Governor every dimension of this currently occupied territory.

Yet I also want to be careful with this sort of talk, not merely because I may be more wary than some about what we should expect of our efforts, but also because this kind of thinking can readily degenerate into a form of triumphalism the world rightly looks upon with suspicion. It is language that can begin to sound like an imperialistic desire for hegemony in the culture. George Marsden says,

> Today's intellectual environment is far more pluralistic and we are fortunate to have available a developed intellectual tradition that is suited to taking account of the implications of that pluralism. Today I think it is much clearer than it was forty years ago that evangelicals do not have to take over the old Protestant agenda of dominating Western civilization or world civilization. Although we have benefited immensely from those who introduced this community to various versions of this Kuyperianism, I think it is clear that we no longer have to talk of remaking the mind of Western civilization. Rather, we should give up our vestigial establishmentarianism and accept our status as one community (or coalition of communities) within civilization. This is, I think, a healthier position for the church anyway.[18]

16. "Toward a Christian View of Things," in *The Making of a Christian Mind,* ed. Arthur Holmes (Downers Grove: InterVarsity Press, 1985), p. 11. For a Roman Catholic understanding of this enterprise, see Francis E. George, "Evangelizing American Culture," in *The New Catholic Evangelization,* ed. Kenneth Boyack (New York: Paulist Press, 1992), pp. 42-55.

17. *The Two Tasks* (Wheaton: Billy Graham Center, 2000), p. 42.

18. George Marsden, "The State of Evangelical Christian Scholarship," *Christian Scholar's Review* 17, no. 4 (1988): 356.

I am highly motivated to be about the business of cultivating our minds and our learning, but it seems to me that our first motives for doing so must be intrinsic rather than instrumental. In other words, we must learn to love God with our minds, to use our artistic gifts for Christ, to embody him in serving our neighbor and our society. But our primary motive for doing so must not be the transformation of culture. Our prime motive must be *obedience to Jesus Christ.* Then, if the living Christ graciously chooses to use our efforts to mold our culture into more of what he wants it to be, we will be grateful. On the other hand, if he does not so choose — and let us be clear about it, he does not always so choose — and the culture remains resistant, even hostile, to our Christian influence, we must not be cast down. Our motivation is not dependent on the acceptance and approval of our culture; in the end we care preeminently about the approval of Jesus Christ. Our goal is to love God with our minds, whether the culture comes to appreciate our efforts or not.

A helpful image here, I think, is that of Daniel in Babylon. This young man, probably still in his teens, was surrounded by an alien culture that had little tolerance for his monotheistic allegiance to Yahweh. Yet that allegiance was not for Daniel negotiable. He was determined to remain faithful to the Lord whatever the consequences. So he set out to make his way in Babylon.

Daniel was not looking for confrontation. He bore no chips on his shoulder and at all times seemed to behave with a lovely respectfulness toward the Babylonians, especially the King. Yet Daniel's preexisting allegiance never wavered. In the opening chapter, for example, that allegiance prevented him from eating meat that had been dedicated to idols. But Daniel looked for a compromise, a strategy that turned out well. He sought only to live faithfully to the Lord in the midst of a people who thought and operated very differently.

And what was the result? Because of his sheer excellence and integrity — characteristics which were the *result* of his unalloyed allegiance to God — by the end of the first chapter Daniel is found to be ten times better than the wise men of Babylon. By the end of the second chapter the Babylonian king is granting him "high honors and many great gifts." In fact, the king sets him as "ruler over the whole province of Babylon, and chief prefect over all the wise men of Babylon." On the other hand, there was also that unpleasant business of Daniel's three friends in the fiery furnace in Daniel 3, and by chapter 6 we find Daniel himself surrounded by ravenous lions. But no matter. He was the same Daniel, driven by the same allegiance, whatever the circumstances. His head was unturned by the shallow tributes of the culture — "You may keep your gifts for yourself and give your reward to someone else," he says to the besotted Belshazzar in chapter 5 — but he was equally undaunted by its ill treatment. Daniel was driven by intrinsic, not extrinsic, motives.

In his beautifully written and insightful book on *The Arctic,* Barry Lopez reports that in the far northern waters different types of ice, though side by side, will sometimes appear to be flowing in opposite directions. This is not, however, merely an optical illusion. The shallow floe ice is often driven by the winds and surface currents, while the icebergs, with most of their bulk hidden beneath the surface, are driven by the deeper currents of the sea. It's a useful image for Christians in our contemporary culture, and it helpfully explains how Daniel managed so well in such a hostile environment. Daniel was driven not by the surface winds of the culture he was living in, but by the deeper currents of his faithfulness to God. Here is a powerful model for today's Christian scholars, and for Christian colleges as well, for as Miroslav Volf reminds us, "In contemporary de-Christianized, pluralistic, and rapidly changing Western cultures, only those religious groups that make no apologies about their 'difference' will be able to survive and thrive. The strategy of conformation is socially ineffective in the short run (because you cannot shape by parroting) and self-destructive in the long run (because you conform to what you have not helped shape). A good deal of courage in nonconformity is needed both to preserve the identity of Christian faith and to insure its lasting social relevance."[19]

Our prime motivation for the cultivation of the Christian mind must therefore be intrinsic, not extrinsic. We do it out of allegiance to Christ, out of obedience to his command to love God with our minds. As children of this "last Adam" (1 Cor. 15:45) we desire to discharge to the utmost our role as his vice-regents within the created order. If we fulfill this task well, God in his grace may allow our work to have a healing, preserving, or enlightening influence on our culture. By its sheer quality, by its integrity and winsomeness, it may force a hearing and move

19. "Theology, Meaning, and Power," in *The Future of Theology: Essays in Honor of Jürgen Moltmann,* ed. Miroslav Volf et al. (Grand Rapids: Eerdmans, 1996), p. 100.

minds and hearts. We can easily think of splendid examples where this has happened. On the other hand, that same work, or other equally fine work, may win no hearing at all. It may be shunned and we may find ourselves ostracized from the guild, treated as outsiders and impostors. Or anything between these extremes. But in the end, though we much prefer the former and dread the latter, the response of the world, whatever it may be, cannot be what drives us. What drives us, however the world may respond, is our allegiance to the Lordship of Jesus Christ.

The best motives for Christian scholarship are thus the most personal ones. These motives do not stem first and foremost from a set of abstract beliefs or a system of thought, or even from the most unselfish aspirations for transforming our culture. Neither are they expressions of our commitment to some particular set of Christian "virtues," or "values," or "Judeo-Christian principles." Our motives grow out of nothing so abstract or depersonalized as dedication to "our Christian heritage," or "the Christian tradition," or "a Christian vision." Nor are they prompted by a vague institutional desire to "maintain a Christian environment" that is somehow, even more vaguely, "informed by the Christian faith." Each of these good things, captured in phrases culled from institutional mission statements, may best be viewed as derived from something deeper. They are penultimate things, but they are not, must not be, cannot be, the Christian's bedrock. Rightly understood, each is a worthy byproduct of that most fundamental thing: our allegiance to a person, the Lord Jesus Christ.

Christian scholars cannot afford, as Eloise Meneses remarks, "to assimilate our Christian perspective to a secular one, much less leave it to the side. This is . . . because we give our ultimate commitment not to truth in any pantheistic sense, but to the Truth who was an Incarnation of God, and who lived, died, and was resurrected in the body in the first century. Our ultimate commitment is to Jesus Christ, and to Him alone."[20] Penultimate commitments are judged by the ultimate commitment, she says. "And since our ultimate commitment is to a person, it is Jesus himself who judges our work."[21]

20. Eloise Hiebert Meneses, "No Other Foundation: Establishing a Christian Anthropology," *Christian Scholar's Review* 29, no. 3 (Spring 2000): 545.

21. Meneses, "No Other Foundation," pp. 545-46. Cf. on this point David K. Naugle, *Worldview: The History of a Concept* (Grand Rapids: Eerdmans, 2002), pp. 338-39.

If such a personalistic emphasis mistakenly strikes some as pietist-ic, we must nevertheless not shy away from it. Jesus demands nothing less than this sort of personal allegiance from those who would be his followers: "Whoever does not bear his own cross and come after me, can-not be my disciple" (Luke 14:27). Jesus was far harder on religious people than the non-religious, and a personal allegiance to Jesus himself is the only thing that raises our practice of religion above the sorts of things Jesus so roundly condemned. It was in fact the most religious of his day whom Jesus censured for abandoning this "key of knowledge" and keep-ing it from others (Luke 11:52). Historian Mark Noll has criticized the ef-fects of a distorted pietism on Christian thought, but as he is also care-ful to point out, there is no inherent conflict between "warm piety and hard thinking."[22] Pietists, says Noll, were the ones who "rediscovered the truth that Christianity is a life as well as a set of beliefs."[23] When piety is understood as a passionate personal allegiance to the Lord Jesus Christ — of the sort demanded by no less than Jesus himself — and that alle-giance is rightly understood to require loving God with our *minds* as well as our hearts, souls, and strength, we discover the deepest and most en-during motives for Christian scholarship.

Distinctively Christian

In his essay on "A Baptist View of the Catholic University," Thomas Morris, a Baptist philosopher who teaches at Notre Dame, says, "Every university exists both for the discovery of new knowledge and for the transmission of the best of human culture and knowledge. It has al-ways been my assumption that a distinctively Catholic university exists for these reasons as well, but that, in addition, it is intended to be pre-dominantly a community of individuals who approach these tasks from the perspective of the historically important and intellectually powerful worldview that forms the foundation of Catholic thought and life — the worldview of traditional Christian theism."[24] While it is

22. "Christian World Views and Some Lessons of History," in Holmes, ed., *The Making of a Christian Mind*, p. 43.

23. Noll, "Christian World Views and Some Lessons of History," p. 42.

24. In *The Challenge and Promise of a Catholic University*, ed. Theodore Hesburgh (Notre Dame: University of Notre Dame Press, 1994), pp. 226.

not clear to me how working from a "worldview of traditional Christian theism" can render an institution distinctively Catholic — would not a Baptist university such as Baylor, for example, meet this criterion? — Morris's stipulation of a specifically Christian theism is a useful one.

But what is it that marks a theistic worldview as *distinctively* Christian? Surely the answer is found in the doctrine of the Trinity, and specifically the Christocentric focus we have been discussing. Yet if this is the case, we may need to tighten our language. Perhaps what we require is a distinction between "Christian" thinking and "*distinctively* Christian" thinking.

To grasp the difference, imagine a Christian scholar involved in three different conversations about some particular discipline — say, history, or philosophy, or biology. The first conversation is with a secular colleague; the second is with a colleague who is a Muslim; the third is with a colleague who is a committed Christian. Let us stipulate that the conversations we have in mind are not those in which the Christian is attempting to give witness to her non-Christian colleagues about her Christian faith; the exchanges are simply discussions of the subject matter of the discipline these three scholars share in common.

With her secular colleague our Christian thinker experiences a fundamental level of intellectual commonality. With the second, her Muslim friend, she shares an additional theistic dimension — a belief in a personal God who created all things. With the third she shares the full complement of Christ-centered convictions. How might these three conversations differ?

We may think of this trio of conversations as three concentric circles of discourse, the largest of which is the third. The first circle of discourse fits within the second, and both of these fit within the third.

Notice that due to a lack of shared presuppositions, what our Christian thinker is able to discuss in the first two conversations may be something more circumscribed — something less than, but not something other than, what she will say in the third. Both of these circles exist within the third. But conversely, the third conversation includes all that our Christian scholar can say in the first two, but also more. Because she is working from a fully integrated, Christ-centered worldview, all of the circles surely represent "Christian" thinking — that is, they contain things a Christian does in fact think — but it is not until we arrive at the unique Christ-centered dimensions of the subject found in the largest circle that we arrive at distinctively Christian ideas.[25] Distinctively Christian thinking involves an exploration of the full Trinitarian implications of what we study, and its Christ-centeredness in particular, for as Karl Barth says, "The doctrine of the Trinity is what basically distinguishes the Christian doctrine of God as Christian . . . in contrast to all other possible doctrines of God."[26] Quoting C. J. Nitsch, Barth goes on to affirm that without the Trinity, theism "only distinguishes God and the world and never God from God." Until we arrive at Trinitarian thinking, our thinking may be factually sound and even generically theistic, and therefore truly within the circle of what a Christian thinks, but it will not yet be *distinctively* Christian.

The image of the three circles is imperfect because in practice what is distinctively Christian about our thought may (or may not) also entail differences within all three circles; that is, the distinctively Christian dimensions of our thought often color in a variety of ways the rest of what a Christian thinks. Genuine Christian thought is more than a mere add-on. Yet our larger point is this: to engage in distinctive Christian thinking is to go beyond. It does not settle for merely "faith-informed" scholarship. George Marsden uses this term but also rightly points out its potential insipidness: "The only disadvantage with that term is that it can be *too* general. 'Faith-informed' has to be qualified by reference to a particular faith."[27] And the particular faith in this instance is the Trinitarian claim of the Lordship, and therefore centrality, of Jesus Christ.

Will there be a price to be paid in the modern academy for main-

---

25. C. Stephen Evans helpfully offers a threefold distinction between "purely vocational Christian scholarship," "implicit Christian scholarship," and "explicit Christian scholarship," where the Christian's distinctive claims become increasingly active and visible as one moves across this spectrum. The drawback of this formulation, however, is that in speaking generically of Christian "scholarship," the important distinction between how Christians must think and how they may communicate in various venues is somewhat lost. See Evans, "The Calling of the Christian Scholar-Teacher," in *Faithful Learning and the Christian Scholarly Vocation*, Henry and Agee, eds., pp. 34-35.

26. *Church Dogmatics*, volume I, "The Doctrine of the Word of God," trans. G. W. Bromiley, ed. G. W. Bromiley and T. F. Torrance (Edinburgh: T&T Clark, 1975), p. 301.

27. "Beyond Progressive Scientific Humanism," in *The Future of Religious Colleges*, ed. Paul J. Dovre (Grand Rapids: Eerdmans, 2002), p. 44.

taining this sort of Christ-centered focus, for both individual Christian scholars and for Christian colleges as well? Jesus himself warned there would be. But if so, that surely must not deter us. As the saying has it, it goes with the territory. Jesus never promised that serving him would be safe, only that he, the Lord of the Universe, would accompany us at every moment, even to the end of the age. Perhaps we need only be reminded of that memorable scene in *The Lion, the Witch and the Wardrobe* in which Mr. and Mrs. Beaver instruct Lucy about the challenges of approaching Aslan, the leonine Christ-figure:

> "If there's anyone who can appear before Aslan without their knees knocking, they're either braver than most or else just silly."
>
> "Then he isn't safe?" said Lucy.
>
> "Safe?" said Mr. Beaver. "Don't you hear what Mrs. Beaver tells you? Who said anything about safe? 'Course he isn't safe. But he's good. He's the King, I tell you."

4 A Centered Education

CHALLENGE *To Keep the Center
at the Center*

S ome slogans are not meant to be taken seriously. They are exercises in silliness with no real point. "Just two days from now, tomorrow will be yesterday," says one. "Emordnilap Is Palindrome Spelled Backwards," says another. Or "Half the People in the World Are Below Average."

But sometimes slogans can be humorous and still carry a point, however humble: "Be Nice to Your Kids — They'll Choose Your Nursing Home." "It's Not Whether You Win or Lose, But How You Place the Blame." "Money Isn't Everything, But It Sure Keeps the Kids in Touch." This last may be especially appropriate for parents of college students.

And then there are those slogans that are not funny at all. They address matters of such weight and consequence that we dare not treat them lightly. The call for "Christ-centered education" surely falls into this category. Why? Because its subject matter is so elevated, and the stakes of which it speaks are so high. Few catchphrases can match the weight of this one.

What can it mean to claim that Jesus Christ is central to all of our teaching and learning? Bible, theology, Christian living, ministry, church history — fine, we may say. But what about the arts, the natural sciences, the humanities? Are we really claiming that Jesus Christ is somehow central to chemistry, to sociology, to the history of music; to English literature, to Western civilization, to abnormal psychology; to physics, philosophy, and French? And if so, what can such a claim possibly mean?

To speak of Christ-*centered* liberal arts education is to make the claim that Jesus is the centerpiece of all human knowledge, the reference point for all our experience. It directs our attention to the only One who can serve as the centerpiece of an entire curriculum, the One to whom we must relate everything and without whom no fact, no theory, no subject matter can be fully appreciated. It is the claim that every field of study, every discipline, every course, requires Jesus Christ to be understood aright. Do we really mean this? Do we really intend what our slogan appears to affirm: a Christ-*centered* education?

For many non-Christians, especially in the academic world, such a notion comes across not merely as absurd but offensive. We may claim Jesus as the cornerstone of our educational enterprise, but for countless others he is a very different kind of stone, "a stone of stumbling, a rock that will make them fall" (1 Pet. 2:8; cf. Rom. 9:33). The Christ of the Bible is scandalous to a great many people. Yet here we are claiming that this One stands at the core of all humans can know or understand. Is this pious hyperbole? Or are we ready to back this radical language, embodying as it does such an astonishing claim? When we affirm that the education to which we aspire is Christ-*centered*, are we in Christian higher education willing to live with the consequences?

It is startling enough to remind ourselves of how far-reaching the claim of a Christ-centered education really is. But the slogan appears all the more shocking when we compare it to the general stance of modern education. The phrase is offensive not only because Jesus Christ is the "great stone of stumbling," but because our commitment to him appears to be a blatant violation of the academic spirit.

The secular academy purports to be about a quest for truth, or at least for knowledge. But the contemporary observer may be excused for thinking that this quest sometimes appears to be all journey and no arrival. In fact, not a few contemporary voices will insist on as much. Arrival implies closure, which in our academic climate seems always premature. Today's Zeitgeist requires skepticism and doubt, a tentativeness toward all things at all times. It reveres "the roaming, free-floating intellectual who has seen through the pretensions or naivete of those who . . . make serious intellectual and moral commitments."[1]

1. Alvin Plantinga, "On Christian Scholarship," in *The Challenge and Promise of a Catholic University*, ed. Theodore Hesburgh (Notre Dame: University of Notre Dame Press, 1994), p. 278.

In such a climate, truth claims, and especially religious truth claims, are viewed at best, in Ralph McInerny's words, as "professionally gauche." At worst they are dangerous and disallowed. In our perspectival world, even claims to knowledge may seem grandiose, much less claims to truth.

Yet Christian higher education — Christ-*centered* education — does not merely arrive at truth claims; it begins with them, and the most staggering truth claims at that. We claim that Jesus Christ *is* the Truth (John 14:6). As the great *Logos* of the universe he is the very embodiment of Truth in every way. We begin with the claim that Jesus Christ stands at the core of all we can know, and follow with an insistence that we cannot grasp anything aright apart from him. Thus the Christian thinker's ultimate task is nothing less or other than to seek out the meaning of the Lordship of Jesus Christ for every dimension of human experience, throughout every discipline. C. S. Lewis says, "There is no neutral ground in the universe; every square inch, every split second, is claimed by God and counterclaimed by Satan."[2] Our goal is therefore to "take every thought captive to Christ" (2 Cor. 10:5). Our subject matter is, at least potentially, in the words of Walter Ong, "the whole of actuality."[3] We want to discover all that is true, how it is true, how it relates to everything else, and ultimately, how it all relates to Jesus Christ. For it is only in this last endeavor that we will truly accomplish the others. This is what it means for Christians to "love God with all our minds" (Mark 12:30), what it means to think *Christianly*. Yet we should allow ourselves no illusions. This is not an enterprise the secular academy is likely to understand or appreciate.

Seeing Christ at the Center

My goal here cannot be to show how such Christ-centered thinking plays itself out across the curriculum or throughout the disciplines. As George Guthrie says, "The process of integrating the Christian view of

2. "Christianity and Culture," in *Christian Reflections,* ed. Walter Hooper (Grand Rapids: Eerdmans, 1967), p. 33.

3. Walter J. Ong, "Realizing Catholicism: Faith, Learning, and the Future," in *Faith and the Intellectual Life,* ed. James L. Heft (Notre Dame and London: University of Notre Dame Press, 1996), p. 40.

the world with academic discipline — that is, working out how the authority of Scripture works with other forms of authority in the academy — has been neither simple nor simplistic."[4] The ways are too many and too complex for that. Consider, for example, the classic approach of just one historic Christian voice, St. Bonaventure:

> Wisdom is written everywhere, Bonaventure insists, and the world is like a book written front and back, or a mirror imaging the presence of God in its order and beauty and light. A rose is not just a rose when it exists to praise its maker. God's good-ness emanates like light diffusing itself throughout the entire creation; he is the exemplar, the Logos of all created things, and he is the one to whom it leads and for whom it all exists. Emanation, exemplarism, and consummation: these are the themes that shaped Bonaventure's worldview and thence his approach to learning. They are all three Christocentric themes, for Christ is the Light of the world, the eternal Logos, and the object of contemplation and love.[5]

Emanation, exemplarism, and consummation: what exactly does this mean? Arthur Holmes spends several pages exploring Bonaventure's approach to Christ-centered learning, pointing out its strengths and weaknesses. Other Christian thinkers have described the task of seeing the Christ-centeredness of things differently. Yet it cannot be our purpose to explore the options here. Even if I were capable of doing so, it would far exceed our present scope. My purpose is more restricted. I desire only to call attention to what we mean when we talk about Christ-centered education. It is an education that rigorously and without apology insists upon looking through and beyond the created order to see the Christ-centeredness of all things.

This sort of looking beyond is what C. S. Lewis had in mind when he drew in a famous passage some extraordinary insight from the most ordinary of situations: "I was standing today in the dark toolshed," he said. "The sun was shining outside and through the crack at the top of

---

4. "The Authority of Scripture," in *Shaping a Christian Worldview: The Foundations of Christian Higher Education,* ed. David S. Dockery and Gregory Alan Thornbury (Nashville: Broadman and Holman, 2002), p. 23.

5. Arthur F. Holmes, *Building the Christian Academy* (Grand Rapids: Eerdmans, 2001), pp. 43-44.

the door there came a sunbeam. From where I stood that beam of light, with the specks of dust floating in it, was the most striking thing in the place. Everything else was almost pitch-black. I was seeing the beam, not seeing things by it." But suddenly Lewis's perspective was transformed. "Then I moved," he says, "so that the beam fell on my eyes. Instantly the whole previous picture vanished. I saw no toolshed, and (above all) no beam. Instead I saw, framed in the irregular cranny at the top of the door, green leaves moving on the branches of a tree outside, and beyond that, 90 odd million miles away, the sun. Looking along the beam and looking at the beam are very different experiences."[6]

Lewis was struck by this experience and saw it as a metaphor for how different people approach the business of thinking.

> As soon as you have grasped this simple distinction, it raises a question. You get one experience of a thing when you look along it and another when you look at it. Which is the "true" or "valid" experience? Which tells you most about the thing? And you can hardly ask that question without noticing that for the last fifty years or so everyone has been taking the answer for granted. It has been assumed without discussion that if you want the true account of religion you must go, not to religious people, but to anthropologists; that if you want the true account of sexual love you must go, not to lovers, but to psychologists; that if you want to understand some 'ideology' . . . you must listen not to those who lived inside it, but to sociologists.[7]

Lewis was addressing here, of course, the tendencies of the modern academic world. When he speaks of the "last fifty years or so" he is referring to the first half of the twentieth century. We need hardly point out that the tendencies he describes have only accelerated since then.

As a Christian, Lewis showed little patience with such a cramped and reductionist approach to thinking, and he rightly refused to give in to it. He viewed such self-imposed limitations — that is, the insistence upon looking merely at, never along — as the equivalent of preparing for one's intellectual task by putting on mental blinders. Lewis understood that there is more to the world than can be grasped under such

6. "Meditation in a Toolshed," in *God in the Dock: Essays on Theology and Ethics,* ed. Walter Hooper (Grand Rapids: Eerdmans, 1970), p. 212.

7. Lewis, "Meditation in a Toolshed," p. 213.

self-imposed restrictions, and he was not shy about pointing out its follies. Indeed, in another place he likens them to a dog sniffing his master's finger: "You will have noticed that most dogs cannot understand *pointing*. You point to a bit of food on the floor; the dog, instead of looking at the floor, sniffs at your finger. A finger is a finger to him, and that is all. His world is all fact and no meaning."[8]

In such a world as ours, Lewis says, we often "find people deliberately inducing upon themselves this doglike mind":

> The extreme limit of this self-blinding is seen in those who, like the rest of us, have consciousness, yet go about to study the human organism as if they did not know it was conscious. As long as this deliberate refusal to understand things from above, even where such understanding is possible, continues, it is idle to talk of any final victory over materialism. The critique of every experience from below, the voluntary ignoring of meaning and concentration on fact, will always have the same plausibility. There will always be evidence, and every month fresh evidence, to show that religion is only psychological, justice only self-protection, politics only economics, love only lust, and thought itself only cerebral biochemistry.[9]

Like Lewis, Christian thinkers — if the thinking they're doing is distinctively Christian — can never settle for merely "looking at." They will always want to combine a rigorous looking at with a determination to look along. Otherwise their work will be no different from that of their secular counterparts. Such undifferentiated contributions would certainly be useful as far as they go, as are those of their secular colleagues, but they will not be distinctively Christian — which is to say, Christ-centered. And for that reason they will fail to grasp the most meaningful dimensions of their own subjects. To probe those dimensions they require the Key to the universe: the person of Jesus Christ.

Our intellectual work is, from a Christian point of view, incomplete until we "look along" our subject matter, asking in what ways what we're seeing relates to the Lordship of Jesus Christ. This is essentially what it means to think Christianly about a subject, and it extends

8. "Transposition," in *The Weight of Glory and Other Addresses,* rev. ed., ed. Walter Hooper (New York: Macmillan, 1980), p. 71.

9. Lewis, "Transposition," pp. 71-72.

into every course in every discipline, across the entire curriculum — including, we should note, the sciences. For "it is the one and the same God who establishes and guarantees the intelligibility and the reasonableness of the natural order of things upon which scientists confidently depend, and who reveals himself as the Father of our Lord Jesus Christ. This unity of truth, natural and revealed, is embodied in a living and personal way in Christ."[10]

Notice that Christ-centered thinking is therefore not necessarily something other than secular thought, but something more. This is why William Dyrness observes, "It is hard to understand how some can insist the Christian faith puts people in a box. The opposite is in fact true — the faith is not a box but a window. Christian convictions about creation and redemption make the world open to its transcendent purpose and to the future that God has planned for it. Through his Spirit, God has revealed to us 'what no eye has seen, nor ear heard, nor the heart of man conceived . . .' (1 Cor. 2:9)."[11]

For the Christian, looking along does not replace looking at; it enhances it. In Walter Ong's words, the Christian faith "does not confront the universe. The faith penetrates the universe."[12] Christian scholars no less than secular scholars are called to give the most rigorous attention to the created order. In fact, Christians enjoy a higher motivation for doing so than the most inspired secular scholar: they are studying the world their Lord made, and which his power sustains, and which he dignified and sanctified by his joining. So their "looking at" will be as careful, disciplined, and dedicated as the most determined secular scholar. The difference is that Christian scholars will not stop there, at least if their contributions are to be distinctively Christian. They want to understand as fully as possible the particular "finger" they're studying; but more than that, they want also to understand what it's pointing toward. They know that it is all in the end related to the person of Christ, and they seek to press beyond the thing itself to understand how this can be. Thus they refuse to settle for merely understanding some particular as-

10. John Paul II, *Fides et Ratio*, 34.
11. William A. Dyrness, "The Contribution of Theological Studies to the Christian Liberal Arts," in *Making Higher Education Christian: The History and Mission of Evangelical Colleges in America,* ed. Joel A. Carpenter and Kenneth W. Shipps (Grand Rapids: Christian University Press, 1987), p. 182.
12. Ong, "Realizing Catholicism," p. 42.

pect of the created order, or even how this aspect relates to other aspects; they insist on reaching further, to its Christ-centeredness. This is what our slogan "Christ-centered education" requires.

Oliver Wendell Holmes reportedly exclaimed, "I would not give a fig for the simplicity this side of complexity, but I would give my very life for the simplicity the other side of complexity." The account may in fact be apocryphal, but no matter. Whoever first uttered it, the thought is a profound one, one with which every Christian thinker can identify. Simplicity this side of complexity is no more than over-simplification; it's not worth much. But the Christian scholar is one who understands that there is indeed a simplicity beyond the complex details of what she is studying, a simplicity which, if she can only discern it, will be found to center upon the person of Jesus Christ. And it is for the knowing of this simplicity, this Christ-centered meaning and significance of what they study, that Christian scholars do in fact give their lives.

"Whatever you do, do it heartily, as to the Lord and not to men, knowing that from the Lord you will receive the reward of the inheritance; for you serve the Lord Christ." So said the Apostle Paul (Col. 3:23-24). Christian scholars delight in their subject matter as much as any secular scholar; they are as motivated by curiosity and a desire to know as any other. But beyond that, they are also motivated by their Christian faith to look not merely at that subject matter but along it, to see in what ways it points them to the Truth who stands at the center of all we can know. John Henry Newman observed that "truth has two attributes — beauty and power; and while Useful Knowledge is the possession of truth as powerful, Liberal Knowledge is the apprehension of it as beautiful."[13] Christians understand both the power and the beauty of truth, and find them both epitomized in Jesus Christ. This is, or ought to be, our supreme motive for scholarship.

Reality Checks

All of this, of course, represents the loftiest of aspirations, relatively easy to articulate, immensely difficult to execute. For there are unfor-

13. John Henry Newman, *The Idea of a University*, ed. Martin J. Svaglic (Notre Dame: University of Notre Dame Press, 1982), p. 165.

giving realities every Christian scholar must navigate. Our goal may be nothing less than plumbing the Christ-centered unity of all things, but living out such an aspiration is anything but a simple task.

First, this approach requires hard work and determination. As Nicholas Wolterstorff reminds us, the task of the Christian scholar "is not a job for hacks."[14] We are not talking about leap-frogging the subject matter to arrive at Christocentric issues, as if we are essentially disinterested in the subject itself and desire only to see its Christological implications. If we are not to settle for merely looking at, but insist also on looking along, by the same token we cannot look along until we have accomplished some degree of looking at. Both are of pressing interest to the Christian.

Second, the effort of looking both at and along one's subject requires a certain depth of biblical and theological insight. It is not enough merely to be a Christian and to know one's discipline; genuinely Christian thinking requires depth on both sides of this ledger. As Willis Glover observed nearly half a century ago, "An intellectual revolution is not likely to be affected by a Mother Goose Christianity dimly remembered from youthful Sunday School experience. The Christian scholar needs to be theologically literate."[15]

For not a few Christian scholars, gaining this theological literacy presents a dilemma. Mary Stewart Van Leeuwen describes their plight this way: "Most Christian scholars come to their tasks with a decidedly lopsided training. On the one hand, their highest academic credentials have usually been obtained in intellectually sophisticated yet highly secularized university settings. On the other hand, their biblical training has largely been confined to what they get from sermons, Sunday school lessons, and lay Bible studies, all of which are aimed at the strengthening of faith but not in a particularly intellectual way."[16] But as Van Leeuwen also observes, these limitations must be overcome: "To bring Christian criteria adequately to bear on academic endeavors, scholars need not just minimal biblical literacy, not just statement-of-faith-based orthodoxy, not just a record of faithful attention to ser-

---

14. *Reason Within the Bounds of Religion* (Grand Rapids: Eerdmans, 1976), p. 103.

15. Willis B. Glover, "The Vocation of a Christian Scholar," *The Christian Scholar* 37, no. 1 (March 1954): 422.

16. Mary Stewart Van Leeuwen, "Bringing Christian Criteria to Bear on Academic Work," in Carpenter and Shipps, eds., *Making Higher Education Christian,* pp. 191-92.

mons and Sunday school lessons, but intellectual sophistication and discernment in their understanding and application of Scripture."[17] Gaining such sophistication and discernment while maintaining hard-won expertise in a particular field often makes the task of the Christian scholar an arduous one, and some accomplish it more effectively than others. But none can avoid its necessity.

Third, this approach requires honesty. There can be no room for forcing one's scholarship into some preset mold so as to make it come out a particular way. "Squeezing lessons out of any subject is bad scholarship."[18] "That would be," as C. S. Lewis once noted, citing Francis Bacon, "to offer to the author of truth the unclean sacrifice of a lie."[19] The Christian scholar is under obligation to seek the truth, and only the truth, confident that when it is adequately and accurately understood it will point to Christ.

Fourth, the very loftiness of our goal demands humility. To borrow Lewis's notable "Weight of Glory" language, the full burden of the Christian thinker's task is so heavy that only humility can carry it, and the backs of the proud will be broken. Isaac Newton changed the world by conjuring epoch-making thoughts no one had thought before him; yet of his own work he said, "I don't know what I may seem to the world, but, as to myself, I seem to have been only like a boy playing on the sea shore, and diverting myself in now and then finding a smoother pebble or a prettier shell than ordinary, whilst the great ocean of truth lay all undiscovered before me." Whole lifetimes of work may touch only the hem of the Christian's intellectual task. It is as vast as the universe, as boundless as the universe's Creator. One day, says the Apostle Paul, we shall know as we are presently known — that is, in full. But "for now," we see only dimly, as if through a darkened glass (1 Cor. 13:12). There can be no room for pride or triumphalist claims of finished truth or knowledge. As Christians we can and should aspire to the highest of Christ-centered intellectual goals, and whatever we achieve in that direction will be more than worth the effort. But we must also maintain at all times a humility and judicious tentativeness generated

17. Van Leeuwen, "Bringing Christian Criteria to Bear," p. 191.

18. Richard A. Riesen, *Piety and Philosophy: A Primer for Christian Schools* (Phoenix: ACW Press, 2002), p. 94.

19. "Learning in Wartime," in Hooper, ed., *The Weight of Glory and Other Addresses*, p. 27.

both by the monumental size of the task and the feebleness of our own capacities.

Fifth, this sort of work also requires patience and cooperation. Looking at and looking along do not always occur simultaneously. The former must by definition precede the latter. The work of one scholar will build upon the unfinished work of others, which in turn will serve as the foundation for still others. Thus Christian scholars must avoid slipping into a hurry-up mode or being forced into it by others. Their work must exhibit a certain patience and communal quality.

Again, C. S. Lewis is helpful here. Humility, he says, may encourage us "to concentrate simply on the knowledge or the beauty, not too much concerning ourselves with their ultimate relevance to the vision of God. That relevance may not be intended for us but for our betters — for men who come after and find the spiritual significance of what we dug out in blind and humble obedience to our vocation."[20] Lewis does not absolve the Christian thinker from a responsibility to "look along"; as we observed above, he was critical of those who settled for less. But he counsels care and patience. Scholarship is typically a communal affair; we are dependent upon one another. What one scholar may contribute, another can build upon. Thus there may be times, Lewis says, when we may pursue our "looking at" for its own sake. But even this is valid only if we understand it "in a sense which does not exclude [it] being for God's sake."[21] In the end, if our work is to be distinctively Christian, it will not dodge the issue of the Lordship of Jesus Christ.

The reader may recall the tale of the king who wished to build the grandest cathedral in the land. He assembled a team of the finest craftsmen and put them to work under the leadership of a brilliant foreman. But when the construction of the cathedral was barely half finished the foreman died. The king was saddened by the loss, and he knew this man would be difficult to replace. His successor would have to be an accomplished craftsman, but he must also be one who shared the king's exalted vision. Thus the king took it upon himself to find a replacement.

Visiting the work site, the king came upon a mason preparing tiles for the mosaics on the floor. The king admired his skill and in-

20. Lewis, "Learning in Wartime," p. 27.
21. Lewis, "Learning in Wartime," p. 27.

quired what he was doing. "Why, your Majesty," the man replied, "I'm cutting tiles for the mosaics on the floor." Next the king found a carpenter constructing beams for the roof. The king admired his craftsmanship too and asked him what he was doing. The man replied, "Oh Sire, I'm fashioning beams for the roof." Next the king found a stonecarver who was fitting stones for the great buttresses. Admiring the beauty and precision of his work, the king again asked what he was doing. "I'm building the grandest cathedral in the land," the man replied.

"Yes!" cried the king. "Here is my new foreman!"

Christian scholars are like the stonecutter who understood his calling. He was not merely an individual artisan going about his craft; his craftsmanship was the servant of something larger and far grander. In the same way, Christian scholars view their work as larger than themselves, larger than itself. They look not only at what they're studying but also along it, so as to see its Christ-centered implications. This tethering of the temporal to the eternal provides meaning and significance and beauty to what they do and generates the highest motivation for excellence. Their study becomes virtually an act of worship. They work not merely to understand the created order, as worthwhile as that goal is within itself; they also study the created order to deepen their understanding and appreciation of, and ultimately their relationship with, the One who fashioned it and who occupies its center, its Creative Orderer, the Lord Jesus Christ.

A Friendly Conversation

How might this work itself out in practice? As we have said, there are as many answers as there are Christian scholars, or disciplines, or methods of study, and our purpose here cannot be to explore them. But perhaps we may venture just this glimpse.

I recall a delightful walk one beautiful fall day with the president of a large, denominational university. During a break in the schedule of the conference we were attending, we strode across the leafy quads of Harvard University, talking about our respective institutions. At one point he inquired whether all of our faculty were Christians. I assured him they were, and then asked whether that was the case at his institution. No, he said, not all of his faculty were Christians. I then asked him whether it was his goal to turn out committed Christians as graduates. He assured me it was. So I asked him how that was possible if his faculty was populated by non-Christians. I reminded him of Jesus' observation that when fully formed, the student will look like his teacher. If his teachers do not live and work from a Christian worldview, I asked, why would he expect it of his students?

As it happens, this president's institution qualifies as what in an earlier chapter I have referred to as an Umbrella institution, which I consider not only a legitimate but an important type of school. Thus the question I was raising was not about the design of his institution but about his stated goal of turning out fully formed Christians. My friend responded as follows: "Well, we would certainly have Christians teaching our theology and religion courses. But in other areas of the curriculum, why should it matter? Take chemistry, for example. Why would it matter whether you have a Christian or a non-Christian teaching the subject?"

"Here is how we view it," I said. And I proceeded to lay out for him the Christ-centered approach to chemistry we aspire to at Wheaton College. "Chemicals," I acknowledged, "obviously behave the same for Christians as they do for non-Christians. At that level you are certainly right; there should be no difference at all. But I want more for our students. I want them to learn to think about chemistry in a fully Christian way. Pagan religions were and are those that focus mainly on the created order, worshiping the earth or sun or moon or some other dimension of that order. But the people of the Book have always been those who were inclined to explore, not simply the created order, but also what it is designed to tell them about the One who made it and sustains it and became part of it. 'The heavens and the earth declare the glory of God,' said the psalmist; I want our students to see God's glory in that dimension of the heavens and the earth we study under the heading of chemistry. I want them not only to be fascinated and delighted by the intricacies of chemical behavior, but also to realize that what they're exploring is the handiwork of the Lord Jesus Christ. Just as we may be enchanted by the exquisite lines and proportions of, say, a beautifully turned vase, we are even more astonished when we look beyond it to consider the eye and imagination and skill of hand of the potter who formed it. In the same way, as St. Augustine said, 'If the work of God's hands is so lovely, how much more beautiful must he be who made them.' I want our students to come to chemistry in just this way; I want them to delight in what they're learning about chemistry, but as Christians I also want them to see at every moment what these things are telling them about the One they know as their Savior, so that in the end they are lifted up to him, even in a chemistry course."

As you might expect, this response led to a lively interchange on the respective advantages and disadvantages of both Umbrella and Systemic educational institutions. It was a profitable conversation for both of us.

Potential for Problems

This radical searching out of the Christ-centeredness of things sometimes forces Christians in higher education into unwanted but inevitable conflicts with the secular world of learning. If our slogan "Christ-centered education" means what it says, it could hardly be otherwise. According to Jesus, "'A servant is not greater than his master.' If they persecuted me, they will persecute you; if they kept my word, they will keep yours also. But all this they will do to you on my account, because they do not know him who sent me" (John 15:20-21). Christian scholars have no business looking for conflict, and belligerence is unworthy of the One they serve. There is every reason to work collaboratively with secular colleagues, to appreciate them and their work and to learn from it. God's common grace at work in these scholars means that whatever is true in their work is just as true as anything else we can know.

But by the same token, we should not expect the phrase "Christ-centered education" to be applauded by the academy. Such a slogan will not be generally understood there, and to the extent it is understood, it is not likely to be widely appreciated. Already by 1968 Harry Smith was chronicling, in his *Secularization and the University,* "the breakdown of any unified metaphysical world-view (if there ever was one) and the multiplicity of truth 'standpoints,' symbol systems, and models for meaning"[22] that had come to characterize American higher education. In the intervening decades these trends have only accelerated.

22. *Secularization and the University* (Richmond, Va.: John Knox Press, 1968), pp. 20-21.

Yet it seems to me this situation should not unduly trouble us. It certainly should not put us on the defensive. Perhaps the best strategy for those of us who aspire to Christ-centered education should be two-fold. First, like Daniel and his friends in a sometimes hostile environment, we should seek to live out our allegiance to Christ with all the diligence and excellence and winsomeness we can muster, seeking to recommend ourselves by the sheer quality and integrity of our lives and work. But second, we should also, like Daniel, refuse to compromise our convictions or apologize for our allegiance. In the end we must stand or fall before Jesus Christ. It is infinitely more important to please him than to satisfy the demands of our secular colleagues.

It is not uncommon to hear members of the academic establishment call Christians into question from its secular presuppositions. But the Christian scholar's task will sometimes be to turn the tables by calling the secular establishment into question from Christian presuppositions. If, as the Christian believes, nothing in the end can be understood aright apart from the person of Christ, then Christian higher education may sometimes have to insist that the academic enterprise give him due consideration. This may not be popular, but it is sometimes required.

Charles Malik's courageous little book *A Christian Critique of the University* calls for just such an effort. Malik was a brilliant Lebanese Christian who earned his Ph.D. in philosophy under Alfred North Whitehead at Harvard. Later he studied at Freiburg with Martin Heidegger. During his long career Malik wrote numerous articles and books on philosophical, religious, and political topics and served on the faculties of several distinguished universities. He also served as Lebanon's Minister of Foreign Affairs and its ambassador to Washington. Malik was one of the original signatories to the Charter of the United Nations, where he served for fourteen years as, variously, president of the General Assembly, president of the Economic and Social Council, president of the Security Council, chairman of the Human Rights Commission, and chairman of that committee of the General Assembly that finalized the text of the Universal Declaration of Human Rights. His was an extraordinary career in the highest echelons of world affairs.

In 1987, Malik delivered a series of lectures that were later published under the above title. Ambassador Malik understood and valued the life of the mind and he knew that what happens in the world of ideas, which he identifies with the university, has profound consequences. Thus he explained the title of his book as follows:

> In view of the unique place and power of the university today I know of no more important question to ask than: What does Jesus Christ think of the university? All other questions without exception are relatively silly when this question looms in the mind.... To the non-Christian or the atheist or the naturalist or the radical secularist this question itself is silly and irrelevant, because what Christ thinks of the university, even if Christ as such existed, makes no difference whatever to the university. The university is wholly autonomous and follows its own inherent laws of development. Christ makes no more difference to the university than he does to the truth or development of physics or mathematics or the course of a raging war. But to a Christian who knows and believes in Jesus Christ as he is given us in the church and the Bible, and who at the same time realizes the unequaled power of the university in the world today, no question compares with this one.... Since the university determines the course of events and the destiny of man more than any other institution or agency today, it is impossible for a Christian not to ask the question: What does Jesus Christ think of the university? To a Christian this question is an absolute imperative.... So from the very start I have put aside all such questionable phraseology as "from the Christian point of view," "in terms of Christian principles," "applying Christian principles or values," "from the standpoint of Christian culture," etc. In fact it is already a concession to entitle this study, *A Christian Critique of the University,* rather than simply and directly, *What Does Jesus Christ Think of the University?*[23]

Charles Malik starts from the point where every Christian thinker must begin: the person of Jesus Christ. He does not presume the validity of the secular academic world and then ask what that world thinks of Jesus Christ; he starts with the most profound truth the race has known, the Lordship of Jesus Christ, and then asks in its light what we

---

23. *A Christian Critique of the University* (Waterloo, Ont.: North Waterloo Academic Press, 1987), pp. 24-25.

are to make of the university. It is altogether the right question and altogether the right way for Christians to go about their intellectual task.

If our goal is to think and act Christianly, Christian scholars must approach the question in just such a Christ-centered manner. Jesus himself left us no other option, for the allegiance he demands of his followers is a radical one: "If any one comes to me and does not hate his own father and mother and wife and children and brothers and sisters, yes, and even his own life, he cannot be my disciple. Whoever does not bear his own cross and come after me, cannot be my disciple. . . . Whoever of you does not renounce all that he has cannot be my disciple" (Luke 14:26-27, 33). Such all-consuming demands would be outrageous if Jesus Christ were not who he claimed to be. But if he is who he claims, and who his Church has always claimed, then he is utterly worthy of such unalloyed allegiance. Christians are precisely those who have decided that these claims are true, and they have already bowed the knee and confessed that "Jesus Christ is Lord, to the glory of God the Father." By this act of obeisance are all other allegiances eclipsed. No other loyalty — not to family, friends, a job, government, a guild, an institution, the academy in general — can be allowed to compete with the Christian's allegiance to Christ. All such competitors become by definition idolatrous when we allow their demands to compromise our obedience to Jesus Christ.

A Christian typically maintains many loyalties, yet all but this one are secondary and derived. They are valid only insofar as they are the *product of,* rather than *in competition with,* our loyalty to Christ. Thus the Christian strives to be a good father, or husband, or employee, or student precisely because Jesus Christ has called him to do so; the Christian scholar works hard at her scholarship and teaching, not in the end out of a misplaced loyalty to the academy, or to a professional guild, or to a discipline, or to a subject matter, or to an institution, or even to her students, but out of obedience to the calling of Jesus Christ. The Lord of the universe will tolerate nothing less: "Whoever does not renounce all that he has cannot be my disciple."

These are the highest possible demands and they sometimes require of Christian thinkers difficult choices. Christian scholars, or for that matter, Christian institutions of higher learning, can often go about their intellectual business without conflict. By their diligence and hard work they may even earn the accolades of the academy. Many within the academy will make room for them and applaud their contribution, even when at points they may not agree. But we should not think it will always be so. There will be other times when Christians and Christian institutions within the academy will be tested as to their allegiance. They will be required to identify themselves in costly ways with Jesus Christ, to "go forth to him," so to speak, "outside the camp and bear the abuse he endured" (Heb. 13:13).

Christian scholars have not always been willing to bear this burden. As Nathan Hatch says, "Like children long rejected, evangelical scholars are still too anxious to be accepted by their peers, too willing to move only in directions that allow them to be 'relevant.'" The result is that "we have been far more inclined to speak up when our Christian convictions are in tune with the assumptions of modern academic life than when they are at odds. It is much easier, for instance, to set oneself in the vanguard of social progress than it is to defend those Christian assumptions that the established and fashionable intellectual circles of our day regard as obscurantist and fanciful. Yet it is this tougher mental fight that we must not avoid."[24]

The Christ of our "Christ-centered education" is a highly controversial figure. "Do not think that I have come to bring peace on earth," he said. "I have not come to bring peace, but a sword. For I have come to set a man against his father, and a daughter against her mother, and a daughter-in-law against her mother-in-law; and a man's foes will be those of his own household" (Matt. 10:34-36). Jesus Christ is a scandalous stone of stumbling to the world. The all-encompassing nature of the Bible's claims for Jesus renders him unique. He is not merely one Lord, one Savior, among many; he is the singular Sovereign of the universe, the only-begotten Son of the Father, the once-for-all God-man. If he is truly the universe's Creator, Sustainer, Redeemer, the very Goal of all things, then there can be no other.

In our day these claims are intolerable, and Christians will be constantly pressured, both directly and indirectly, to tone them down.[25] If we do not, there will be a price to pay, in reputation or prestige if no

---

24. Nathan O. Hatch, "Evangelical Colleges and the Challenge of Christian Thinking," in Carpenter and Shipps, eds., *Making Higher Education Christian*, pp. 166-67.

25. For example, see John Hick, "The Non-Absoluteness of Christianity," in *The Myth of Christian Uniqueness: Toward a Pluralistic Theology of Religions*, ed. John Hick and Paul F. Knitter (Maryknoll, N.Y.: Orbis Books, 1987), pp. 16-36.

other. No matter how winsomely we manage to handle ourselves, if we in Christian higher education are determined to live out our allegiance to Christ we will, as Jesus himself instructs us, experience some of his reproach. We certainly are not greater than our master; if the world resented him, to the extent we identify ourselves with him we may well experience some of the same. And under such duress it is always tempting to play down our relationship with him. We will still speak of God, but we find ourselves doing so in only the most generic terms. We will refrain from using Jesus' name, lest that name offend. Or if we do use that name, as in the slogan "Christ-centered education," we may be tempted to dilute its content.

Sometimes such challenges will be direct and outright. I was asked not long ago to offer the invocation at a secular academic gathering. Since I'm a Christian, the only way I pray is in the name of Jesus, "for there is one mediator between God and men, the man Christ Jesus" (1 Tim. 2:5). Yet knowing the current social climate and the power of Jesus' name to divide, I did not want to put the convener in jeopardy. So I asked him, "Do you think it will be a problem in this gathering for me to pray in Jesus' name?"

The convener thought for a moment and then replied that, yes, he thought that would be a problem. What was I to do? Though my prayers are always in Jesus' name, God has nowhere ordained that I must explicitly use those words, and I do not always do so. Yet here was a case where I was being asked to distance myself from Jesus for the sake of the sensibilities of others, and to acquiesce in that unspoken premise of American civil religion that stipulates that all ways to God are equally valid. Should I do so, and settle for some such formulation as "in your name," or no formulation at all, so as to avoid mentioning the offensive name of Jesus?

I make it sound as if I was confronted with a dilemma; in fact, I faced no dilemma at all. I'd long ago worked out what to do in such situations and had, in fact, done it before. A moment's thought makes the required response clear: Suppose the convener had said to me, "Look, we want you to come to this meeting, but please do not bring your wife. Some at this gathering find her offensive. We're happy to have you, but please don't mention her name." What would have been my response to such a proposition? In the same way, this situation was requiring of me that I disassociate myself from the name of Jesus. I was being forced to choose, which meant that I had no choice at all, precisely because, as in my marriage, that choice was made long ago. Jesus said, "Whoever is ashamed of me and of my words in this adulterous and sinful generation, of him will the Son of man also be ashamed when he comes in the glory of his Father with the holy angels" (Mark 8:38). I informed the convener it would probably be best if he found someone else to give the invocation, which with obvious relief he gratefully agreed to do.

Here was a case where the challenge, though a minor one, was direct. More often the challenges are subtle and indirect. Jesus Christ, we discover, is the Rock of Offense; we sense the resistance and, if we are not careful, we flex accordingly. We find ourselves less and less often uttering his name. We learn to speak in terms generic enough to offend only the most ardent atheists. It is in just such a climate that we are in the greatest danger of losing the substance of the phrase "Christ-centered education."

Nothing could be more vital for Christian higher education than that we continue to revel in our allegiance to Jesus Christ, and in the fact that the education we offer is both *Christ*-centered and Christ-*centered*. We must refuse to water down either side of this important slogan. We must insist upon keeping Jesus Christ at the core of all we do.

Conclusion

So what does it mean for our education to be *centered* on the person of Christ? Stephen Monsma says, "A Christian university that is truly, fully Christian does not offer an essentially secular education with some Christianity tacked on in the form of some courses in religion, some chapel services or Bible studies, or faculty who are examples of Christian living. Instead it is marked by courses and curricula which are rooted in and are permeated by a Christian worldview, rather than a secular worldview (often disguised as a supposedly neutral worldview)."[26] Monsma is right, provided we keep in mind the profound Christ-centeredness of the Christian worldview of which he speaks.

26. Stephen V. Monsma, "Christian Worldview in Academia," *Faculty Dialogue* 21 (Spring-Summer 1994): 146.

Understanding this Christocentric claim leads directly to the awareness that Jesus Christ is the only One who can serve as the centerpiece of an entire curriculum, the One to whom we must relate everything and without whom no fact, no theory, no subject matter can be fully grasped or appreciated. Christocentrism is what renders our thinking distinctively Christian. It is thinking that asks and seeks to answer, systemically, throughout every dimension of the curriculum, reaching to every corner of every discipline, this searching question: What difference does it make here, for this aspect of our living or learning, to affirm that Jesus Christ is Lord? The pursuit of this question across the curriculum (and for that matter, the co-curriculum) is what makes for a uniquely Christ-centered education.

5 It's All God's Truth

CHALLENGE *To Strengthen the Foundations*
of Christian Thought

"All truth is God's truth." So goes another of the well-worn shib-
boleths we hear often in the world of Christian higher education — so often, in fact, that many have become weary of it.

This aphorism is an old one and it sports a noble history. For a
long time it has been wielded by Christian educators like a double-
edged sword. Its blade flashes back and forth, on the one side slicing all
who would argue that the Bible is our only source of truth, on the
other warding off any critics who might count us among that crowd.
We recite the phrase almost as a mantra, as if we needed regular reas-
surance that the battle between science and religion, reason and faith,
really is a phony war.

But these days there is good reason to wonder whether this
motto too has much life left in it. A declaration such as "All truth is
God's truth" takes on the status of a slogan only because it is so useful. There is a freshness to it, a brevity, a conciseness. The claim is
punchy, pointed; it says so much in only five one-syllable words. Yet
like every other powerful expression, its very pithiness condemns it to
a lingering death. Precisely because it is so useful the sentence be
comes a slogan and is used over and again. With time this repetition
reduces it to a cliché, and we tire of hearing it. Someone begins the
sentence and can scarcely finish it — we all nod our heads and chime
in to complete it for him.

Like a dead metaphor, this slogan hasn't actually disappeared. Its
ghost lingers in the language of those who are unembarrassed by

85

clichés. But the phrase has largely lost its substance. We continue to haul it out, but it lacks its former punch. It no longer conjures up the ideas that prompted its users to consider it effective in the first place. If anything, the slogan now appears to serve a quite different function, that of appearing to say something without perhaps saying very much at all.

I don't know that there is value in trying to recover the vitality of a venerable slogan. Breathing life into dead expressions is probably not possible in any case. But I do think we should make sure the important ideas this slogan has long emphasized are not lost. They are crucial to a biblical, Christ-centered worldview, and to the work of Christian higher education in particular. We may be able to dispense with one particular expression of these ideas, but we must not lose our purchase on the ideas themselves.

Necessary Implications

The slogan "All truth is God's truth" became widely used in Christian higher education because it encapsulated a set of convictions that are vital for the Christian's intellectual task. These ideas lie embedded in the slogan as entailments, necessary implications. To embrace the slogan was to embrace these implications. My purpose here is to surface these entailments so that, even if we may allow an overworked catchphrase to rest in peace, we will not lose the truths it was designed to express. They are so important that, even if our slogan no longer works, we shall have to find other, if less pithy, words to capture them.

What follows is an unpacking of ten important ideas embedded in the phrase "All truth is God's truth."[1] Each of these ideas is massive in its own right; each has far-flung implications of its own. In combination these ideas cast us out onto limitless intellectual seas, both philosophical (theories of knowledge, theories of truth, theories of language) and theological (the nature of God, the nature of general and

---

1. It is worth noting that the concept undergirding this slogan, that of "the unity of truth" (34), is one of the working premises of John Paul II's Encyclical Letter on the relationship between faith and reason, *Fides et Ratio*. Although I haven't attempted to isolate them, a careful reading of this document would, I suspect, demonstrate that each of the following entailments may be found implicitly or argued explicitly there.

special revelation, the nature of humans and the *imago dei*). Over the centuries entire libraries have been written on these ideas, and I hold no illusion that we will give them their due here. Our only recourse will be to keep our present purposes modest, precisely because these ideas are so expansive. What follows is therefore designed as an exercise in recollection, a refreshing of our memories.

Ten Fundamental Ideas

1. God exists.

This is the most basic idea of all. It is the foundation for all that a Christian can know. It's a given, a truth merely assumed by the Scriptures, never defended. The first verse of the Bible simply says, "In the beginning God created the heavens and the earth." Before there was anything of the created order, God existed. If that is not true, nothing else a Christian believes makes sense. But if it is true, then all of what follows becomes possible.

2. Through the agency of his Son, God created the universe and all that is in it.

As we saw in an earlier chapter, the Triune God created all that exists. He himself is not a created being; he is the eternal uncreated Creator. But everything else that is exists because God called it into existence. Through Christ God made everything, and everything he made remains utterly contingent upon him at every point and at all times. Were God to cease upholding it, it would instantly cease to exist. This created order is not merely an extension of God; he is distinct from it and transcends it in every way. But he is also immanent at every point within it. He is present everywhere in his creation and he knows it exhaustively.

3. We can therefore entertain an intellectual construct called "reality."

Apart from the existence of God we can make little sense of a concept such as *reality*. We are locked into merely our own perceptions of things, none of which can be labeled reality. Were there such a thing as reality, the ancient and contemporary skeptics agree, we could not know it exists; and even if we could know it exists, we could have no access to it. Thus such a concept can play no real part in our intellectual system; we

87

lose the intellectual permission to entertain a strong notion of reality. Not wanting to give up the term, we nostalgically speak about "multiple realities," all of them constructed by us, but by this we cannot mean anything more nor other than our perceptions. If we remove God from the picture, the word "reality" loses its capacity to mean much.

But if God does exist, everything changes. If there is a God, one who knows himself and the world he created exhaustively, a concept such as reality can, quite literally, make sense. As a shorthand definition we can think of reality as simply "things as God knows them to be." Such a formulation remains, to be sure, only a theoretical construct, but what an important construct it is. Such a construct makes it possible for us actually to mean something by the term.

We should pause for a moment with this last point. Some may be tempted to dismiss anything so ephemeral as a theoretical construct, assuming it to be little more than a hopeless abstraction. But that would be a serious mistake. Coherent thinking often requires the presence of theoretical constructs. Without them entire structures of thought and behavior collapse.

Consider, for instance, the science of textual criticism. Textual criticism (the attempt to reconstruct a lost ancient document from later copies with as much accuracy as possible) is utterly dependent on a crucial theoretical construct: the notion of an "original text." This construct is theoretical because we do not possess the original (called the *autograph*), and no one, least of all the textual critic, expects it to show up. If it did suddenly appear, the textual critic would immediately be out of a job. Textual criticism focuses instead on the copies of the ancient text that have come down to us. Through a process of selecting and examining all the available manuscript evidence (called *recension*), and following tested principles of correction (called *emendation*), the textual critic strives to reconstruct the original text as far as may be possible from the manuscript evidence. The textual critic knows the original text itself is unobtainable and holds no illusions that it will ever be perfectly reconstructed. Yet the theoretical construct called the original text still drives the critic's every effort and makes it possible. Imagine trying to do textual criticism if one were to do away with the concept of original text. What would one be striving toward? How would one order one's steps? To what end? Despite the unobtainability of the autograph — or perhaps the reverse, just *because* of it — the process of textual criticism depends from beginning to end upon the premise that an "original text" once existed and in a sense exists still in the form of the theoretical *telos* of the effort. Without such a theoretical construct the enterprise can make no sense.

In the same way, it is crucial for Christian thought that we be able to speak of the concept of reality. The existence of God as the Creator and Knower of all things makes this possible. Reality for the Christian is simply, "things as God knows them to be." If this idea seems at first abstract and irrelevant, so does the concept of an "original text" that everyone acknowledges we do not possess and never will — until one realizes how essential it is to the process of textual criticism. In the same way, while a God-centered definition of reality does not by itself grant *us* access to that reality — that issue arises later — it is nonetheless what makes it possible to talk about reality in the first place. If an un-mediated access to reality is unobtainable to me, it is not unobtainable to God. Thus there exists an actual state of things, grounded in and known exhaustively by God, and this is what we mean by reality. Thus far it is only a theoretical construct, but as we shall see, it is a vitally important one for Christian thought.

4. This reality is complex and multi-dimensional.
The *cosmos* God created is not simple. It is multi-faceted. It has physical, spiritual, and moral dimensions to it, but each dimension is fully real because its reality is anchored in the fact that it is part of what God knows to be the case. Thus Christian thinkers like Arthur Holmes can speak of the "truth" of Christian ethics.[2] The wrongness of child abuse is just as "real" as the physical composition of steel or the spiritual component of a human being. Though profoundly different from one another in one sense, in another sense each is part of God's design and each is perfectly known by him. Their realness or actuality stems from the fact that they are known by God to exist or to be the case: "The Creator, not the human creatures, gives form to matter, animation to dust, order to chaos. The Orderer and the activity of ordering precede humanity."[3] This includes the moral and ethical realms as well as the

---

2. *All Truth Is God's Truth* (Grand Rapids: Eerdmans, 1977), p. 6.
3. Mark R. Schwehn, *Exiles from Eden: Religion and the Academic Vocation in America* (New York: Oxford University Press, 1993), p. 128.

physical. Thus the Christian can argue, as does J. Budziszewski, that "the root of the enacted law is the moral law, . . . the root of the moral law is the design of the created order, and . . . the root of the created order is the Creator." Conversely, "Enacted law, severed from moral law, is tyranny"; "ethics, severed from the design of the moral order, is chaos"; and "creation, severed from the Creator, is an idol."[4]

5. This reality, though complex and multi-dimensional, is also coherent and unified, centered upon the person of Jesus Christ.
We have spoken at length of the Christocentricity of all that we can know. This Christ-centeredness brings a coherence and unity to the universe. When properly understood, as by God himself, Jesus Christ is seen to be the Source, the Sustainer, and the Goal of all created things. The entire universe is in the process of being "summed up" in him. He is the Alpha and the Omega, the first and the last, the beginning and the end, the divine *Logos* who is at once the eternal principle and principal of the universe. Thus it is a created "order" God has made, a *cosmos* ("an apt and harmonious arrangement"). Rightly understood it constitutes a unity, all centered on the person of Jesus Christ.

6. God has created humans with the capacity to apprehend, however fallibly and incompletely, this reality.
As part of his creation God made human beings and assigned them as stewards over his handiwork. To equip them for this task, and for fellowship with himself, he created them "in his own image." Humans do not merely bear the *imago dei* (image of God); they in a sense constitute the *imago dei*. The presence of this Godlikeness in humans has profound implications for the race, including the fact that humans have in limited ways been granted the unique capacity to apprehend and describe some aspects of the reality God knows.[5] More important still, they possess the capacity to worship and communicate with God himself.

4. "The Roots of Law," *Religion and Liberty* II (September-October 2001): 10.
5. Cf. Alvin Plantinga, *The Twin Pillars of Christian Scholarship* (Grand Rapids: Calvin College and Seminary, 1990), pp. 47-48.

7. Genuine knowledge is therefore feasible for humans.

Because of our finiteness and sinfulness, humans can never know any aspect of reality as God knows it — that is, perfectly and infinitely. But to whatever extent humans are able to apprehend that reality, to that extent they bear the capacity to do so accurately because of the mark of the *imago dei* upon and within them. Thus genuine knowledge becomes a possibility: in *some* ways, humans are able to *some* extent, to know and describe *some* dimensions of the reality God knows. Being made in his image, they are enabled in limited ways to think God's thoughts after him. As Jonathan Edwards put it, true knowledge consists of the "agreement of our ideas with the ideas of God"[6] — which is to say, with reality, or "things as God knows them to be."

8. Human knowledge of reality stems from two prime sources: special revelation and discovery.

In earlier ages Christian thinkers sometimes spoke of the two books of God: the Book of God's Words and the Book of God's Works. They were acknowledging the two avenues — what John Henry Newman referred to as our "double creed, natural and revealed"[7] — by which humans can arrive at knowledge of "things as God knows them to be," including knowledge of God himself. Humans can come to know that something is the case because God has told them by special revelation it is so (for example, that Jesus Christ is God's Son); or they can know something is the case by discovering it for themselves — that is, by applying their God-given capacity for apprehension to those dimensions of the created order that are available to them (for example, that the earth revolves around the sun). Faith is here best juxtaposed therefore not with reason per se, but with learning, since learning requires the application of reason, but so does faith.[8] All of which leads to the interesting observation by Ralph McInerny that one "paradoxical result of [contemporary thought] will be the realization that it has now fallen to believers to come to the defense of reason in order to defend the faith. This task is particularly urgent because of the way faith presupposes reason and

6. "The Mind," in Jonathan Edwards, *Scientific and Philosophical Writings*, ed. Wallace E. Anderson (New Haven: Yale University Press, 1980), pp. 341-42.

7. *The Idea of a University*, ed. Martin J. Svaglic (Notre Dame: University of Notre Dame Press, 1982), p. 355.

8. Cf. Plantinga, *Twin Pillars*, pp. 51-52.

would be unintelligible without a robust confidence in the capacity of our mind to know the world and enunciate truths about it."[9]

9. We can therefore maintain a distinction between truth and error.
Because of their finiteness and sinfulness, humans do not always or even typically understand God's reality accurately. Either or both of God's books may be misapprehended. Humans may misunderstand what God has said in his Word, or they may misconstrue what they discover within the created order. In either case, to the extent their apprehensions, or their expressions of those apprehensions, accord with reality as God knows it to be, their apprehensions or expressions may be said to be truthful. To the extent they do not accord with that reality, they are in error.

I am not interested in propounding a view of truth that, in A. C. Thiselton's words, citing Hans-Georg Gadamer, is "bound up too narrowly with theoretical reason alone. Such a view . . . belongs essentially to the outlook of the Enlightenment and its rationalism."[10] But the operative words here are "too narrowly" and "alone." If we are to avoid the extremes we shall have to work hard to retain that *legitimate* cognitive dimension of truth so often sacrificed in the jumble of modern theories of truth and language.[11] To accomplish this requires finding and maintaining a balance between the objective and personal dimensions of truth. But this also appears obvious to me: in the end, some version of a representational theory of language and of a correspondence theory of truth must remain in play if we are to conceive of truth in a fully biblical way.

In his encyclical *Fides et Ratio* (56), John Paul II defines truth as the "consonance between intellect and objective reality." Yet Alister McGrath argues that "it is a travesty of the biblical idea of 'truth' to equate it with the Enlightenment notion of conceptual or propositional correspondence."[12] McGrath wants us to remember that for Christians, truth is

9. Ralph McInerny, *Characters in Search of Their Author*, The Gifford Lectures, 1999-2000 (Notre Dame: University of Notre Dame Press, 2001), p. 123.

10. "Truth," *New International Dictionary of New Testament Theology*, ed. Colin Brown, vol. 3 (Grand Rapids: Zondervan, 1986), p. 898.

11. Thiselton, "Truth," pp. 894-901.

12. *A Passion for Truth: The Intellectual Coherence of Evangelicalism* (Downers Grove: InterVarsity Press, 1996), p. 177.

much more than mere "cerebralized information." Says McGrath, "The statements of John's Gospel must be taken with the utmost seriousness: Jesus does not merely show us the truth, or tell us the truth; *he is the truth* — and any concept of 'truth' which is unable to comprehend the fact that truth is personal is to be treated with intense suspicion."[13]

Is there a necessary conflict between John Paul's notion of "consonance" and McGrath's concern for the personal? A stress on the personal dimension of truth for Christians may arrive from two distinguishable directions. On the one side, it may stem from a concern for the personal appropriation of Christian truth — *"an appropriation-process of the most passionate inwardness,"* to use Kierkegaard's phrase[14] — such that what is objectively true quite apart from me is appropriated by me in such a way that it also becomes subjectively true for me. This is a point many evangelicals grew up being reminded of on a regular basis: namely, that for the Christian a mere "head knowledge" of the truth is not enough; genuine Christianity requires a "heart knowledge" as well.

This observation is sometimes set forth as an argument for the personal nature of truth, but it could more accurately be viewed, it seems to me, as addressing the personal dimension of faith. It is a way of stressing the crucial subjective aspect of Christian faith, wherein the fact that, say, the gospel is objectively true whether I believe it or not does me little good ("even the demons believe, and tremble") until I personally appropriate it with a sort of "passionate inwardness." In this sense truth is very personal indeed.

But more to our point is the notion expressed by McGrath. His is a familiar and important argument. Since the God who is the author of truth is a person, and only persons are capable of apprehending his truth, the point seems inescapable: truth is profoundly personal. Stones or fish or cyclones know nothing about truth. Only persons care about issues of truth. Yet none of this contradicts what we have said about the fundamental nature of truth. When Jesus says, "I *am* the truth," he is speaking precisely as the great *Logos,* the Word, the ultimate expression of God to the *cosmos.* "No one has seen God at any

---

13. McGrath, *A Passion for Truth,* p. 178.

14. Here is Kierkegaard's full statement: *"An objective uncertainty held fast in an appropriation-process of the most passionate inwardness is the truth,* the highest truth attainable for an *existing* individual." Søren Kierkegaard, *Concluding Unscientific Postscript,* trans. David F. Swenson and Walter Lowrie (Princeton: Princeton University Press, 1941), p. 182.

time," says John; "the only begotten God who is in the bosom of the Father, he has *explained* him" (John 1:18). The verb "explained" here is the Greek *exegeomai,* from which we derive our term "exegesis." The verb means to recount, to unfold, to declare. Jesus is the exact "representation" ("likeness, image," *eikon,* Col. 1:15) of the invisible God. In him dwells all the fullness of the Godhead *bodily* (Col. 2:9). Everything he embodies or does or expresses is in exquisite accord, absolute oneness, with the Father (John 10:30). Whatever is true about God, Jesus expresses it, declares it, incarnates it perfectly. Truth is not merely a set of cognitive propositions or ideal Platonic forms, living out their abstract existence in isolation from and without need of God. Truth has no independent existence whatsoever. Truth is utterly contingent upon the personal God of the universe. All truth comes from God and is given its ultimate expression in God's Son, Jesus Christ. The idea that Jesus *is* the truth does not work against our understanding of truth as a feature of apprehensions or expressions; it is in fact the ultimate instance of this very thing. "In many and various ways God spoke of old to our fathers by the prophets; but in these last days he has spoken to us by a Son" (Heb. 1:1-2). Everything about Jesus and his teaching perfectly expresses God to the world. He himself *is* the very Word of God. Thus Jesus Christ may be the ultimate instance of a "picture *(eikon)* theory" of language at work within a "correspondence theory" of truth.[15]

10. All that is truthful, from whatever source, is unified, and will cohere with whatever else is truthful.
Because God's reality is unified and coherent, centered as it is on the person of Christ, all truthful apprehensions of that reality, or truthful expressions of those apprehensions, will cohere and contribute to an integrated, unified, Christ-centered vision of all things. Thus no Christian need fear truth from any source. As Cardinal Newman said, "Truth is bold and unsuspicious; want of self-reliance is the mark of falsehood."[16] What humans may discover in one place, if it is true, will always — at least, in the end — cohere with what is known truly from another place,

---

15. Cf. Miroslav Volf, "Theology, Meaning, and Power," in *The Future of Theology: Essays in Honor of Jürgen Moltmann,* ed. Miroslav Volf, Carmen Krieg, and Thomas Kucharz (Grand Rapids: Eerdmans, 1996), pp. 106-8.
16. *The Idea of a University,* p. 55.

and all will ultimately manifest their Christ-centeredness. That is because all truth, whatever its source, can be said to be true only by virtue of the fact that it accords with "things as God knows them to be." And "things as God knows them to be" form a unified, Christ-centered whole.

It is in this sense that "All truth is God's truth." All truth is sourced in God — it is his truth, which is to say, it accords with what he has designed, what he knows to be the case, and what he has made available to us. This is what renders it truthful. Thus Arthur Holmes can sum up the Christian's intellectual task this way: "If [all truth] ultimately fits into a coherent whole, then our task is to interpret it as such by developing Christian perspectives in the natural and social sciences and the humanities, so as to structure a Christian worldview that exhibits plainly the principle that truth is one and all truth is God's."[17]

Needful Ideas

We have rushed through these ten ideas. Thoughtful readers may have wanted to stop and explore, or perhaps object, at a dozen points along the way. These ten ideas are massive and complex, and over the centuries each has engendered long and tangled discussions. But my purpose here is not to defend these ideas; that would be, as Walter Metzger said in another context, "a project which, if I were ever brave enough to tackle, I would never be brave enough to do in haste."[18] Even were such a task within the reach of my expertise, it would certainly be beyond the scope of this work.

Nor do I claim that these ideas exhaust a Christian way of viewing the several topics they touch. For instance, Kierkegaard and other thinkers like him typically refuse to settle for the above definition of truth but want instead to build into their definitions the importance of an inward or subjective embracing of it as well. I do not wish to quibble over such definitions or what should or should not be emphasized. My goal here is merely to make explicit the key ideas implicit in our well-worn slogan, "All truth is God's truth," ideas summarized by Arthur Holmes as follows:

17. *The Idea of a Christian College,* rev. ed. (Grand Rapids: Eerdmans, 1975), p. 63.
18. Walter P. Metzger, "Academic Freedom in Delocalized Institutions," in *Dimensions of Academic Freedom* (Urbana: University of Illinois Press, 1969), p. 6.

Long before the Enlightenment and postmodernity, Christian theology taught that God created in wisdom, with archetypal ideas in mind, that truth exists in God's own knowledge and is revealed in his creation. This is part of the metanarrative about Jesus Christ, the Logos of creation and redemption, and his kingdom that awaits fulfillment. It means that truth comes ultimately from God, no matter by what divinely provided means it is discovered. It gives epistemic confidence, confidence in the existence of truth and confidence in reason as well as revelation. Epistemic modesty is important, to be sure, because of finiteness and sin, but epistemic confidence is needed in facing postmodernity.[19]

The adage "All truth is God's truth" represents an attempt to encapsulate each of these fundamental ideas, or relatively close approximations of them, including a core realism and some version of a correspondence theory of truth wherein human ideas or expressions are the truth-bearers and God's knowledge is the ultimate truth-maker. The slogan either assumes these ideas or it represents them within itself and constitutes an affirmation of them. They are entailed in its five pointed words. They are what has made this catchphrase so useful and given it such a punch. As an aphorism it may be brief, but it carries a heavy wallop.

I do not think we in Christian higher education can do without some version or variation of these essential ideas. Together they constitute a position which may be called, not a "naive realism," but a "sophisticated realism,"[20] "unified realism,"[21] "chastened realism,"[22] or "critical realism." Darrell Bock describes the critical realist's stance as follows: "By 'critical realism' I mean that there is a reality external to us:

19. Arthur Holmes, *Building the Christian Academy* (Grand Rapids: Eerdmans, 2001), pp. 106-7. For some important contrasts of this position with Platonic thought, see Holmes, *All Truth Is God's Truth* (Grand Rapids: Eerdmans, 1977), pp. 32ff.

20. "Christians will be (sophisticated) realists because they are theists. There is one God and therefore one world and one truth about that world (i.e., God's knowledge of the world)." Alan Padgett, "Christianity and Postmodernity," *Christian Scholar's Review* 26, no. 2 (1996): 131.

21. See Paul Helm, *Faith and Understanding* (Grand Rapids: Eerdmans, 1997), pp. 53-54.

22. George Marsden, "Beyond Progressive Scientific Humanism," in *The Future of Religious Colleges,* ed. Paul J. Dovre (Grand Rapids: Eerdmans, 2002), p. 46.

We have awareness and knowledge of it, so that our accounts of that reality at least roughly correspond with it, though we're not infallible or exhaustive in our understanding of it. Our awareness of our fallibility makes us critical about the realism within the world. Thus we must constantly examine and reexamine our understanding to check our penchant to understand incompletely if not erroneously."[23]

Such a stance gives meaning to concepts such as knowledge, truth, and an integrated, Christ-centered worldview. I make no claim of being able to answer all the philosophical or theological objections our modern or postmodern world may raise against these ideas. But this much I do know: the day we in Christian higher education lose the right to speak of God's existence, or of the real world he has created, or of our finite capacity for knowing that reality, or of a unified Christ-centered worldview, or of such things as the actuality of truth and error, on that day we will have to stop calling the education we offer historically Christian.

Conclusion

In 1966 the Danforth Commission published its Report on *Church-Sponsored Higher Education in the United States.* As part of that report the commission asked, "What is the most valuable contribution an institution can hope to make to the lives of its students?" Their reply:

> Our answer is a reasoned framework of belief that gives meaning to human existence. It should be a faith that has something to say about the inescapable realities of life — good and evil, joy and suffering, death, history, God — a faith that will stand the test of time. It should be the student's own in the sense that it is a part of him — he has thought it through — though probably not his own in the sense that he invented it.
>
> Higher education cannot, even if it would, "give" the student a

23. *Purpose-Directed Theology: Getting Our Priorities Right in Evangelical Controversies* (Downers Grove: InterVarsity Press, 2002), p. 22. Cf. David K. Naugle, *Worldview: The History of a Concept* (Grand Rapids: Eerdmans, 2002), p. 106; N. T. Wright, *The New Testament and the People of God: Christian Origins and the Question of God,* vol. 1 (Minneapolis: Fortress Press, 1992), p. 35.

faith. An adequate faith is a product of many influences. . . . But a college can at least inform the student about the principal alternatives and help him acquire the intellectual tools and a disposition to consider maturely fundamental questions. Through curricular means it can encourage him to organize and unify his knowledge and strive for depth of understanding. It can hold up wisdom and commitment as goals to be sought.[24]

This is a powerful vision, but it is one to which no secular education these days could or would aspire. It is, however, the very kind of education promised and made possible by the ideas entailed in the phrase, "All truth is God's truth." These ideas are invaluable, and they must be cultivated, lest we allow them to atrophy through inattention. They are both ancient and as up-to-date as this morning's newspaper. In every generation they will be challenged, but if we are to preserve the educational goals stated above, they must not be lost.

Could ideas so fundamental to historic Christianity truly be in jeopardy? They are so basic and have held their own for so long that, in the end, the answer must surely be No with regard to the ideas themselves. But with equal certainty we must say Yes with regard to our faithfulness in maintaining them and living them out. The ideas themselves will not disappear, but our commitment to championing them may. The following chapter examines one such core idea that in our generation appears vulnerable.

24. *Church-Sponsored Higher Education in the United States,* ed. Manning M. Pattillo, Jr., and Donald M. Mackenzie (Washington: American Council on Education, 1966), p. 69.

6 A Balanced Epistemology

....

CHALLENGE *To Preserve the Idea of Truth*

O f the several ideas embedded in the slogan, "All truth is God's truth," the most endangered within Christian higher education may be those which touch on the nature of truth and the human capacity to apprehend it. One can see this in the frequency with which we hear those who, one would think, should know better, embracing a perspectivist epistemology, one of the pillars of so-called postmodernity.

Postmodern Reservations

I draw upon the notion of postmodernity only with reluctance. I truly dislike the term, for several reasons. First, there is the question of definition. It is scarcely possible to speak of postmodernity as a single thing, as if it were monolithic. As Thomas Haskell has observed, the term is rather a catchall label used to refer to a "multifaceted explosion of interest in theoretical and epistemological issues in the human sciences."[1] Thus generalizations about postmodernity are inherently precarious and fragile things, susceptible to refutation by the merest citation of some particular postmodernist who may not agree. The term

---

1. *Objectivity Is Not Neutrality: Explanatory Schemes in History* (Baltimore: Johns Hopkins University Press, 1998), p. 8. But see Robert C. Greer's attempt to make sense of the landscape in *Mapping Postmodernism: A Survey of Christian Options* (Downers Grove: InterVarsity Press, 2003).

often appears hopelessly ambiguous, and as a result, may have already outlived its usefulness.

But my greater reservation lies deeper. I find myself increasingly resistant to the way such language inexorably sets the terms of the discussion. This idea is "pre-modern," we say; that one over there is "modern"; another along the way is "post-modern." Must everything be measured against the Enlightenment? How long must we hear modes of thinking that have been around forever characterized only in terms of how they relate to modernity, pre- or post-? What about ideas that long predated modernity? Is it not possible that we should use them to measure modernity, or its offspring postmodernity, rather than the reverse?

For centuries after the Enlightenment Christian thinkers working from a historic Christian worldview called modernity's hubris into question. What sense can it make, then, to refer anachronistically to their critique as "postmodern," as some seem to want to do? Or again, is our analytical framework so impoverished that a simple argument from evidence must *ipso facto* be a sign of having made undue concessions to modernity? When the Apostle Paul summarizes the Gospel — "Christ died for our sins according to the Scriptures, he was buried, he was raised on the third day according to the Scriptures" — and then proceeds to cite extended historical evidence for its credibility — "he appeared to Cephas, then to the twelve, then to more than five hundred brethren at one time, most of whom are still alive, then he appeared to James, then to all the apostles" (1 Cor. 15:1-7) — is this a sign he had been co-opted by modernity's bent toward historicism? One might think so given how often we hear contemporaries rebuked for not much more than following the Apostle's lead.[2] Anyone who knows the history of rhetoric knows that such argumentation has been around from the beginnings of human discourse. If modernity's thinkers became overly enamored of it, they certainly did not invent it. Nor should they be granted proprietary ownership.

What we require, it seems to me, is a modicum of historical perspective. Part of my resistance to the term "postmodernity" lies in con-

---

2. For example, as if no one prior to the Enlightenment cared about such things, see an interest in historicity treated as an automatic indicator of modernity in Greer, *Mapping Postmodernism*, pp. 148-49; cf. pp. 81-86.

tributing to the impression that anything so stylish and trendy — so very "post" — must be new and fresh. The term is trendy enough, but one thing is certain: its ideas surely are not new. The complex of ideas the term typically conjures up, with a radical perspectivalism at their center, are as old as the ancient Sophists, the movement against which in one way or another virtually all of Plato's dialogues were written. Reading an account of these early thinkers — for example, *The Sophists,* by W. K. C. Guthrie[3] — is like reading a *fin de siècle* account of our own academic environment.

The notion that postmodernity represents something novel is therefore shortsighted. Most of its proposals are as old as the history of ideas. Were the ancient Sophists postmodern? Or are postmoderns merely neo-Sophists? The truth is, throughout the centuries these sophistic ideas have repeatedly seen the light of day, and each time they have been weighed and found wanting by Christian thinkers, as they should be again today.

But if we are to use the term intelligibly, we must mean something by it. So let us borrow Alister McGrath's summary description. McGrath identifies postmodernity's leading general feature as "the deliberate and systematic abandonment of centralizing narratives." Says he,

> The general differences between modernity and postmodernity have been summarized in terms of a series of stylistic contrasts, including the following:

Modernism	Postmodernism
Purpose	Play
Design	Chance
Hierarchy	Anarchy
Centering	Dispersal
Selection	Combination

> Note how the terms gathered together under the "modernism" category have strong overtones of the ability of the thinking subject to analyze, order, control and master. Those gathered together under the "postmodernism" category possess equally strong overtones of

3. *The Sophists* (Cambridge: Cambridge University Press, 1971).

the inability of the thinking subject to master or control, with the result that things need to be left as they are, in all their glorious and playful diversity. This applies just as much to the religions as to everything else.

It will thus be clear that there is an inbuilt precommitment to relativism or pluralism within postmodernism in relation to questions of truth. To use the jargon of the movement, one could say that postmodernism represents a situation in which the signifier has replaced the signified as the focus of orientation and value.[4]

Radical Perspectivism

No part of this ancient and postmodern mix is more inimical to a Christian worldview, it seems to me, than the radical perspectivism that lies at its core. Says Merold Westphal, perspectivism "is the dual claim that our insights . . . are relative to the standpoint from which they are made, and that the standpoint we occupy . . . inevitably betrays that it is not an absolute standpoint, an all-inclusive 'totalizing' point of view that sees everything and is blind to nothing. In short, perspectivism is the relativism that insists that we are not God, that only God is absolute."[5] According to Westphal, such perspectivism constitutes a common thread among postmodern as well as other contemporary philosophers. Significantly, Guthrie makes precisely the same point about the ancient Sophists. Thus he speaks of the "one epistemological standpoint which all shared, namely a scepticism according to which knowledge could only be relative to the perceiving subject."[6]

It is not uncommon nowadays to hear Christians herald this sort

---

4. Alister McGrath, *A Passion for Truth: The Intellectual Coherence of Evangelicalism* (Downers Grove, Ill.: InterVarsity Press, 1996), p. 185.

5. Merold Westphal, "Postmodernism and the Gospel: Onto-theology, Meta-narratives and Perspectivism," *Perspectives* 15 (2000): 10. For an insightful critique of this central, indeed identifying, premise of postmodernism, see Douglas Sloan, *Faith and Knowledge: Mainline Protestantism and American Higher Education* (Louisville: Westminster/ John Knox Press, 1994), pp. 212ff.

6. Guthrie, *The Sophists*, p. 50; see also pp. 4ff. for the full complex of sophistic thought. Cf. Plato, *Cratylus* 385E.

of perspectivism as a positive development. Perhaps the epitome, or na-dir, of this sort of thinking was Mark McLeod's argument in his article, "Making God Dance: Postmodern Theorizing and the Christian College." McLeod rejects the very existence of a knowable "thing-in-itself" reality. Says he, "My thesis is that there is no . . . mind-independent world; there are, instead, many worlds that are created by human theo-rizing and creative work." Thus a concern for what is true is replaced by a search for what is "interesting" — and in particular for the Christian, what is "interesting" to God:

> What makes our theories objective is not some world external to our minds but rather that God takes delight in them, that they make God dance. Our theories can be wrong — note that I did not say false. They can be wrong if God does not approve of them, if God finds them uninteresting. Furthermore, there can be more than one theory that is right, since God can find more than one thing interesting. And beliefs can be true, but only within the the-ory or, more broadly speaking, worldview in which the belief is held. But what is true given the conditions of one theory or worldview may not be true in another. Of course one cannot say that they contradict one another across the worlds, for that as-sumes a third-person point of view, a noumenal world. That is pre-cisely what is rejected on this account. None of this means that just anything will go, for God will not approve of just anything. Some theories do not make God dance.[7]

This sort of radical perspectivism, though seldom stated in such cavalier form, appears to have made significant headway in Christian academic circles. After all, it is claimed, the epistemic humility repre-sented by such an approach is just the Christian's cup of tea. Moreover, postmodernity's perspectivism "actually serves to open the academy to the voices of Christian scholars and others with a theistic approach to teaching and scholarship. If all views are considered equal in a postmodern world, then the Christian voice must be as welcomed as any other."[8] Thus, it is argued, a perspectivist stance may afford Chris-

7. "Making God Dance: Postmodern Theorizing and the Christian College," *Christian Scholar's Review* 21, no. 3 (March 1992): 286.
8. Dennis A. Sheridan, "Modern and Postmodern Challenges to Liberal Educa-

tians a new place at the academic table, a place which was often denied by modernity.

An Alluring Half-Truth

Yet as David Livingstone warns, "The very pluralism that gets Christian thinking to the table can too easily tend to extract the teeth of its cognitive claims."[9] Here is the question: If we embrace such an all-encompassing perspectivism, what happens to the notions of "reality," "truth," and "knowledge"? If we are utterly unable to see any dimension of anything in any way as it really is, if all we ever have is our own point of view, what happens to the ancient claims of the Bible, of the Gospel? What happens to the Church's willingness (or ability) to say to the world, as it has from its inception, "Thus saith the Lord"? Is the good news of Jesus Christ really no more than "my point of view," something that works for me? Have we no access whatever to the real, to the absolute, to that which transcends us all and is therefore as true for one as it is for the other? As Lesslie Newbigin reminds us, "The church witnesses to that true end for which all creation and all human beings exist, the truth by which all alleged values are to be judged. And truth must be public truth, truth for all. A private truth for a limited circle of believers is no truth at all."[10]

Radical perspectivism — whether in its Kantian, Emersonian, or Nietzschean forms — has always seemed to me a half-truth masquerading as the whole truth. Half of the truth surely is that we take in everything through our own perceptual grid, and this point must be taken seriously. As I will argue in a later chapter, experience, presuppositions, and paradigms color everything. They affect what we look for or don't look for; how we look or don't look; what we see or don't see. There can be no such thing as value-free, theory-free, paradigm-free facts, the so-called "view from nowhere." The lens through which we peer is impli-

tion," in *The Liberal Arts in Higher Education: Challenging Assumptions, Exploring Possibilities*, ed. Diana Glyer and David L. Weeks (Lanham, Md.: University Press of America, 1998), p. 44.

9. David N. Livingstone, "The Idea of a University: Interventions from Ireland," *Christian Scholar's Review* 30, no. 2 (December 2000): 202.

10. *Foolishness to the Greeks: The Gospel and Western Culture* (Grand Rapids: Eerdmans, 1986), p. 117.

cated in everything we see. But this is no new postmodern insight. Clear-eyed thinkers have acknowledged as much for a very long time. Nearly half a century ago, for example, Willis Glover argued that "no one can be fully conscious of his own perspective. . . . Objective scholarship is an abstraction; it can never be realized in concrete fact."[11]

Yet this observation, as important as it is, does not represent the whole picture. It must be balanced with its counterweight: namely, the idea that because of the *imago dei* within us, and because of the way God has made the world, we also possess the capacity to see some things, in some ways, to some extent as they really are. "Every truth — if it really is truth — presents itself as universal, even it if is not the whole truth."[12] Thus Stephen Toulmin says, "The view that each of us has of the events through which we have lived is inevitably *incomplete*, but that is not the same as being *slanted*: that is, biased to the point of actual distortion. So the claim that there is no way to avoid bias or distortion . . . elevates a practical problem to the level of an outright impossibility."[13]

The matter of transcending one's own perspective does indeed present a practical obstacle to seeing anything "as it really is." But as Toulmin notes, we need not elevate this practical problem to the level of impossibility. We do possess the capacity to see some things, in some ways, to some extent as they really are. As Amos Yong says, "Evangelicals can and should acknowledge the fallibilistic nature of knowledge and the relative or contextual form of all interpretation, without surrendering to a skeptical or nihilistic relativism with regard to truth."[14] If we are to maintain a genuinely biblical and historically Christian epistemology, we must find ways to uphold both ends of this tension.

A Balanced Stance

Mark Schwehn is one who, in his discussions of Christian higher education, has resisted the demands of an unbridled perspectivism. He

11. Willis B. Glover, "The Vocation of a Christian Scholar," *The Christian Scholar* 37, no. 1 (March 1954): 423.

12. John Paul II, *Fides et Ratio*, 27.

13. *Return to Reason* (Cambridge, Mass.: Harvard University Press, 2001), p. 7.

14. "The Demise of Foundationalism and the Retention of Truth: What Evangelicals Can Learn from C. S. Peirce," *Christian Scholar's Review* 29, no. 3 (March 2000): 580.

says, "Christians . . . should insist that all human beings share a capacity for self-transcendence, an ability to bring their own narrative identities under some measure of critical scrutiny. Part of what it means for humankind to be fashioned in the image of God is that we are imbued with a capacity for critical self-consciousness."[15] Schwehn calls for an objectivity "properly refurbished under Christian auspices." It would not be an objectivity that involves the "the notion of an unmediated access to reality" or "the view that we could ever become free from bias or purified of distortions." Rather, what he has in mind is historian Thomas Haskell's notion of the "ascetic dimension" of the intellectual life. He quotes Haskell as follows:

> The very possibility of historical scholarship as an enterprise distinct from propaganda requires of its practitioners that vital minimum of ascetic self-discipline that enables a person to do such things as abandon wishful thinking, assimilate bad news, discard pleasing interpretations that cannot pass elementary tests of evidence and logic, and, most important of all, suspend or bracket one's own perceptions long enough to enter sympathetically into the alien and possibly repugnant perspectives of rival thinkers. All of these mental acts — especially coming to grips with a rival's perspective — require detachment, an undeniably ascetic capacity to achieve some distance from one's own spontaneous perceptions and convictions, to imagine how the world appears in another's eyes, to experimentally adopt perspectives that do not come naturally — in the last analysis, to develop, as Thomas Nagel would say, a view of the world in which one's own self stands not at the center, but appears merely as one object among many.

It seems to me that the Christian must stake out the territory somewhere near the midpoint between a strong epistemological realism and a strong epistemological idealism, bearing the full tension of the two while succumbing to neither side. For the full truth lies at neither end of the spectrum. If the naive realist makes too little of the human role, the full-blown idealist makes too much.[16] Yet upholding both sides

15. "The Christian University: Defining the Difference," *Current Issues in Catholic Higher Education* 20, no. 2 (Spring 2000): 17.

16. Alvin Plantinga: "[Perennial naturalism] vastly underestimates the place of

of this tension is precisely what a radical perspectivism does not do. It capitulates to the idealist side, allowing it to eclipse the realist. It is as if we were to become polytheists by allowing the "God is Three" affirmation of the Trinity to drown out the "God is One," or Docetists by allowing the deity of Christ to overwhelm his humanity. Our task is to hold the twin tensions of our epistemological stance. Neither can be allowed to dominate the other. We must concede neither the radical objectivism of modernity nor the equally radical subjectivism of postmodernity. As David Naugle argues, "If held in balance, this position can avoid the excesses of both modernist dogmatism and postmodern skepticism and terminate in a kind of critical realism which recognizes the role of both objectivist and subjectivist factors in the knowing process."[17]

The Appeal to Humility

An unbalanced perspectivism represents a particularly seductive half-truth for Christians because of its susceptibility to being declared the whole truth by virtue of its appeals to humility. Yet this half truth *qua* whole truth represents postmodernity's grounds for humility, not the Christian's.[18] For Christians to capitulate to it is to embrace the spirit of our age at the expense of the historic stance of biblical Christian-

---

human beings in the universe, and [creative anti-realism] vastly overestimates it." "On Christian Scholarship," in *The Challenge and Promise of a Catholic University,* ed. Theodore Hesburgh (Notre Dame: University of Notre Dame Press, 1994), p. 275.

17. Naugle, *Worldview: The History of a Concept* (Grand Rapids: Eerdmans, 2002), p. 106. Holding these two tensions is not quite the same as George Lindbeck's post-liberal attempt to "split the difference" between them; see Greer, *Mapping Postmodernism,* p. 148.

18. For example, see Mark Schwehn's contrast of Richard Rorty's "indictment of objectivism" with Parker Palmer's (*Exiles from Eden: Religion and the Academic Vocation in America* [New York, Oxford: Oxford University Press, 1993], p. 25). The Christian side of this contrast, as applied, for example, to the study of history, sounds something like this: "I have implicit confidence that, because of how God has configured the world, teaching about the past may actually uncover the truth about the past. Or at least some of the truth some of the time in some circumstances, for the epistemological assurance provided by Christian belief is a confidence attended with much humility." Mark Noll, "Teaching History As a Christian," in *Religion, Scholarship and Higher Education,* ed. Andrea Sterk (Notre Dame: University of Notre Dame Press, 2002), p. 163.

ity;[19] it is for the Church to abandon her ancient obligation to say to the world, "Thus saith the Lord." Why? Because such a statement inherently purports to be speaking for God, something a full-blown perspectivism not only renders impossible but deems reprehensible and worthy of censure.

Some seem to hold out the hope that Christians can embrace a full-blown perspectivist's stance without sacrificing our ability to "bear witness to the Absolute," or without descending into an "all views are equally valid" type of relativism.[20] But it is not clear to me how this could be. If we insist that the Absolute exists, but also that we can in no way know it or profess it as such, since all our judgments are perspectival and relative, of what value is our insistence that it exists? What does it mean to claim that we can "bear witness to an Absolute"

---

19. Philosopher Alvin Plantinga portrays this perspectivist epistemology as the product of a prominent worldview he calls "creative anti-realism." Along with Judeo-Christian theism and "perennial naturalism," Plantinga describes creative anti-realism — the notion that it is we the speakers of language or users of symbols or thinkers of categorizing thoughts who are responsible for the fundamental lineaments of reality — to be one of if not the prime contender in the contemporary "arena in which rages a battle for our souls." Speaking of this complex of ideas, Plantinga says, "Suppose you think our world is somehow created or structured by human beings. You may then note that human beings apparently do not all construct the *same* worlds. . . . Here it is an easy step to another characteristically contemporary thought: the thought that there simply is not any such thing as *the* way the world is, no such thing as objective truth, or a way the world is that is the same for all of us. Rather, there is my version of reality, the way I've somehow structured things, and your version, and many other versions: and what is true in one version need not be true in another. . . . There is no such thing as *the* way the world is; there are instead many different versions, perhaps as many different versions as there are persons; and each at bottom is as acceptable as any other. (From a Christian perspective, part of what is involved here, of course, is the age-old drive on the part of fallen humankind for autonomy and independence: autonomy and independence, among other things, with respect to the demands of God.) Thus a proposition really could be, as some of our students are fond of saying, true for me but false for you. Perhaps you have always thought of this notion as a peculiarly sophomoric confusion; but in fact it fits well with this formidable and important, if lamentable, way of thinking. The whole idea of an objective truth, the same for all of us, on this view, is an illusion, or a bourgeois plot, or a sexist imposition, or a silly mistake. Thus does anti-realism breed relativism" ("On Christian Scholarship," p. 276).

20. For example, Merold Westphal, "Postmodernism and the Gospel," pp. 6-10; or Gary John Percesepe, "The Unbearable Lightness of Being Postmodern," *Christian Scholar's Review* 20, no. 2 (1990): 118-35.

when the most we can ever say about it is the absolutely relative, "This is the way it looks to me"? Such perspectivism renders us utterly unable to claim, on the basis of God's Word, what Christ's Church has always claimed: "Here is not merely what we say; here is what God says." Indeed, it locks us out from ever positing *anything* as true, in the strong sense of transcending individual perspectives so as to be true for one in the same way it is for the other.

If the existence of God and the Absolute (as against their absence) makes no practical difference in our understanding of what we as humans are able to know and speak, what is the point of affirming them? In other words, if no one has any access in any way to God's understanding of things — if the Absolute is equally inaccessible to all because we are all restricted to the merely perspectival — of what value is it to insist that the Absolute does in fact exist? And why wouldn't such an insistence itself have to be construed not as a statement about God's actual existence — all such absolute statements being disallowed — but merely another instance of a purely relative statement about "the way things look to me"? And how can such a position lead to anything *but* the morass of relativism? If humans cannot to any degree know and speak truth, in the thick sense of the term, how *could* one person's point of view be any more "true" than another's? Why *aren't* all viewpoints equally valid, or for that matter, equally invalid? In fact, what keeps the notion of validity in play at all?

Robert Hauptman published an article in *Academe* entitled "Dishonesty in the Academy." The article begins with these words: "Academics are committed to the discovery, propagation, and dissemination of truth. They seek it out, confirm it, publish the results of their quest, and teach it to their undergraduate, graduate, and postdoctoral students and protégés. Truth may vary depending on perspective, gender, culture, agenda, zeitgeist, and a host of other factors, but the unequivocal goal of the college or university professor is to ascertain the truth and share it with students and peers."[21] Hauptman then proceeds to lament in detail the widespread loss of integrity found not merely among today's students, but among professional academicians as well. He complains that students in particular "are dishonest because their role models (parents, instructors, doctors, lawyers, clerics,

---

21. "Dishonesty in the Academy," *Academe,* November-December 2002, p. 39.

police, and society in general) offer little to stimulate principled action. Consequentialist ethical theories that care more about results than principles take precedence over traditional moral thinking. As a result, unethical activity becomes acceptable when it is convenient or whenever one can get away with it."[22]

What Hauptman fails to observe, of course, is that one of the key reasons these role models have so little to offer is that they have embraced Hauptman's own confused view of truth. How can it be the "unequivocal goal" of a professor to ascertain and share truth if truth itself "varies" according to gender, culture, agenda, Zeitgeist, and a host of other factors? Whose truth is this professor "unequivocally" ascertaining and propagating? And if truth itself is no more than a dependent variable, how could any other dimensions of one's ethical system escape a similar relativizing effect? What then is left but a "consequentialist ethic" whereby one merely does what is convenient, or whatever one can get away with? Hauptman's appeal to "principles" is pure nostalgia; his perspectivist views won't permit it. And Christians who believe they can embrace a full-blown perspectivism — "perspectival all the way down" — without jeopardizing Christian truth are, I think, equally mistaken.

The Task Ahead

It seems to me that we Christians have our work cut out for us in the realm of epistemology. This is Douglas Sloan's appeal at the end of his extended discussion of mainline Protestantism's engagement with higher education throughout the first half of the twentieth century. Sloan documents the failure of neo-orthodox theology to provide a workable alternative to the shortcomings of both modernity and postmodernity, and then chides evangelicals for more lately embracing the same approach. "Indeed," he says, "the correspondences and similarities between the neoevangelical and the earlier stages of the neo-orthodox engagement with American higher education are striking."[23]

Several of the similarities Sloan sees are unproblematic, even

22. Hauptman, "Dishonesty in the Academy," p. 41.
23. Sloan, *Faith and Knowledge,* pp. 229-37.

commendable. First, he says, there is the emphasis "on the importance of the intellectual life." Second, like the neo-orthodox voices before them, evangelicals are willing to criticize the academy for its "fragmentation and balkanization," and its failure, even its inability, to deal with the larger questions of life such as death, evil, and meaning. In this regard, Sloan says, "evangelicals have one step on the neo-orthodox. They can now appeal to the postmodern breakdown of objectivity, whereas the neo-orthodox had to mount their attack on 'the cult of objectivity' while its devotees were in full sway." Third, evangelicals "conceive of their task as one of bringing a biblically based concept of the Christian faith to bear on modern culture and intellectual life by demonstrating that, of all possible alternatives, such a view of the Christian faith makes the best sense of the human condition." But Sloan is unsure how radically evangelicals intend this. He criticizes the inability of neo-orthodoxy's existentialist approach to keep faith in play with knowledge, and he chides the later narrative theologians for a similar shortcoming. Are evangelicals falling into the same trap? "How different [their approach] is from, say, Reinhold Niebuhr's understanding of the church's task of interpreting the modern predicament in the light of biblical images and stories is not clear." Finally, Sloan argues that "the main emphasis of the neoevangelicals in their engagement with higher education, just as it was for the neo-orthodox, is the need to uncover and criticize the hidden presuppositions of modern consciousness and its intellectual endeavors." In this appeal, he says, the evangelicals "sound almost indistinguishable from the neo-orthodox."

So far, so good. But if in some important ways evangelicals have "caught the falling banner of the mainline Protestant engagement with American higher education" and are "renewing the battle in their own turn," Sloan is not optimistic for their success, primarily because of their inability to propose in convincing terms "actual new ways of knowing, new epistemological possibilities." Evangelicals have "identified the importance of the hidden assumptions at work in modern consciousness, and they have emphasized the need to bring these to light and to demonstrate that other assumptions about the world, with far different implications, are also available and worthy of being considered. Simply proposing alternative worldviews for interpreting the world, however, is not enough." Sloan cites Huston Smith to the effect that "worldviews arise from epistemologies," and then drives home the point with his own observation that "the ultimate hold of any worldview rests in its having its own accompanying epistemology." Evangelicals, he says, "have necessarily rejected the narrow scriptural literalism, along with what George Marsden accurately identifies as the 'early modern' epistemology — a nineteenth-century Baconian common sense realism — with which the evangelical tradition has been yoked for much of its existence." But does it have anything to put in its place? Will not "modern thought forms by their nature make it impossible" to develop an epistemology that will enable faith to hold its own in the academy with knowledge? "Barring their reversion to an earlier, more hardened fundamentalism, the survival of the neoevangelicals would seem to depend directly on the extent to which they succeed in moving beyond the neo-orthodox option in trying to join faith and knowledge. This would require a radical epistemological transformation." But on this count Sloan is skeptical. Says he in conclusion, "Such a radical epistemological turn on their part seems unlikely."

Sloan's skepticism on this point is justified. The particular turn he is angling for is almost certainly one evangelicals will not find compelling, at least not as an answer to the epistemological challenges of our day. Nor will the secular academy. It is an appeal, as he sees it, to the importance of "non-sensory, qualitative knowledge," and to "intuitive imagination" as an avenue to gaining it. If this is impossible, he says, "it is difficult to see that there can be any real future, certainly for religion. And, without the development of qualitative ways of knowing, there can be little hope ultimately (and perhaps proximately) for the future of a living earth, and for the human being overall."

We can agree with Sloan that the stakes in our contemporary epistemological struggle are high, if not quite as apocalyptic as he makes them out, even if we are also concerned that, from a Christian point of view, he has not quite captured them aright. But Sloan's otherwise insightful book is marred by such an unworkable proposal for a solution. What could conceivably prompt our contemporary intellectual world, held in thrall as it is to the common materialist assumption that the question of the existence of God is irrelevant and must be bracketed from the frame, to decide that "the immaterial, non-sensory realm" is just as real as the sensory world we all live in, and that the human "intuitive imagination" is the means of coming to genuine knowledge of it? Even if we were to conclude that Sloan was on the right track — a conclusion I do not share, though I am sympathetic to the need for a more biblically-based, holistic approach to knowing[24] — the approach Sloan sets forth was tried long ago and found ineffectual.[25] The prospects of such a shift are not, we may surmise, very promising.

But more important for our purposes, Sloan's solution represents a certain sleight of hand. True enough, the issues of faith and learning do boil down to two ways of knowing, but by the lights of historic Christianity those two ways of knowing are not *imagination* — something akin to Kant's "aesthetic intuition," or even George Santayana's "animal faith"[26] — and *science*. They are *revelation* and *human discovery*. Sloan's *science/imagination* analysis actually mirrors and thus embraces the very fact/value or knowledge/faith divide his book discredits. What we require is something more radical, a historically Christian approach that challenges the reigning paradigm and refuses to leave its lines in place, an epistemology that begins with God and his image within his creatures. Whether this will prove persuasive to a secularized academy is not the question. The academy's reigning presuppositions may preclude it from even considering such a thing. But that must not deter us. What we require is an epistemology that helps us think holistically *as Christians*. If secular critics do not approve, then we shall have to live without their approval:

> The point of Christian scholarship is not recognition by standards established in the wider culture. The point is to praise God with the mind. Such efforts will lead to the kind of intellectual integrity that sometimes receives recognition. But for the Christian that recognition is only a fairly inconsequential by-product. The real point is valuing what God has made, believing that the creation is as "good" as he said it was, and exploring the fullest dimension of what it meant for the Son of God to "become flesh and dwell among us." Ultimately, intellectual work of this sort is its own re-

24. What Parker Palmer calls "wholesight," or "rounder ways of knowing," in *To Know as We Are Known: A Spirituality of Education* (San Francisco: Harper, 1983), p. xii; cf. Naugle, *Worldview*, p. 334.

25. See James Turner, *Without God, Without Creed: The Origins of Unbelief in America* (Baltimore: Johns Hopkins Press, 1985), pp. 187ff.

26. Cf. George Santayana, *Scepticism and Animal Faith: Introduction to a System of Philosophy* (New York: Dover Publications, 1955).

ward, because it is focused on the only One whose recognition is important, the One before whom all hearts are open.[27]

Finding the Balance

What we must articulate — precisely because it is so profoundly entailed in biblical Christianity[28] — is an epistemological stance that avoids the pitfalls of both modernity and postmodernity. It refuses to capitulate to modernity's radical "objectivist, disinterested onlooker conception of knowing" with its false claims to human certainty; but it also refuses to succumb to the radical subjectivism or perspectivism of postmodernity, with its equally bogus claims of humility. A biblical stance requires something between these two extremes, what Mark Schwehn calls a "through the glass darkly" thesis: "The thesis holds that there really is a way things are that is distinct from any and all of our versions of it, but that we are forever barred for all sorts of reasons from grasping the way things are completely,"[29] with the operative word here being "completely." It is a position that says, in effect, "Though I am finite and sinful and surely 'see through a glass darkly,' and can never in this life know anything as God knows it — which is to say, completely — yet because I am made in the image of God and bear something of his likeness I can nonetheless know some things to some extent in some of their dimensions as they really are." We can make no claims of mastery or of exhaustive knowledge of anything. But neither should we relinquish all claims whatever to knowledge. We seek instead the balance of that historic Christian understanding of knowledge[30] that furnishes us not with certainty, but with confidence; not sight, but a genuine knowing that some things are so because God has dis-

---

27. Mark A. Noll, *The Scandal of the Evangelical Mind* (Grand Rapids: Eerdmans, 1994), pp. 248-49.

28. Ralph McInerny: "One of the convictions of the believer is that nothing he believes can be in conflict with what he knows to be true. . . . So too, in arguing that some things that are revealed entail something else, one must abide by the common rules for valid reasoning." *Characters in Search of Their Author*, The Gifford Lectures, 1999-2000 (Notre Dame: University of Notre Dame Press, 2001), p. 61.

29. Schwehn, *Exiles from Eden*, p. 91.

30. And that of the Catholic church today: see John Paul II, *Fides et Ratio*, 82.

closed them to us, and has made us creatures such that we are able to apprehend to some degree that disclosure, whether from revelation or through our own discovery.

Interestingly, such a balanced epistemological tension constitutes a direct counterpart to the hermeneutical stance of thinkers such as Kevin Vanhoozer. The contemporary world of hermeneutics is plagued by the same postmodern viruses as the realm of epistemology. There, postmodern thinkers have been at pains to overturn any notion of language that could bear the weight of representing truth or reality. In the bargain they also, therefore, overturn any possibility of an inscripturated divine revelation such as the Bible. Significantly, their arguments against such "logocentric" views of language mirror precisely those of the radical perspectivists. Replying to this attack on "the entire Western metaphysical tradition — classical, medieval, and modern — with its confidence in language to mimic or imitate reality truthfully,"[31] Vanhoozer develops a hermeneutical stance that yields not exhaustive but "adequate knowledge." Says he, "Interpretation is not an all-or-nothing affair. We need not choose between a meaning that is wholly determinate and a meaning that is wholly indeterminate. Neither need we choose between a meaning that is fully present and a meaning that is forever deferred." Rather, though for now we see through the text darkly, "we *do* see. There is something in the text that can be known, though perhaps not exhaustively. We must therefore distinguish between the *inexhaustibility* of meaning and its *indeterminacy*. The former need not imply the latter; it is one thing not to know everything, quite another to know nothing."[32]

Certainty versus Confidence

I have noted that for Christians certainty, at least in the Enlightenment sense, is not required for genuine knowledge. This of course depends on what we mean by "certainty" and "knowledge." Yet I do not wish to burden our current discussion with a complex discussion of theories of

---

31. Naugle, *Worldview*, p. 176.

32. *Is There a Meaning in This Text? The Bible, the Reader, and the Morality of Literary Knowledge* (Grand Rapids: Zondervan, 1998), p. 139.

knowledge. What I am interested in is the less technical biblical distinction[33] the Apostle Paul makes when he says, "We walk by faith, not by sight" (2 Cor. 5:7). In this contrast sight stands for the kind of certainty so valued by modernity; it is the result of seeing things for oneself. According to Paul, this is just what the Christian often does not have, and more importantly, must not demand. What the Christian discovers, by contrast, is *confidence,* that confidence that comes through trusting the Word of God (Heb. 11:1-2). Thus the contrast Paul has in mind here is not the common one between certainty and doubt; it is the contrast between certainty and confidence. A simple example serves to illustrate the point.

Mr. A happens upon a crime in progress. He observes Mr. B, whom he knows, pull out a gun and shoot an unarmed man. Mr. A rushes to the victim and discovers that his heart has stopped beating. He's dead. Mr. A has witnessed a murder.

At Mr. B's trial, Mr. A is called to the witness stand. As part of his examination the prosecutor asks Mr. A whether he is sure it was the defendant, Mr. B, who shot the victim. Mr. A says yes, he is "certain" it was Mr. B.

The trial ends with the jury convicting Mr. B of first-degree murder, and he receives a harsh sentence. After the trial a reporter interviews Mrs. C, who was one of the jurors. "You knew your decision would have grave consequences for the defendant; yet you brought back a guilty verdict," the reporter says. "How could you be sure that Mr. B was the one who committed this crime?" To which Mrs. C replies, "The evidence demonstrated beyond a shadow of a doubt that Mr. B was guilty. I became certain of his guilt."

Both Mr. A and Mrs. C speak of being "certain" of Mr. B's guilt. Mr. A's certainty was based on first-hand observation ("sight"), while Mrs. C's was based on a body of evidence centering on the testimony of Mr. A. But both, using the term as most do in its non-technical sense, are "certain" that Mr. B was the murderer. If you were to ask them, "Do you 'know' Mr. B to be guilty?" both would likely answer yes.

---

33. One similar to Augustine's, who understood the more technical distinctions between knowledge and belief, but also observed, "When we utter words more suited to common usage, as, indeed, the Holy Scripture uses them, we should not hesitate to say that we 'know' both what we perceive with our bodily senses and what we believe on the authority of trustworthy witnesses" (*Retractations,* I.xiii.3).

Yet there is an important distinction between their respective "certainties," so much so that we do well to use different terms for their two kinds of knowing so as to avoid confusing them. Mr. A had "certainty" in the sense of seeing for himself; this is essentially what the Apostle Paul means by "sight." Mrs. C, by contrast, had what may more usefully, so as not to confuse the two, be termed "confidence." She came to this confidence — a confidence so strong that it was "beyond reasonable doubt" — primarily because of the testimony of another who knew the truth firsthand. This sort of confidence is akin to what the Apostle Paul means by "faith," or "taking God at his word." We may call Mrs. C's confidence "certainty" if we are using the term colloquially, but if we are trying to make careful biblical distinctions, we would say what Mrs. C experienced was "confidence" rather than "certainty."

Postmodern voices are at pains to call into question modernity's so-called "Cartesian anxiety" — that is, its quest for and pretentious claims to "certainty" — even in the technical realms of science, much less elsewhere. Christians should be sympathetic to this critique. In fact, thoughtful Christians were saying similar things about modernity long before postmodernity came on the scene. For example, Arnold Nash six decades ago argued,

> In theory the liberal university rejects the attempt to teach a unified conception of the world. But it has not failed to teach a *Weltanschauung*. On the fundamental questions of life and destiny, as Kierkegaard has reminded modern man, neutrality is impossible. Even to take up a *neutral* position is to take up *some* position. However, the contemporary university has not even been unconsciously neutral, for it has taught more or less explicitly a philosophy whose fundamental tenets are that man, if not perfect, is, like the world itself, slowly getting better, and that pre-suppositionless science, as the only way of reaching truth, is the main agent whereby — through education — this progress can be maintained. This creed . . . is now shattered beyond all possible hope of repair.[34]

34. Arnold S. Nash, *The University and the Modern World: An Essay in the Social Philosophy of University Education* (London: S.C.M. Press, 1945), pp. 183-84. In this connection, see Sloan's *Faith and Knowledge* for a detailed account of mainline Protestant higher education's extended critique of modernity throughout the first half of the twentieth century. Unfortunately, as Sloan demonstrates in detail, this movement's attempt to re-

The hubris of human claims for this sort of certainty, dispensing as it does with any need for God, deserves to be highlighted. But this critique must not lead us to the opposite conclusion that we cannot therefore know or profess anything as true in the strong sense. Using the term again colloquially, both Mr. A and Mrs. C could genuinely say that they "know" that Mr. B was guilty. Mr. A could know it with something approaching "certainty."[35] Mrs. C could know it with "confidence." When it comes to the truths of Christianity, it is this latter kind of knowing to which Christians aspire, not the former.

Proper Provisionality

What we require, then, is the disentangling of two ideas; namely, that if we cannot know anything as God knows it (that is, perfectly and exhaustively, with "apodictic foundations and absolute totality"[36]), then we cannot truly know anything at all, even partially. We must cut ourselves free from this all-or-nothing idea. "Incomplete" need not automatically imply "false." Nor must it follow that, if we lack God's all-inclusive "totalizing" vision, which sees everything and is blind to nothing, all we are left with is our opinion. These are not our only options.

In his revisiting of John Henry Newman's *The Idea of a University*, historian Jaroslav Pelikan helpfully distinguishes between two types of relativism. An *ex post facto* relativism, he says, is only another way of expressing intellectual humility; "It represents the admission that after thinkers or scholars or judges have done their best to be honest and not to intrude themselves and their prejudices on their material, the results

---

place the ill effects of modernity's radical objectivism with a neo-orthodox approach to relating faith and knowledge failed utterly. Says Sloan, "By the end of 1969, along its entire front, the major twentieth-century engagement of the Protestant church with American higher education had collapsed, and its forces were in rout" (p. 206).

35. Even in Mr. A's case we do not have absolute certainty. Eyewitnesses are sometimes mistaken. Perhaps Mr. A saw an unknown identical twin pull the trigger; perhaps what he saw was an elaborate hoax. Only God has absolute knowledge and therefore absolute certainty.

36. Merold Westphal, "The Ostrich and the Boogeyman: Placing Postmodernism," *Christian Scholar's Review* 20, no. 2 (1990): 116.

of their research and thought will still be flawed and will bear the marks of the time and place and personality in which they have arisen. This is an admission that keeps scholars honest."[37] But an *a priori* relativism, wherein a radical perspectivism is itself deemed a first principle, is a different matter. This kind of relativism, says Pelikan, bankrupts the entire intellectual enterprise.

Pelikan is right in his assessment of *a priori* relativism, but there is substantial risk of confusion, it seems to me, in using the term "relativism" to describe simple intellectual humility. Both Christianity and postmodernity call for humility in our claims of knowing. Yet they part company in the reasons for that humility. Radical perspectivism claims that all we can ever achieve is our own point of view, but this line of thought comes up short when measured against the Scriptures. What the Bible claims, by contrast, is that, though we can in fact know some dimensions of some things to some extent as they really are, we can never know even these things exhaustively — that is, as God knows them. This need not mean that we know nothing, much less that all of our human knowing, because of its limitations, is therefore false. It means only that our human knowing is always dramatically partial and incomplete. This stance too furnishes more than sufficient grounds for humility, or for what N. T. Wright calls "provisionality."[38] With the Preacher we say, "I have seen the burden God has laid on men. He has made everything beautiful in its time. He has also set eternity in the hearts of men; yet they cannot fathom what God has done from beginning to end" (Eccles. 3:10-11). But this need not leave us mired in relativism. As the Apostle Paul put it, "For now we see in a mirror dimly, but then face to face. Now I know in part *(ek meros);* then I shall understand fully, even as I have been fully understood" (1 Cor. 13:12). Paul would surely have insisted that only God "sees everything and is blind to nothing." But with equal confidence we can say that such an insight did not lead the Apostle to the conclusion that he was left with nothing more nor other than his own opinions.

---

37. Jaroslav Pelikan, *The Idea of the University: A Reexamination* (New Haven & London: Yale University Press, 1992), p. 29.

38. *The New Testament and the People of God: Christian Origins and the Question of God,* vol. 1 (Minneapolis: Fortress Press, 1992), p. 35.

Challenging the Paradigm

But what of the argument that postmodernity's perspectivism at least forces its proponents to afford Christians a place at the intellectual table? Is this not at least one of the happy byproducts of postmodern thought? Nathan Hatch answers this way: "The modern intellectual world is adrift, incapable or unwilling to allow any claim of certainty to set the coordinates by which ideas and commitments are to be judged. The positive side of this situation, of course, is that toleration and subjectivity have become the principal virtues of our age, meaning that marginal groups — even evangelicals — are accorded far more respect than they were earlier in the century. The danger . . . is that the gentle lamb of toleration often returns as the wolf of relativism. Christians, then, are both better off and worse off: better in that they are tolerated like everyone else, worse in that no claim to truth carries weight any longer."[39]

The tradeoff Hatch cites is a crucial one. That postmodernity's relativism represents a boon for Christians has always appeared to me a painfully naive idea.[40] What its advocates do not seem to grasp is this: to join the discussion on postmodernity's terms requires anteing up postmodernity's full-blown perspectivism. All who are willing to grant this starting point will be allowed admission; those who do not comply will not be offered a spot at the table.

Were the academy's constructivist assumptions themselves open

39. Nathan O. Hatch, "Evangelical Colleges and the Challenge of Christian Thinking," in *Making Higher Education Christian: The History and Mission of Evangelical Colleges in America*, ed. Joel A. Carpenter and Kenneth W. Shipps (Grand Rapids: Christian University Press, 1987), p. 163; cf. Hatch, "Christian Thinking in a Time of Academic Turmoil," in *Faithful Learning and the Christian Scholarly Vocation*, ed. Douglas V. Henry and Bob R. Agee (Grand Rapids: Eerdmans, 2003), p. 95.

40. See Michael McConnell, "'God Is Dead and We Have Killed Him': Freedom of Religion in the Post-Modern Age," *Brigham Young University Law Review* 163 (1993), Section IV. After citing the argument that postmodernism would "appear to augur a revitalization of religious freedom," McConnell asks, "Why, then, does it seem not to work out that way? Why is it that most of the post-modernist movements that we see in law — critical legal studies, feminism, critical race theory and so forth — seem by and large in their actual political activity to be hostile and detrimental to religious freedom? Postmodernism, it turns out, represents not just a critique of liberalism but an intensification and exacerbation of the very features of liberalism that created the conflict with the freedom of religion."

to discussion, the picture would be different. Nicholas Wolterstorff, for example, has argued that in this postmodern moment religious perspectives can no longer be denied a rightful place at the academy's table. "As I see it," he says, "what ought to replace the old picture of the academy as a generically human, foundationalist enterprise, is a picture of the academy as a locus of what might be called 'dialogic pluralism': a plurality of entitled positions engaged in dialogue which is aimed at arriving at truth. Those who see the world through religious eyes belong in that dialogue."[41] Yet, as his reference to an arrival at truth indicates, Wolterstorff is not willing to grant postmodernity's constructivist assumptions. In fact, he explicitly rejects them in a series of repudiations: "It is regularly said nowadays that reality is never present to us, forever screened from view by concepts. I disagree. . . . It is regularly said or assumed nowadays that embracing the legitimacy of particularism in scholarship requires becoming a global antirealist — requires holding that there is no way things are except relative to our conceptual schemes. I disagree. . . . It is regularly said or assumed nowadays that each 'perspective' is as good as any other. I disagree."[42]

In our final chapter I will argue for a position similar to what Wolterstorff here calls "dialogic pluralism." But it must be noted that, as illustrated by Wolterstorff, that argument involves challenging the reigning perspectivist paradigm, not embracing it. We find the same challenge in Richard Bernstein's arguments for a similar position he calls "engaged fallibilistic pluralism."[43] Alvin Plantinga and others (including Wolterstorff) have attempted to rise to this challenge by arguing for an epistemological alternative to the radical perspectivism of our day.[44] Similarly, F. LeRon Shults has argued for a "postfoundationalist" middle way be-

---

41. "Scholarship Grounded in Religion," in Sterk, ed., *Religion, Scholarship and Higher Education,* p. 14.

42. Wolterstorff, "Scholarship Grounded in Religion," p. 14.

43. "Religious Concerns in Scholarship: Engaged Fallibilism in Practice," in Sterk, ed., *Religion, Scholarship and Higher Education,* pp. 150-58.

44. For example, Alvin Plantinga, *Warrant: The Current Debate* (New York: Oxford University Press, 1993); *Warrant and Proper Function* (New York: Oxford University Press, 1993); *Warranted Christian Belief* (New York: Oxford University Press, 2000); see also W. Jay Wood's work on the role of properly ordered emotions and virtues in the epistemological task, *Epistemology: Becoming Intellectually Virtuous* (Downers Grove: InterVarsity, 1998).

tween the extremes of modernity and postmodernity.[45] Whether such contributions will suffice remains to be seen, but some such challenge must be mounted. The academy's constructivist presuppositions must be brought to light and opened for debate. What we must not do is acquiesce to, much less embrace, those assumptions under the illusion that they will make a place for Christian thinking at the academy's table. The fact is, they will do the opposite; these assumptions will emasculate genuine Christian thinking or stifle it altogether.

The Academy's Standards

That this epistemological question remains the ultimate issue in the Christian's participation in the secular academy emerged in the epilogue of the summary volume of the thee-year Lilly Seminar on Religion and Higher Education, *Religion, Scholarship and Higher Education: Perspectives, Models and Future Projects*. In this epilogue Nicholas Wolterstorff attempts to identify some of the recurring themes of the sprawling multi-year conversation among a diverse assortment of scholars. In the end, he says, the group generally came together around a position approximating Bernstein's "engaged fallibilist pluralism," or as he might have said, his own "dialogic pluralism." They agreed that the academy, "rather than favoring any particular comprehensive perspective, and also rather than favoring the elimination from any role in the academy of the comprehensive perspectives of its members, should be pluralistic in this regard. Allow, and even encourage, a plurality of voices: the Catholic, the Protestant, the Jewish, the Muslim, the humanist, the naturalist, all of them and more. Give faculty and students the freedom to let their comprehensive perspectives shape their work in whatever way seems to them appropriate, provided it satisfies the standards of the academy."[46] But where the consensus broke down, significantly, was over this last issue: the standards of the academy. Says Wolterstorff, "It was that matter of the *standards of the academy* that caused the most disagreement in the group."

45. *The Postfoundationalist Task of Theology: Wolfhart Pannenberg and the New Theological Rationality* (Grand Rapids: Eerdmans, 1999), pp. 38-42.

46. Sterk, ed., *Religion, Scholarship and Higher Education*, p. 250.

The question apparently boiled down to whether there will be one and only one set of epistemic rules for operating in the academy, or whether those rules themselves must be part of the debate between and among competing comprehensive perspectives. Says Wolterstorff, "The seminar ended with some participants expressing unhappiness over the fact that we had not been able to deal satisfactorily with this fundamental epistemological issue." Yet the directors of the project were at least pleased that the seminar "was able, with such insistence and acuity, to identify this issue as among the most important of those that remained to be analyzed and discussed in depth."[47]

The definition of "the standards of the academy" is indeed the key question. Yet it is not clear to me that the issue is much debated in the academy as a whole; at least, it's not debated in the ways Christians need to see it debated. Despite the courageous forays of scholars such as George Marsden seeking to clear a space in the academy for the purportedly "outrageous" idea of Christian scholarship,[48] the academy appears to be perking along on a set of unwritten but ironclad presuppositions that leave little room for religious claims to truth.

A candid assessment of this state of affairs was drawn by one of the most conspicuous voices in the contemporary academy, the former dean of the College of Liberal Arts and Sciences at the University of Illinois at Chicago, Stanley Fish, in his aptly titled article in *First Things*, "Why We Can't All Just Get Along."[49] Religionists cannot be granted a place at the academic table, argues Fish, because of their insistence upon making religious truth claims. To join the academic discussion one must give up such things. But religionists cannot do so without pulling the rug out from under their own stance, and so they should not even try to join the discussion. But since they foolishly seem to want to join in anyway, they must be told they are not welcome. The two sides, religion and the academy, cannot "just get along." They must occupy separate spheres.

Fish is particularly skeptical of George Marsden's appeal, in *The Soul of the American University*, to the very perspectivism we have been

47. Sterk, ed., *Religion, Scholarship and Higher Education*, pp. 253-54.

48. *The Outrageous Idea of Christian Scholarship* (New York: Oxford University Press, 1997).

49. "Why We Can't All Just Get Along," *First Things*, February 1996, pp. 18-26.

discussing. To offer this as a rationale for why Christians should have a place at the academic table is foolish, says Fish. Marsden's is "a self-defeating argument because it amounts to saying that when it comes to proof, religious perspectives are no worse off than any other. It is an argument from weakness — yes religious thought is without objective ground, but so is everything else; we are all in the same untethered boat — and if a religious perspective were to gain admittance on *that* basis, it would have forfeited its claim to be anything other than a 'point of view,' a subjective preference, a mere opinion. It would have joined the universe of liberal discourse but at the price of not being taken seriously."[50]

Stanley Fish is something of an academic gadfly, but the forthrightness of his assessments is refreshing. And it is typical of him; Professor Fish often writes what others are thinking but decline to say so pointedly. Yet thankfully, neither Stanley Fish nor those he describes have the final word on who will be permitted membership in the academic community. I will argue in a final chapter that the concept of the marketplace of ideas on which Fish and others like him are operating is dangerous, unhistorical, and unnecessary. But Fish is right about one thing: the contemporary academy's epistemological rules appear to leave little room for historic Christianity.

Postmodernity has come late to Christianity's long-running critique of modernity, and the two are agreed that the vaunted claims of the Enlightenment and her children were overblown and doomed to failure. For centuries thoughtful Christian thinkers (though by no means all)[51] were saying as much — and were written off as old-

---

50. Fish, "Why We Can't All Just Get Along," p. 26.

51. As Gregory Alan Thornbury says of many Christians in the academy during the rise of modernity, "Instead of launching a full-scale orthodox critique of modernity, theologians accepted the philosophical terms of the debate and sought to show that Christianity could keep current with new intellectual trends. Ironically, a reverse trend occurred. Even as conservative theologians jockeyed for academic respectability, they continued to lose credibility among their peers. As the theologians conceded epistemological and theological ground, they hemorrhaged older expressions of doctrine for newer ones more amenable to modernity. As the academy grew more alienated from traditional forms of metaphysical speculation, theologians continued to lose face, in part, it seems, because they gave up their beliefs so easily." "The Lessons of History," in *Shaping a Christian Worldview: The Foundations of Christian Higher Education*, ed. David S. Dockery and Gregory Alan Thornbury (Nashville: Broadman and Holman, 2002), p. 56.

fashionedly "pre-modern" for their efforts. Now postmoderns have come to agree. But once we move past this common critique, there opens up a profound parting of the ways. What historic Christianity would put in the place of modernity and what postmodernity wants to put there clash dramatically. In fact, the two are in many ways inimical to one another, particularly when it comes to the question of the nature of truth.

Conclusion

In the end, of course, postmodernity does have something important to say to our generation. Like a contemporary Baalam's ass, its criticisms of modernity need to be heard, and perhaps will be heard in a way the Church's have not. But as Marsden observes, "We ourselves do not have to hold to postmodern epistemologies to see the force of their critiques of old-style liberalism."[52]

What puzzles me, though, are Christians who seem to miss this point. They appear to think that both postmodernity's dethroning of modernity and what it would erect in modernity's place are of equal value, and they seem to want to baptize both as Christian. Such a strategy seems shortsighted at best. Not a few in recent years, with Christian proponents of a radical perspectivism among them, have criticized earlier generations of Christian theologians and philosophers for cozying up too close to modernity. How can they not see that in the decades to come, when postmodernity has long since been eclipsed by some New Latest Thing, the critics will be saying something similar about them?

A wiser stance, it seems to me, is to join Thomas Haskell in his skepticism about our postmodern moment:

> I am not among those who believe that, on a certain day in the 1960s, the path of human development darted off in an unprecedented new direction, producing a so-called linguistic turn that relieves us of any further need for words such as "objectivity," "rationality," "logicality," or "truth." It is mere presumptuousness to

---

52. "What Can Catholic Universities Learn from Protestant Examples?" in Hesburgh, ed., *The Challenge and Promise of a Catholic University*, p. 196.

think that ours is the first generation to see how things really are, and presumptuousness on stilts to think that how things really are is that nothing but language or discourse is real. Although I have no quarrel with those who remind us that history and fiction are not easily separable, I do resist those who glibly dismiss the distinction, as if it made no difference to the conduct of life or scholarship. The fallibility of all truth claims I readily concede, but I have little patience with those who go beyond fallibility to attack the idea of truth itself.[53]

To claim postmodernity as an unmitigated boon to Christianity is to court a dangerous and foolish illusion. Its radical perspectivism mercilessly undercuts the Christian's ability to make truth claims. What we must champion instead are the classical ideas embedded in the slogan "All truth is God's truth." The phrase itself may have outlived its usefulness, but the ideas it was designed to convey remain timelessly pertinent. They have already outlasted "modernity." In the same way, long after "postmodernity" has come and gone, they will still be giving strength and structure to serious Christian thought.

53. Haskell, *Objectivity Is Not Neutrality*, p. 9.

7 Integrative Thinking: Prolegomena

CHALLENGE *To Understand the Integrative Mandate*

We have examined two of the most common catchphrases of Christian higher education, "Christ-centered education" and "All truth is God's truth." Yet another is the equally ubiquitous reference to "the integration of faith and learning." In many circles this slogan represents the best shorthand description of what Christian colleges are about.[1]

But once again, not a few in recent years have found themselves asking whether we may be losing our grasp on what this venerable slogan was designed to convey. One sometimes hears Christian scholars using the phrase while almost in the same breath espousing some of

---

1. This slogan is often lengthened nowadays to include the integration of "faith, learning and living," or of "faith, learning and service." One hears this extension not only from expected quarters, such as Anabaptist (for example, Douglas Jacobsen and Rhonda Hustedt Jacobsen, eds., *Scholarship and the Christian Faith: Enlarging the Conversation* (Oxford: Oxford University Press, 2004) or Wesleyan (for example, V. James Mannoia, *Christian Liberal Arts: An Education That Goes Beyond* [Rowman and Littlefield, 2000]) circles, but from Reformed voices as well. These additions are designed to stress the importance of a more holistic vision of a fully integrated Christian life, not merely an integrated mind or intellect. While I embrace this broader biblical emphasis, the particular challenges to integration I wish to address here remain those of the intellectual sort, and these relate primarily to the first two concepts in the slogan, faith and learning. For a helpful discussion of the broader vision, that is, the challenge of faithfully living out one's integrated, Christ-centered worldview in service to God and others, see Cornelius Plantinga, *Engaging God's World: A Christian Vision of Faith, Learning, and Living* (Grand Rapids: Eerdmans, 2002).

what it was intended to counteract. Could it be that this slogan, too, is failing us?

Sorting out an answer will require us to explore the phrase's three crucial terms, to which we will turn presently. But first we must focus on some preliminary concerns, concerns that raise the question of whether we should be aspiring to integration in the first place. Do we really need the term "integration"? If so, what do we mean by it? To what does it apply? Is it for all Christian thinkers, regardless of their theological orientation? Doesn't an aspiration to integrative thinking lead to a cookie-cutter approach to Christian scholarship?

Necessary Language

Some have argued over the years that the language of integration is unfortunate. It appears to suggest an exercise in forcing together disparate things. That is not what the intellectual task of the Christian is about, say these critics. Christian thinking is about discovering the Christ-centered unity of all knowledge. Thus the term "integration" is misleading and should be replaced.[2]

I am sympathetic to this criticism. I, too, often wish we could dispense with the notion of integration and speak only of the unity of knowledge. But I do not think we can, or should, for this reason: We may be looking to discover the unity of knowledge, but in doing so we are inevitably involved in bringing together not disparate things, but things that since the Enlightenment have been perceived to be or portrayed as disparate.

The language of integration was from the beginning designed to make a statement: What others have put asunder, we want to *re-integrate,* so that we can see it for the harmonious, Christ-centered whole it is. This terminology was targeted specifically against the intellectual disintegrations perpetrated by the Enlightenment. Thus, as William Hasker observes, we have ample justification for speaking of

---

2. For example, the mission statement of the Council for Christian Colleges and Universities, which formerly spoke of the integration of faith and learning, now speaks more generally of transforming lives "by faithfully relating scholarship and service to biblical truth."

integration. "We as human knowers *are* confronted by diverse and apparently unconnected bodies of knowledge achieved through different means; it is precisely and only by 'integrating' such diverse bodies of knowledge that the vision of a unity of truth is gained."[3]

> It hardly needs pointing out that the leadership of the academic disciplines is not in the hands of those who share the vision that "all truth is God's truth." While many Christian colleges provide a good undergraduate education and some offer limited graduate study, leadership in the various academic fields is vested in "prestige" graduate programs at leading secular universities. Christian faculty members, having been trained in such institutions, have typically received little or no guidance in relating their graduate training to their Christian faith. As they begin their professional careers, then, they are *in fact* confronted with two "separate and disjoint bodies of knowledge and belief," simply because the graduate program has not assisted, and may have actively discouraged, the establishment of connections between them. Under these circumstances, to object to talk of "integration" is simply to deny the realities of the situation.[4]

Breadth of the Term

If the language of integration is for Christians all but unavoidable, we will do well to make the effort to keep clear on what we mean, and do not mean, by it. The term will gain fuller definition as we go, but at the outset we should note that when Christians use this language to describe the intellectual task, they are using it somewhat more broadly than did Ernest Boyer in his celebrated 1990 report, *Scholarship Reconsidered: Priorities of the Professoriate.*

Seeking to provide a new vocabulary by which the academic world might more usefully conceive its work, Boyer attempted to distinguish "the scholarship of integration" from what he called "the scholarship of discovery" (original research), "the scholarship of application," and "the

---

3. "Faith-Learning Integration: An Overview," *Christian Scholar's Review* 21, no. 3 (March 1992): 237.

4. Hasker, "Faith-Learning Integration," p. 237.

scholarship of teaching." In this way Boyer used the term "integration" to refer to only part of the scholar's task; that is, that "serious, disciplined work that seeks to interpret, draw together, and bring new insight to bear on original research."[5] This involves, he said, "making connections across the disciplines, placing the specialties in larger context, illuminating data in a revealing way, often educating nonspecialists, too."[6]

By contrast, our use of the term encompasses each of Boyer's categories of scholarship. As Boyer says, summarizing the larger picture, "Surely, scholarship means engaging in original research. But the work of the scholar also means stepping back from one's investigation, looking for connections, building bridges between theory and practice, and communicating one's knowledge effectively to students."[7] As will become clear, we are using the term "integration" to refer to the application of Christian thinking to any or all of these dimensions of the scholar's task.

Thinking versus Communicating

We must also emphasize that the focus in what follows is on the demands of Christian *thinking*. It is crucial to distinguish these demands from the challenges Christians face in communicating with their non-Christian colleagues. The two issues should not be confused. Yet they often are, not least in discussions of whether and how Christian scholarship makes a distinctive contribution to the world of ideas. In such discussions the question of how we think about something in genuinely Christian ways is often conflated with how we communicate about that same thing publicly. The result, predictably, is confusion.

In a *Christianity Today* piece on how Christian historians approach the writing of history, Tim Stafford addresses both of these issues. On the question of communicating with secular peers, Stafford noted that "all evangelical historians find themselves living between two communities. Professionally they are oriented toward the academy. All are stu-

---

5. *Scholarship Reconsidered: Priorities of the Professoriate* (Princeton: The Carnegie Foundation for the Advancement of Teaching, 1990), p. 19.
6. Boyer, *Scholarship Reconsidered*, p. 18.
7. Boyer, *Scholarship Reconsidered*, p. 16.

dents of a rigorous secular training. . . . To be in dialogue with peers inevitably means speaking in a secular voice."[8] In support of this point Stafford quotes historian Grant Wacker: "The nub of the issue is, how do you talk about God in history in a public university? Does that kind of language have any credibility? If language is likely to repel, or to bemuse, there's no point raising it."

But Stafford also cites the Christian scholar's obligation to integrative *thinking*. Thus he speaks of the task facing Christian historians and "the evangelical Christian college, which bases its existence on the possibility of providing uniquely Christian learning. The word integration is supposed to describe the process that professors at Christian schools follow, bringing their faith and their learning together into a coherent whole."

The difficulties inherent in both of these tasks — thinking Christianly and communicating effectively with non-Christian colleagues — are daunting, but they may be somewhat less so if we at least avoid confusing the two. By definition, but also somewhat counterintuitively, the broad realm of secular scholarship represents the *smallest* of the three circles of discourse we discussed in Chapter Three. When speaking in that more circumscribed venue, Christian thinkers will typically restrict themselves to what can be said from those many aspects of their subject they hold in common with their secular colleagues. One way to describe this limitation is to say, as does George Marsden, that in secular settings Christian scholars must "pull their punches."[9] Yet the image of pulling one's punches carries pejorative overtones, overtones I think are unfortunate and unnecessary in the present instance. Perhaps we can improve the picture by conceiving of our communication strategy as an exercise in *transposition,* analogous to the argument of C. S. Lewis in his essay of the same title.

In communicating with his or her secular colleagues, what the Christian scholar is about, to use Lewis's terms, is a "kind of transposition or adaptation from a richer to a poorer medium,"[10] that is, a

---

8. "Whatever Happened to Christian History?" *Christianity Today,* April 2, 2001, p. 42.

9. "Beyond Progressive Scientific Humanism," in *The Future of Religious Colleges,* ed. Paul J. Dovre (Grand Rapids: Eerdmans, 2002), p. 42.

10. "Transposition," in *The Weight of Glory and Other Addresses* (New York: Macmillan, 1980), p. 60.

transposition from a fuller Christ-centered understanding that is charged with meaning, to the secularist's more circumscribed understanding that may be strong on facts but weak on meaning. "The strength of such a critic," says Lewis, "lies in the words 'merely' or 'nothing but.' He sees all the facts but not the meaning. Quite truly, therefore, he claims to have seen all the facts. There *is* nothing else there; except the meaning."[11] Lewis's genius stemmed from his ability to distinguish these two levels of thinking and experiencing, not to mention his insistence upon keeping us straight on their relative merits. Thus we find him constantly reminding us about which is which, as for example when he says things like this: "If flesh and blood cannot inherit the Kingdom, that is not because they are too solid, too gross, too distinct, too 'illustrious with being.' They are too flimsy, too transitory, too phantasmal."[12]

To illustrate the principle of transposition Lewis introduces the familiar example of drawing. "The problem here is to represent a three-dimensional world on a flat sheet of paper."[13] The Christian scholar's challenge in communicating with a secular audience is akin to one who lives in a three-dimensional world trying to communicate with an imaginary figure who lives in only two dimensions:

> If we can imagine a creature who perceived only two dimensions and yet could somehow be aware of the lines as he crawled over them on the paper, we shall easily see how impossible it would be for him to understand. At first he might be prepared to accept on authority our assurance that there was a world in three dimensions. But when we pointed to the lines on the paper and tried to explain, say, that "this is a road," would he not reply that the shape which we were asking him to accept as a revelation of our mysterious other world was the very same shape which, on our own showing, elsewhere meant nothing but a triangle. And soon, I think, he would say, "You keep on telling me of this other world and its unimaginable shapes which you call solid. But isn't it very suspicious that all the shapes which you offer me as images or reflections of the solid ones turn out on inspection to be simply the old two-

11. Lewis, "Transposition," p. 71.
12. Lewis, "Transposition," p. 69.
13. Lewis, "Transposition," p. 60.

dimensional shapes of my own world as I have always known it? Is it not obvious that your vaunted other world, so far from being the archetype, is a dream which borrows all its elements from this one?"[14]

In a similar way, the nature of the Christian scholar's audience may legitimately circumscribe what he or she is able to communicate in a given venue. For the purposes of communication, Christians in purely secular venues often restrict themselves, temporarily and in an ad hoc way, to a flatlander's perspective. Such adaptations are justifiable and by no means useless. Within their limited purposes and as far as they go, these can be wonderfully rewarding academic conversations. After all, three-dimensional characters live not just in the third dimension but in the other two as well. To learn all we can of these two dimensions, and in fact to contribute fruitfully to that body of knowledge ourselves, is not only legitimate for Christians but important.

But it is crucial to see that these same restrictions — the restrictions imposed by the communication setting — must not be allowed to constrain the way Christians *think*, at least not if their thinking is to be distinctively Christian. It is certainly legitimate to try to think integratively and holistically as Christians, but then restrict the sorts of things we communicate when speaking with those who do not share our Christian presuppositions. What we must not do is allow those flatlander restrictions to establish the standards and parameters for our *thinking*.

There is something sad, and dangerous too, about watching Christian scholars sanitize not merely their communication, but their very thought processes to satisfy the demands of their secular guild. Writing of Christian philosophers, Ralph McInerny says, "Many believers, under the influence of the current prejudices of the profession, accept the judgment that they are somehow suspect and anomalous. . . . This leads to the distressing spectacle of believers proceeding as if they did not believe, taking a working skepticism to be a condition of doing philosophy. But a faith thus set aside may not be there when one goes back for it."[15] Along with Lewis, McInerny holds that the Christian

14. Lewis, "Transposition," pp. 61-62.
15. *Characters in Search of Their Author,* The Gifford Lectures, 1999-2000 (Notre Dame: University of Notre Dame Press, 2001), p. 11.

thinker actually holds a "tremendous advantage" over his secular colleagues. Why? "The reason is that his antecedent attitude is not based on hearsay, the idols of the tribe, what the most respected thinkers hold, etc., but on the Word of God. The believer holds as true what God has revealed to be true and has the sanction of God himself for them. Collective human wisdom may be fallible, but God is not."[16]

This line of thinking is why Alvin Plantinga, another Christian philosopher, argues that Christians have no business embracing standards that prevent them from thinking in distinctively Christian ways. In fact, Plantinga argues that such distinctively Christian thinking should show up even in a Christian's public scholarship:

> What we need . . . is scholarship that takes account of all that we know, and thus takes account of what we know as Christians. . . . What we must do . . . is use all that we know, not just some limited segment of it. Why should we be buffaloed (or cowed) into trying to understand these things from a naturalistic perspective? . . . As Christians we need and want answers to the sorts of questions that arise in the theoretical and interpretative disciplines; in an enormous number of such cases, what we know as Christians is crucially relevant to coming to a proper understanding; therefore we Christians should pursue these disciplines from a specifically Christian perspective.[17]

Plantinga's point appears to challenge Grant Wacker's argument above. What is the point, Wacker asks, of using language — much less taking recourse to ideas — that in a secular setting have no credibility? If such language "is likely to repel, or to bemuse, there's no point raising it." Plantinga, by contrast, seems to argue that we should use it anyway. We should do our thinking as Christians and let the chips fall where they may. If our Christian scholarship repels or bemuses, so be it. We are seeking truth, not approval.

But must we choose between these options? Surely there is a case to be made for both as appropriate. There are times when Christian presuppositions must and should come to the fore in public scholar-

16. McInerny, *Characters in Search of Their Author,* p. 12.

17. "On Christian Scholarship," in *The Challenge and Promise of a Catholic University,* ed. Theodore Hesburgh (Notre Dame: University of Notre Dame Press, 1994), pp. 292-93.

ship; the subject matter simply demands it. At such times the Christian scholar may be found standing over against her secular colleagues. As George Marsden says, "Religious scholars can play by the prevailing rules of the academic game only up to a point. At some point or points they will run into real differences that are ideologically based."[18] At other times, however, Christian scholars can without compromise limit themselves to what they hold in common with secular colleagues. As D. G. Hart observes, the distinction between general and special revelation often "removes the inherent antagonism between believing and unbelieving minds by recognizing that they share a world of inquiry in common."[19] In such cases it may be workable for Christian scholars to keep the discussion at a flatlander's level, a level they inhabit along with their secular colleagues. The subject matter, the venue, and the audience will dictate which approach is appropriate.

Yet it is crucial to remember that this is a communication strategy, nothing more. In her *thinking*, the Christian scholar must always remain willing to be distinctively Christian. As Nicholas Wolterstorff comments, the task of thinking as a Christian "requires . . . all the qualities of the competent, imaginative, and courageous scholar. To contribute to the development of theory, sometimes in defiance of the academic establishment, obviously requires such qualities. But equally, to discern that some part of the belief-content of one's authentic Christian commitment ought to be functioning as control within some particular piece of theory-development requires such qualities."[20]

But the inevitable question arises: If Christians make such concessions in their public communication — that is, if we are thinking one way, and, in certain public settings, communicating another — does that not lead to intellectual schizophrenia at best and duplicity at worst? The answer is that it would if our adaptation involved compromising something we genuinely believe. But that is not what I am counseling here. We do not say different things to our secular colleagues from what we truly believe; we are talking only about grounding our communication with our colleagues whenever possible on those as-

---

18. Marsden, "Beyond Progressive Scientific Humanism," p. 41.

19. "Christian Scholars, Secular Universities, and the Problem with the Antithesis," *Christian Scholar's Review* 30, no. 4 (Summer 2001): 400.

20. *Reason Within the Bounds of Religion* (Grand Rapids: Eerdmans, 1976), p. 103.

pects of our thought we hold in common with them. We are speaking of no more than a communication strategy. Marsden labels this sort of accommodation "methodological secularization," which he defines this way: "For limited ad hoc purposes we will focus on natural phenomena accessible to all, while not denying their spiritual dimensions as created and ordered by God or forgetting that there is much more to the picture."[21]

Significantly, the New Testament offers a useful model of this communication strategy. Pauline scholars have long observed the differences between Paul's speeches to his synagogue audiences and the two recorded occasions where we hear him addressing gentile audiences (Acts 14 and 17). With the former he could assume both an acceptance and an understanding of the Old Testament; hence his typical approach to these audiences was anchored in a "Thus saith the Lord" exploration of the Scriptures. But with gentile audiences he could assume no such points of contact. Thus his addresses to them are quite different, and markedly free of references to Scripture. Paul was adapting himself to his audience by restricting himself, at least in these initial efforts, to the points of commonality he shared with them.

Sometimes this is precisely what Christian thinkers should do. In fact, such an approach is often more effective than its alternative. In his discussion of "Christian Apologetics," C. S. Lewis says,

> I believe that any Christian who is qualified to write a good popular book on any science may do much more by that than by any directly apologetic work. The difficulty we are up against is this. We can make people (often) attend to the Christian point of view for half an hour or so; but the moment they have gone away from our lecture or laid down our article, they are plunged back into a world where the opposite position is taken for granted. As long as that situation exists, widespread success is simply impossible. We must attack the enemy's line of communication. What we want is not more little books about Christianity, but more little books by Christians on other subjects — with their Christianity latent. You can see this most easily if you look at it the other way round. Our

21. *The Outrageous Idea of Christian Scholarship* (New York: Oxford University Press, 1997), p. 91; cf. Jacobsen and Jacobsen, *Scholarship and the Christian Faith*, p. 155.

Faith is not very likely to be shaken by any book on Hinduism. But if whenever we read an elementary book on Geology, Botany, Politics, or Astronomy, we found that its implications were Hindu, that would shake us. It is not the books written in direct defence of Materialism that make the modern man a materialist; it is the materialistic assumptions in all the other books. In the same way, it is not books on Christianity that will really trouble him. But he would be troubled if, whenever he wanted a cheap popular introduction to some science, the best work on the market was always by a Christian.[22]

Notice that Lewis is not calling for Christian scholars to adopt the non-Christian presuppositions of their secular counterparts; he is not asking us to cease *thinking* as Christians. On the contrary, he is calling for rigorous Christian thinking, so much so that one could write a "good popular book" on a subject wherein our Christian thinking is so integral that it is latent in the entire treatment. What he is recommending is a *communication* strategy.

The strategy Lewis recommends will not be everywhere useful or possible. But it serves to reinforce our point that we must keep distinct the issues of Christian thinking and Christian communication in a secular setting. In other words, as Christians, our thinking may include more than we attempt to communicate to a secular audience, though it will not include something other. What we must not do, on the other hand, is to allow the limitations of that secular setting to establish the assumptions or parameters for our thinking. The secular setting may dictate what or how much we may say as Christians, but it must not dictate what or how we think.

The Theological Roots of Integration

But isn't this business of integrative thinking, some may ask, a uniquely Reformed or Calvinist affair?[23] I believe we should resist this notion. It's fair to say that Calvinists — from Calvin himself, to the influential work

22. C. S. Lewis, "Christian Apologetics," in *God in the Dock,* ed. Walter Hooper (Grand Rapids: Eerdmans, 1970), p. 93.
23. See Jacobsen and Jacobsen, *Scholarship and the Christian Faith,* p. 25.

of the Dutch thinkers Abraham Kuyper and Herman Dooyeweerd, to the contemporary voices associated with, say, Calvin College and Seminary — have done the most effective job of championing the integrative task,[24] but there can be no thought of proprietary ownership. The rationale I have argued is not a uniquely Calvinist one; it rises out of a *biblical* rationale, one that belongs to all Christians everywhere. It stems from that profound central affirmation of every Christian from whatever tradition that Jesus Christ is Lord. As such it does not depend upon any particular group's distinctive beliefs, and it is certainly not exclusively Calvinist. Hence the expressly non-Calvinist scholar Walter Ong can nonetheless say of Catholic scholarship, "If the scholarship is truly Catholic, it will seek to understand the whole of actuality."[25] In his own life, says Ong, "the biblical and Catholic conviction that, however vast the universe in time and space, God made it all, has . . . been the sustaining force uniting faith and science and scholarship of all the kinds with which I have been in contact. . . . However overwhelmingly huge and complex that universe may be, this is the universe in which the humanity of Jesus Christ is rooted, the universe in which the Son of God became a human being who died for us and rose to bring us to a new life. Our scholarship, like all else in our lives, rests on trust in the living and loving God."[26] Here is a biblical, Christ-centered vision of integration, but one which is by no means uniquely Calvinist.

Consider a Wesleyan approach. Contemporary Wesleyans have not typically stressed the language of integration in describing the Christian's intellectual task. They sometimes speak of applying the so-called "quadrilateral" of Scripture, tradition, reason, and experience. Yet for our purposes this way of describing the Christian's intellectual task takes us in the same direction as the language of integration. The

24. See, for example, James Bratt, "What Can the Reformed Tradition Contribute to Christian Higher Education?" in *Models for Christian Higher Education: Strategies for Success in the Twenty-first Century,* ed. Richard T. Hughes and William B. Adrian (Grand Rapids: Eerdmans, 1997), pp. 125-40; Ken Badley, "The Faith/Learning Integration Movement in Christian Higher Education: Slogan or Substance?" *Journal of Research on Christian Education* 3, no. 1 (Spring 1994): 13-33.

25. "Realizing Catholicism: Faith, Learning, and the Future," in *Faith and the Intellectual Life,* ed. James L. Helft (Notre Dame and London: University of Notre Dame Press, 1996), p. 40.

26. Ong, "Realizing Catholicism: Faith, Learning, and the Future," pp. 40, 42.

scholar who coined the term "quadrilateral" to describe Wesley's intellectual method, historian Albert Outler, makes the point that Wesley's focus was always "firm and clear in its Christocentric focus."[27] What's more, it was rigorously revelation-based; Wesley's "first appeal was to the Holy Bible." Scripture, his "pre-eminent norm," was "truly his second language. His rhetoric throughout is a tissue woven from the Biblical texts. . . . His appeal to Scripture goes far deeper than the use of texts in support of his own views. His larger concern was to let each part of Scripture be pondered in the light of the whole, obscure texts in the light of the more lucid ones."[28] Yet Wesley also understood that there was more to the picture: "Holy Scripture is clearly unique. But this in turn is illuminated by the collective Christian wisdom of other ages and cultures between the Apostolic Age and our own. It also allows for the rescue of the Gospel from obscurantism by means of the disciplines of critical reason. But always, Biblical revelation must be received in the heart by faith: this is the requirement of 'experience.'" What then is needed for genuinely Christian thinking? "A familiarity with Scripture that is both critical and faithful; plus, an acquaintance with the wisdom of the Christian past; plus, a taste for logical analysis as something more than a debater's weapon; plus, a vital, inward faith that is upheld by the assurance of grace and its prospective triumphs in this life."[29]

If there is more to this Wesleyan intellectual tradition than the term "integrative thinking" typically implies, there is not less. Nothing we will say works against this Wesleyan approach to thinking Christianly, and nothing in this approach cuts against the integrative aspiration. If Wesleyans have not emphasized the language of integration,[30] neither does a Wesleyan way of describing the task negate it. In-

27. "The Wesleyan Quadrilateral — In John Wesley," *Wesleyan Theological Journal* 20, no. 1 (Spring 1985): 9. Cf. on Wesley's understanding of human reason, Thomas C. Oden, *John Wesley's Scriptural Christianity* (Grand Rapids: Zondervan, 1994), pp. 74-76.

28. Outler, "The Wesleyan Quadrilateral — In John Wesley," p. 13. So strong was Wesley's commitment to the Bible that some Wesleyan scholars have taken to speaking, not of a quadrilateral, but of the trilateral of reason, experience, and tradition, all under the over-arching authority of Scripture.

29. Outler, "The Wesleyan Quadrilateral — In John Wesley," p. 17.

30. Though the philosophy department chair at one Wesleyan institution uses precisely this language; see Michael L. Peterson, *With All Your Mind: A Christian Philosophy of Education* (Notre Dame: University of Notre Dame Press, 2001), p. 208.

INTEGRATIVE THINKING: PROLEGOMENA

deed, the Wesleyan fourfold approach to Christian thinking is one a Calvinist Presbyterian such as historian Richard Lovelace can recommend for its intellectual balance.[31] Wesleyan notions of human freedom, the capacity of human reason, or the sovereignty of God may well distinguish them from their Calvinist counterparts, but these differences do not lead to a repudiation of the Christian's integrative task. That is because the impulse to a Christ-centered integration is anchored in premises so basic to Christian thought that it transcends such sectarian differences.

One exception to this rule might appear to be the Anabaptist tradition. According to Paul Keim, the distinctive features of Anabaptist-Mennonite colleges are based

> first of all on a shared faith identity connected to Anabaptist history, a core theological vision, and close relationship with distinctive churches. Mennonite historian Harold S. Bender identified the central teachings of the Anabaptist theological vision as "first a new conception of the essence of Christianity as discipleship; second, a new conception of the church as a brotherhood; and third, a new ethic of love and nonresistance." This understanding of Christian faith as incarnational ecclesiology, the mandate to follow Jesus' example in word and deed (discipleship), and the ethic of peace remain the core theological assumptions of the Mennonite church and its colleges.[32]

Thus Richard Hughes concludes, "The starting point for Mennonites has more to do with holistic living than cognition, more to do with ethics than intellect."[33]

Hughes is no doubt correct in this assessment, but we would conclude too much from it if we were to take it to mean that integrative thinking stands in conflict with Anabaptist convictions. While the distinguishing features of the Anabaptist tradition have allowed Anabap-

31. Richard Lovelace, "Recovering Our Balance," *Charisma*, August 1987, p. 80.
32. "The Ethos of Anabaptist-Mennonite Colleges," in Dovre, ed., *The Future of Religious Colleges*, p. 270.
33. "Christian Faith and the Life of the Mind," in *Faithful Learning and the Christian Scholarly Vocation*, ed. Douglas V. Henry and Bob R. Agee (Grand Rapids: Eerdmans, 2003), p. 9.

tist scholars to bring to the table of Christian higher education some badly needed emphases, it probably is the case that they are not the emphases that have typically nourished the hard intellectual work of integration. In fact, one Anabaptist scholar, Rodney Sawatsky, goes so far as to declare, "A coherent philosophy of Mennonite higher education still waits to be written."[34] Yet this does not require us to conclude that Anabaptist emphases somehow militate against the business of integration, much less preclude it. Such emphases may account for why the language of integration has not loomed large within the Anabaptist tradition, but there are any number of Anabaptist scholars who have contributed wonderfully to the integrative task. Being thoroughly Anabaptist and caring about the integration of faith and learning need not be mutually exclusive. The rigors of the Christian's intellectual task should be viewed not as somehow foreign to what it means to be Anabaptist, but as one of the important parts of the holistic approach to Christian living Anabaptists want to stress.

By contrast, the Lutheran tradition is more problematic. It has shown some outright resistance to the notion of integration. In his book *Lutheran Higher Education,* Ernest Simmons grants that the integrative model "deserves consideration." "In this model," he says, "religion and science as well as faith and learning, function in intrinsic complementarity with a common worldview.... There are educational traditions, such as the Roman Catholic and the Reformed, which see this as their ultimate goal. The ideal of the unity of truth drives these traditions to bring all understanding into relationship with the Christian worldview under the Sovereignty of God. It is a beautiful vision of wholeness, which is certainly an ideal of education."[35] Nonetheless, for Lutherans, says Simmons, not integration but *"dialogue* is the intrinsically Lutheran way of approaching the relationship of faith and learning."[36] The worlds of faith and learning engage one another, but without aspiring to the more ambitious goal of an integrated worldview. Why? In a word, humility. "For the most part, ... the Lutheran tradition has opted for a more limited approach, acknowledging that we see

34. "What Can the Mennonite Tradition Contribute to Christian Higher Education?" in Hughes and Adrian, eds., *Models for Christian Higher Education,* p. 192.

35. *Lutheran Higher Education: An Introduction* (Minneapolis: Augsburg Fortress, 1998), p. 6.

36. Simmons, *Lutheran Higher Education,* p. 6.

only through a glass darkly and that all our thought and action is subject to human frailty and sin. It affirms a dialectic of nature and grace
that can mutually inform one another but which in this life can never
fully coincide."[37] This Lutheran preference for a dialogic rather than an
integrative model, says Simmons, "is a direct expression in education
of Luther's understanding of the two kingdoms."[38]

It is not clear to me why the differences must be stated as starkly
as Simmons suggests, since even the most ardent proponents of integrative Christian thinking insist on the requirement of humility. After all, who would not agree with Simmons that "in this life" faith
and learning are never likely to "fully coincide"? Moreover, there is
reason to qualify Simmons's conclusion even on his own terms. He
himself refers to the aspiration for an integrated worldview as "a
beautiful vision of wholeness, which is certainly an ideal of education." Further, in discussing the contribution of religious colleges, he
says, "One of the most important services that colleges can render to
the church is to sustain its faith tradition in dynamic interrelation-
ship with contemporary thought and life. . . . To see all life and
thought within the context of God's law and governance can provide
a basis for holistic integration at a time in society when fragmentation is the norm."[39] Holistic integration? Simmons in fact advocates
a notion not far from the slogan "All truth is God's truth" when he

---

37. Simmons, *Lutheran Higher Education,* p. 6.

38. Simmons, *Lutheran Higher Education,* p. 6. Arthur Holmes attributes Luther's
reticence about integrative thinking to his nominalist background: "Although Luther
emphasized the usefulness of liberal learning in both church and society, he was not optimistic about any further relationship between faith and learning. Human reason, he
allowed, can show that God exists and that he is able to help us, but it cannot reveal who
he is or that he is willing to help. Its main functions are in temporal affairs rather than
in contemplating eternal truths in the mind of God or tracing the unity of truth — a
crucial change from both monastery schools and scholastic universities. Luther's nominalist background was involved here since, if universal terms only designate similar particulars rather than eternal realities, then human reason is basically equipped only for
earthly affairs. Unresolved tensions will remain, and Luther's two kingdom theology
found expression in the relationship between faith and secular learning generally as well
as in the relationship between logic and theology. He refused to integrate them in an
overall logical system as the scholastics did." *Building the Christian Academy* (Grand
Rapids: Eerdmans, 2001), pp. 63-64; cf. pp. 67-68, 115.

39. Simmons, *Lutheran Higher Education,* p. 70.

says, "If the world is God's creation, then there is surely no inhibition to the pursuit of inquiry, for any truth discovered is yet another truth about what God has done."[40] Thus Simmons is able to speak of the "integrity of creation."[41] Why, then, would we not want to pursue an understanding of that integrity as far as our finite and sinful limitations will allow us?

Simmons is right to speak of the unity of truth as an ideal — it *is* an ideal, one we will never in this life achieve. But in our broken world we face a similar dilemma with many of our ideals, such as justice, peace, and love. Does our inability to implement fully such ideals mean that we should abandon the attempt to live them out? Surely, as Jerald Brauer once observed, we should harbor "no illusions about the ease with which a unification of the educational process is to be achieved; nevertheless [we should] stubbornly cling to the ideal that at some point an effective belief in ultimate unification will bring a tentative order and continuity out of a seemingly chaotic enterprise."[42]

Simmons speaks repeatedly of bringing faith and learning into "relationship." But to what end? Surely it is to gain as much as we are able, from both faith and learning, about the "beautiful vision of wholeness" which is available to us in Jesus Christ. One day, so the Scriptures tell us, we shall know fully even as now we are known. But in this age we see as through a darkling glass. Thus all our study requires humility. We must all learn to live with mystery, with the unexplained and the unexplainable. If Mark Schwehn is right, that "Lutheran colleges and universities strive to achieve a perfect synthesis between faith and reason, and then distrust all such final solutions of fallen human intelligence,"[43] then we must all become Lutherans in our tolerance for and even appreciation of paradox and ambiguity. But none of this is an argument for abandoning our aspiration toward "the beautiful vision of wholeness." That vision is not just something for the future; God has graciously given us access, albeit limited access, to aspects of that vision today. Why would we forsake the effort to envision whatever of it

---

40. Simmons, *Lutheran Higher Education,* p. 14.

41. Simmons, *Lutheran Higher Education,* p. 14.

42. Jerald C. Brauer, "The Christian College and American Higher Education," *The Christian Scholar* 41, no. 1 (March 1958): 239.

43. "Lutheran Higher Education in the Twenty-first Century," in Dovre, ed., *The Future of Religious Colleges,* p. 221.

we are presently able to gain by eschewing our aspirations toward integrative thinking?

A Worrisome Problem

Perhaps the differences really are starker than this analysis would suggest. Perhaps there are Christians, Lutheran or otherwise, who do not agree that the truth of Christ is all-redeeming and all-transforming; or at least, they might say, not in this age. They believe we must settle for holding what may be known of the two kingdoms in separate compartments, reserving for heaven any notion of a unified vision. But if so, I find this worryingly reminiscent of an earlier episode in the history of the Church, namely, the collapse of Scholasticism due to its inability to bridge a similar compartmentalization.

"In a world where the gap between Christianity and the common life is paralleled only by that between Christian thinking and secular knowledge," said Arnold Nash, "it is salutary to remember that . . . the medieval synthesis collapsed because the Thomistic separation between the truths discovered by human reason and those given in revelation was the reflection in the sphere of knowledge of the gulf which Thomas Aquinas placed between secular work *(opus manuale)* and specifically religious activities *(opera spiritualia).*" The Church intuitively understood that such a division must be overcome. Yet its approach to doing so turned out to be altogether the wrong one. Instead of seeking the unity of truth to which both ways of knowing speak, it settled for merely trumping the one with the other. Says Nash, "The method adopted by the medieval Church to bridge the gulf was as disastrous in life as it was in learning for it meant that theologians claimed the right to dictate to scientists what they should discover and ecclesiastics assumed the power to dictate to merchants the prices at which they could buy and sell their goods, while, in politics, Hildebrand, rightly claiming that political activities should be subordinate to spiritual principles, wrongly thought that that meant that force could be used by the Church to coerce kings and people alike." As a result, Nash continues, "there could be only one end to this senselessness. In R. H. Tawney's apt phrase, the Church soon ceased to count because it ceased to think." When its own approach to bridging the Thomistic gulf proved unworkable, the gulf was left unbridged and every realm of life was affected. "As the dams of medieval restriction broke, each sphere of human activity: scientific investigation, artistic endeavor, business enterprise and political effort developed along autonomous lines."[44]

This is a sobering tale. The Church's inability or unwillingness to work at bringing faith and learning together meant that it ceased to think Christianly about all the realms of life, which in turn meant that in those realms it ceased to matter. This was Mark Noll's worry in his *Scandal of the Evangelical Mind*. To refuse the challenge to think Christianly about every dimension of life, to allow the realms of faith and learning to remain sealed off from one another, is to cease to think, and thus to cease having any contribution to make. But this, it seems to me, would make for a sad state of affairs. As Lutheran Robert Benne argues, reminding us along the way of another sobering tale,

> Were this version of Lutheran theology taken to its logical conclusion it would deprive the gospel of any intellectual content and the law of any moral content. The biblical narrative and theological reflection on it would not be given any epistemological status to engage secular learning. It would champion a form of Lutheran quietism in the realm of education. Much as German Lutherans in the 1930s separated the two kingdoms (government under law separated from Christianity under the gospel) and allowed the Nazi movement to go unchecked by appeal to the intellectual and moral content of the Christian vision, so this approach would allow modern secular learning to go unchallenged by that vision.[45]

If Jesus Christ is who the biblical record and his Church proclaim him to be, then surely the Apostle Paul is right that we cannot leave faith and learning stranded on separate islands. We must strive to "take every thought captive to obey Christ," however imperfectly we accomplish the task. Our unmitigated allegiance to him, combined with our desire to count for something in our world for his sake, would seem to demand nothing less.

44. Arnold S. Nash, *The University and the Modern World: An Essay in the Social Philosophy of University Education* (London: S.C.M. Press, 1945), pp. 181-82.

45. *Quality with Soul: How Six Premier Colleges and Universities Keep Faith with Their Religious Traditions* (Grand Rapids: Eerdmans, 2001), p. 133.

Is this somehow a uniquely Reformed or Calvinist concern? I shouldn't think so. It grows out of the "central Christian conviction that the entire universe and all of life belong to Christ, and that it is from this conviction that thought and action must begin."[46] We can expect differences among Christians over their understanding of how available in this present age the "beautiful vision of wholeness" may be, but such a debate will be over matters of degree. It would be difficult to make a case from Scripture that it is not available at all. Hence the question may devolve to one of proportion. All Christians can aspire to an integrated, Christ-centered worldview, but to what extent can we expect to achieve it in this present age? On that question we can let the debate continue. In the meantime, Christians of all stripes should be able to rally around this common intellectual mission:

> Colleges in the holiness traditions may start their educational philosophy by thinking that "a holy life means a whole life," in education as anywhere else. Colleges in Lutheran and Anabaptist traditions may center their thinking on Christ's suffering servanthood and a Christian's "strength in weakness" that flows from Christ. But no matter how a Christian college plans to integrate faith, learning, and service, it will never just conduct education-as-usual with prayers before class, or education-as-usual with a service-learning component and a ten o'clock chapel break. No, a solidly built Christian college will rise from its faith in Jesus Christ and then explore the height and depth, the length and breadth of what it means to build on this faith — not just for four years at college, but also for a lifetime of learning and work within the kingdom of God.[47]

Multiple Approaches

Finally, it is important to remember that while our discussion focuses on the task of integrative thinking, it does not address the question of

46. Arthur Holmes, *Building the Christian Academy*, p. 104. Interestingly, Holmes's point is that this was how the Dutch theologian Abraham Kuyper used the term "Calvinism," at least in his discussion of the Christian's intellectual task, over against using it to refer to some "particular theology."
47. Cornelius Plantinga, Jr., *Engaging God's World*, p. xiv.

how such an aim may be pursued across the disciplines. To speak of a common Christ-centered goal does not imply a cookie-cutter approach to Christian scholarship; in fact it requires the opposite. Virtually infinite are the methods required to explore the manifold dimensions of God's complex world and our place within it. Christian scholars employ a wide variety of useful approaches across the several academic divisions, across the many disciplines, even within each discipline.[48] Yet the conviction behind the integrative task is that each of these approaches, if pursued aright, aim toward a common end: a unified, Christ-centered understanding of the world. This is the promise of the slogan, "the integration of faith and learning."

John Henry Newman offered a distinctly nineteenth-century, yet still interesting, description of both the unity and the complexity of what we study. "All that exists," he said, "as contemplated by the human mind, forms one large system or complex fact, and this of course resolves itself into an indefinite number of particular facts, which, as being portions of a whole, have countless relations of every kind, one towards another."

> Knowledge is the apprehension of these facts, whether in themselves, or in their mutual positions and bearings. And, as all taken together form one integral subject for contemplation, so there are no natural or real limits between part and part; one is ever running into another; all, as viewed by the mind, are combined together, and possess a correlative character one with another, from the internal mysteries of the Divine Essence down to our own sensations and consciousness, from the most solemn appointments of the Lord of all down to what may be called the accident of the hour, from the most glorious seraph down to the vilest and most noxious of reptiles.[49]

Inevitably, the study of such a complex unity requires a wide range of approaches. The approach of the natural sciences will look different from the humanities; the arts need not try to emulate the so-

---

48. For a helpful summary of some of these approaches, see Hasker, "Faith-Learning Integration: An Overview," pp. 239-48.

49. *The Idea of a University*, ed. Martin J. Svaglic (Notre Dame: University of Notre Dame Press, 1982), pp. 33-34.

cial sciences. In fact, even within disciplines there will develop many variations. Within applied areas the task will appear different from more theoretical realms. But in each case, we seek to "understand the height and depth, the complexity and startling simplicity, the richness and the stark nakedness, the consistency and the impenetrable paradox of reality as revealed by the manifold paths of the educational search."[50] This variety stems not from artificial disciplinary boundaries but from the fact that different scholars are attempting to think Christianly about wondrously different facets or dimensions of "things as God knows them to be," and they rightly require diverse methods to do so. To try to impose a common approach here would be to deny the astonishing complexity of what God has made.

With these important preliminary considerations on the table, we are now in a position to examine more closely the subject of integrative thinking itself.

50. Brauer, "The Christian College and American Higher Education," p. 239.

8   Doing Integration

CHALLENGE   *To Sustain Our Commitment*
to the Integrative Task

As a rule we generally do better when we talk about what we are for
rather than what we are against. Yet we can sometimes see things
more clearly if we set them in contrast. Inform a jeweler, for example,
that you would like to see a strand of her most beautiful pearls. She will
retreat for a moment to a place of safe-keeping, then bring out some of
her most exquisite treasures. And you may be sure she will not stretch
them across the glass counter. She will first lay out a contrasting background, then display the pearls against it, confident that only then will
you fully appreciate their elegance and simplicity.

Similarly, to understand our integrative aspirations more fully it
may be useful to set them against a strong background, that of their
most prominent rival. So let us examine a common alternative to integrative thinking, one, in fact, which repudiates the very possibility of
integration. It's an approach that reaches back to Kantian distinctions
that have shaped all of modern thought, but more specifically, it stems
from David Hume's stringent fact/value dichotomy.

The classic fact/value dichotomy is grounded in a subject/object
cleavage wherein *objective* thinking is thought to focus on the object of
inquiry, leading to factual statements, while *subjective* thinking is focused upon the subject doing the inquiry, leading to interpretive or
evaluative judgments. We are thus left with two types of statements:
objective "how things are" statements (facts), and subjective "how
things ought to be" statements (valuations).

This conceptual gap between objective *is-claims* and subjective *ought-claims* leads to a deep bifurcation of thought, an uncrossable boundary between issues of fact and issues of value, all the while engendering the illusion that we can nicely distinguish between the two. This represents classic Enlightenment thought and as such, it is the line followed by many within the secular academy throughout much of what has become known as modernity. This dichotomist approach is popular because it holds out a seductive intellectual promise: that of eliminating all conflict between reason and faith, or science and religion. It fulfills this promise, however, only by exacting a hefty price from religion. It relegates religion to the subjective side of the dichotomy, rendering it incapable of speaking to the factual.

A Prime Illustration

We can see the full effects of this dichotomist model by examining a prominent example. In 1999 the late Harvard palaeontologist Stephen Jay Gould published a book entitled *Rocks of Ages: Science and Religion in the Fullness of Life.*[1] It is a prime illustration of the dichotomist model at work. In this book Gould displays the intellectual consequences of starting with a fact/value dichotomy, a division he traces to Hume and which he attributes, not implausibly, to most thinking people today both within and without the academy.[2]

Gould begins by assuming the classic dichotomist's stance: "The distinction of 'is' from 'ought' ranks as . . . a central principle."[3] As a result, he is forced to repudiate any notion of a "synthesis," "unification," or integration of knowledge. In the fundamentally bifurcated world posited by the dichotomist model such aspirations must be laid aside. Instead, Gould argues for what he calls "NOMA," or "Non-Overlapping Magisteria" (domains), and the domains he has in mind are facts and values:

> I do not see how science and religion could be unified, or even synthesized, under any common scheme of explanation or analysis;

1. *Rocks of Ages: Science and Religion in the Fullness of Life* (New York: Ballantine, 1999).

2. Gould, *Rocks of Ages,* p. 55; cf. pp. 64, 68ff., 129.

3. Gould, *Rocks of Ages,* p. 57.

but I also do not understand why the two enterprises should experience any conflict. Science tries to document the factual character of the natural world, and to develop theories that coordinate and explain these facts. Religion, on the other hand, operates in the equally important, but utterly different, realm of human purposes, meanings, and values — subjects that the factual domain of science might illuminate, but can never resolve. . . . Science covers the empirical realm: what is the universe made of (fact) and why does it work this way (theory). The magisterium of religion extends over questions of ultimate meaning and moral value. These two magisteria do not overlap.[4]

Facts and values can coexist, says Gould, because they occupy two "utterly different" realms. Thus the two must be kept distinct from one another; they are simply "immiscible."[5] "NOMA," Gould insists, "demands separation between nature's factuality and humankind's morality."[6] Moreover, Gould is clear about the sorts of conclusions such a separation requires: "The first commandment of all versions of NOMA might be summarized by stating: 'Thou shalt not mix the magisteria by claiming that God directly ordains important events in the history of nature by special interference knowable only through revelation and not accessible to science.' In common parlance, we refer to such special interference as 'miracle.'"[7] The same fate awaits Christ's incarnation, virgin birth, and resurrection; or any suggestion that prayer might actually affect something in the natural order (e.g., a prayer for healing); or any other past, present, or future interference by God on the factual side of the dichotomy. Religion and faith will be allowed to speak to subjective values, but they can never be permitted any claims on the objective side. That is the sole preserve of science and reason.

4. Gould, *Rocks of Ages,* pp. 4, 6.
5. Gould, *Rocks of Ages,* p. 65.
6. Gould, *Rocks of Ages,* p. 189; cf. pp. 210-11.
7. Gould, *Rocks of Ages,* p. 85; cf. pp. 93-94.

Too High a Price

For many Christians this is far too high a price to pay for embracing the dichotomist model. They recognize that accepting such a bargain is akin to thirsty sailors drinking seawater. They may find temporary relief, but in the end what they're drinking will kill them. And seawater for the Christian this dichotomist's approach surely is. That's why it has long been found repugnant by historic Christian standards, not least because it has the effect of reducing Christianity to little more than an ethical system.

Unfortunately, the dichotomist's approach has proven less repugnant to two centuries of theological liberalism in the church. Or perhaps it was the reverse: this approach became a progenitor of classical theological liberalism, which in one sense may be viewed as what's left after Christianity has been domesticated by a fact/value dichotomy.[8] At

---

8. See Basil Mitchell, *Faith and Criticism* (Oxford: Clarendon Press, 1994), pp. 67-87. Mitchell here traces the same line — from Hume to Barth — as Jeffrey Stout in his book, *The Flight from Authority: Religion, Morality, and the Quest for Autonomy* (Notre Dame: University of Notre Dame Press, 1981), pp. 128-48. Stout concludes this section with the following observations:

> Theology since Barth is a sad story. The radical theologies of the 1960s served finally as the *reductio ad absurdum* of the premises with which Bultmann and Tillich tried to save theology from Barth's *Dogmatics*. Those theologians who continue to seek a way between the horns, and thus to remain within the secular academy without abandoning the community of faith, have often been reduced to seemingly endless methodological foreplay. This foreplay, when it leads anywhere, typically leads toward disguised versions of liberalism. But the pathos of liberalism, as Van Harvey has shown case by case over the last two decades, is alienation from both the community of faith and the secular academy — a nearly complete loss of audience being the least painful major consequence.
>
> Harvey has used the problem of faith and history, in particular, to show how theologians — despite their attempts to reformulate Christian theism in terms acceptable to a secular academic audience — continue to skirt the issues implicit in Hume's dictum that a wise man proportions his belief to the evidence (as defined by the new probability and as manifested institutionally in the modern academic disciplines). It is hard to imagine a Christian, Jewish or Islamic theologian abandoning the historical claims central to his own tradition without also alienating himself from his own community of faith. But the task of making the traditional claims seem probable has become increasingly difficult in the period defined by Port-Royal, D. F. Strauss, and Ernst

any rate, theological liberals have found this dichotomy useful due to its effectiveness in sealing off faith claims from scientific and historical attack. If the Christian faith is only about subjective values, not facts, it then becomes impervious to modernist criticisms. But such a move has proven spiritually and theologically disastrous for the Christian faith,[9] a faith that is utterly dependent upon God's interventions with real people, places, and events in time/space history, a faith which considers not merely the materialistic realm but the moral and spiritual dimensions of reality as well to be integral parts of an objective order created and known by God.

Categorical Effects

Among the worst defects of a fact/value starting point is the one most relevant to our present discussion. This approach begins by requiring the opposite of the unity posited by a biblical worldview. It forces not a oneness of thought but a fundamental partitioning of things. It is thus disjunctive in nature, disintegrative rather than integrative. It calls for the compartmentalization of one's thought rather than its unification.

Troeltsch. Yet the only alternatives to accepting this task involve either "giving the atheist less and less in which to disbelieve" or a direct (nonapologetic) appeal to the authority of revelation. The problem is that revelation, according to the major Western traditions, is itself a historical event.

It is symptomatic of the state of academic theology that essentially critical essays like Harvey's are among the most enduring theological accomplishments of recent years. Contemporary theology, like an empty pile in solitaire, is waiting for a new king to come along and get things moving again. It could be that Barth was the last. Barth's point, of course, was that theology, by its own best lights, should have been waiting for a king of another sort. (pp. 147-48)

9. See James Turner, *Without God, Without Creed: The Origins of Unbelief in America* (Baltimore: Johns Hopkins University Press, 1985). Turner set out to answer the question, "How did the practically universal assumption of God disappear?" His thesis, which came as an unexpected result of his research, is that unbelief in America was not something that happened *to* religion. "On the contrary," he says, "religion caused unbelief. In trying to adapt their religious beliefs to socioeconomic change, to new moral challenges, to novel problems of knowledge, to the tightening standards of science, the defenders of God slowly strangled Him. If anyone is to be arraigned for deicide, it is not Charles Darwin but his adversary Bishop Samuel Wilberforce; not the godless Robert Ingersoll but the godly Beecher family" (p. xiii; cf. pp. 184-87).

Embracing this categorical mistake leads to two common intellectual faults. First, dichotomist thinking often leads to dualistic analyses that are, from a biblical point of view, naive and oversimplified. The fact/value dichotomy is based upon a now-discredited positivist confidence in objectivity, a "just the facts" approach to learning. But as we have noted, such a notion has been widely debunked not just by Christians but by postmodern voices too. As Nicholas Rescher says in *The Limits of Science,* "No deity has made a covenant with us to assure that what we take to be adequately established theories must indeed be true in these matters of scientific inquiry."[10] We live in a post-Kuhnian age in which even secularists acknowledge that the pristine objectivity imagined by the Enlightenment's children was unachievable. Presuppositions and paradigms affect all of our thought. They affect what we look for or don't look for; how we look or don't look; what we see or don't see. Thus there can be no such thing as a value-free, theory-free, paradigm-free fact. The lens through which we peer is implicated in everything we see. Facts and values are entwined and cannot be hermetically sealed from one another, the one solely objective, the other purely subjective. A unified Christian worldview requires us to see things in a much more nuanced way — one that, in the words of George Marsden,

> emphasizes that crucial to the differences that separate Christian worldviews from non-Christian ones are disagreements about pretheoretical first principles, presuppositions, first commitments, or basic beliefs. Thus, without denying the value of human rationality, it denies the autonomy or competence of reason alone to adjudicate some of the decisive questions concerning the context within which rationality itself will operate. . . .
>
> The prevailing view now emphasizes that Christian thought and non-Christian thought, being founded on some opposed first principles, reflect wide differences in total worldviews. So those who presuppose that the universe was created by the God of Scripture are going to have many differences in viewpoint from those who suppose we have a chance universe. Since Christian principles will thus relate to all of thought and life (though not to all in the same degree), an important activity for such scholars is to define a Chris-

10. *The Limits of Science,* rev. ed. (Pittsburgh: University of Pittsburgh Press, 1999), p. 36.

tian worldview or worldviews in contrast to the prevailing outlooks of our day.[11]

Dichotomist thinking has the effect of rendering one's intellectual work not merely naive, but also, from a Christian point of view, misleading. It is founded upon the illusion that there are facts and there are values, and the two not only can but must be distinguished, because the one is scientific and the other non-scientific. As such, the value side must always remain optional and non-binding because it is subjective — that is, it is about the subject doing the valuing, not about any dimension of objective reality. But facts by definition become obligatory. They are to be received at face value because they have been objectively generated and are thus, well, just facts.

For the Christian this is much too facile. Truly integrative Christian thinking refuses, in Ralph McInerny's words, to "accept the fact/value dichotomy as good money."[12] It will not settle for a compartmentalization of thought that ghettoizes Christianity into the world of subjective values and renders it incapable of having anything useful to say about objective reality, time/space or otherwise. On the contrary, genuinely integrative thinking requires the rigorous sifting of ideas at every level, bringing them to the bar of all that we know as Christians. As Arthur Holmes observes, such thinking "requires a thorough analysis of methods and materials and concepts and theoretical structures, a lively and rigorous interpenetration of liberal learning with the content and commitment of Christian faith."[13] Says Alvin Plantinga,

> We must work at the various areas of science and scholarship in a way that is appropriate from a Christian or more broadly theistic point of view. We should not assume, automatically, that it is appropriate for

11. "The State of Evangelical Christian Scholarship," *Christian Scholar's Review* 17, no. 4 (1987): 355.

12. *Characters in Search of Their Author,* The Gifford Lectures, 1999-2000 (Notre Dame: University of Notre Dame Press, 2001), p. 91. Stanley Hauerwas: "Nor is it sufficient to identify the religious with the 'value' dimensions of knowledge, since that will only privilege the 'factual.'" "On Witnessing Our Story: Christian Education in Liberal Societies," in *Schooling Christians: "Holy Experiments" in American Education,* ed. Stanley Hauerwas and John H. Westerhoff (Grand Rapids: Eerdmans, 1992), p. 225.

13. Arthur F. Holmes, *The Idea of a Christian College,* rev. ed. (Grand Rapids: Eerdmans, 1975), p. 7.

Christians to work at the disciplines in the same way as the rest of the academic world. Take a given area of scholarship: philosophy, let's say, or history, or psychology, or anthropology, or economics, or sociology; in working at these areas, should we not take for granted the Christian answer to the large questions about God and creation, and then go on from that perspective to address the narrower questions of that discipline? Or is that somehow illicit or ill-advised? Put it another way: to what sort of premises can we properly appeal in working out the answers to the questions raised in a given area of scholarly or scientific inquiry? Can we properly appeal to what we know as Christians? In psychology . . . must the Christian community accept the basic structure and presuppositions of the contemporary practice of that discipline in trying to come to an understanding of its subject matter? Must Christian psychologists appeal only to premises accepted by all parties to the discussion, whether Christian or not? I should think not. Why should we limit and handicap ourselves in this way? . . . If we take for granted a Christian explanatory background, we might come up with an entirely different view.[14]

Plantinga speaks broadly of work in the humanities, arts, and sciences, realms wherein a dichotomist model offers little more than the benign coexistence of objective facts and Christian values. But genuine integration views each of the disciplines as exploring in its own way, not one or the other of disjunctive categories, but the infinite variability in how God deals with, is intertwined with, is transcendent to and immanent within the created order. Christian integrative thinking views all of that created order as Christ's handiwork and thus insists that the reach of such thinking be pervasive and systemic. It will not settle for an unreflective acceptance of any proposed "facts" without attempting to think Christianly about the system of thought that generated them. As Howard Lowry once put it, "Christianity is no little 'plus' added on to secular life and thought. . . . It is normative. It has to do with the essence of life and with the whole of life. To compartmentalize it is to imprison it, and to nullify it."[15]

14. "On Christian Scholarship," in *The Challenge and Promise of a Catholic University,* ed. Theodore Hesburgh (Notre Dame: University of Notre Dame Press, 1994), pp. 291-93.
15. *The Mind's Adventure: Religion and Higher Education* (Philadelphia: The Westminster Press, 1950), p. 104.

Emphasizing this point does not require us to conclude, of course, that all areas of human learning are equally affected by a Christocentric focus, or that all are affected in the same way. In fact, the opposite is true. As David Naugle argues, "Some disciplinary areas are more directly impacted by worldview than others":

> The epistemic implications of worldview vary per discipline. Worldviews seem to be least influential (which is not to say noninfluential) in the so-called exact and formal sciences, but are much more telling in the humanities, the social sciences, and the fine arts. For example, the impact of worldview assumptions seems to be much less in the practice of chemistry than in history, far less pervasive in mathematics than in philosophy. This seems intuitive, unless one is talking about the philosophy of chemistry or mathematics, for then one has slipped away from the practice of these disciplines into a discussion of their first principles. When this occurs, worldview factors become quite significant.[16]

In this light, says Naugle, disagreements among practitioners of the harder sciences "is likely to be less *despite* worldview differences, and disagreements among practitioners of the [softer sciences] is likely to be more *because* of worldview differences." Naugle explains this disparity as follows:

> Because worldviews have to do with . . . fundamental realities and the most basic questions about the meaning of the universe, the closer any discipline is to these realities and questions of meaning, the greater the likelihood that a worldview will affect theorizing in that disciplinary area. . . . The idea is that the closer a discipline stands to the center of existence, viz., the divine, the greater the impact ultimate commitments will have on that area of life. Hence theology is primary (at least for theists), then philosophy, followed by the humanities, the arts, and the social sciences, after which come the natural sciences, and finally basic, symbolic studies of mathematics, grammar, and logic.[17]

16. *Worldview: The History of a Concept* (Grand Rapids: Eerdmans, 2002), p. 328.
17. Naugle, *Worldview*, p. 329.

These disciplinary differences must not be underestimated. What Naugle observes about worldviews in general is true of a Christian worldview as well: the implications of the Lordship of Jesus Christ will vary across the disciplines and even within them, depending on what we may be exploring.[18] But though those implications are varied, they are never absent or irrelevant. In one way or another, truly integrative Christian thinking touches everything we study: the subject matter itself; our understanding of the history, philosophy, and methods of the discipline; the attitudes we bring to the task and the ethics with which we pursue it. Precisely because the Christian thinker works from a Christocentric reference point, and nothing can be irrelevant to the person of Christ, by the same token Jesus Christ cannot be irrelevant to anything we study. Nothing evades his touch, and so nothing should escape ours. Not even the natural sciences.

Integrative Science

Since the natural sciences deal only with the factual side, the dichotomist will say, there can be neither place nor need for God in the picture. Religion is about subjective values, so it must be allowed no role in the discussion of natural phenomena. It will perhaps be permitted a role in influencing such subjective issues as the personal ethics of the scientist, but it must remain silent about the objects she is studying.

Over the years some Christian institutions have capitulated to these dichotomists' demands. They have agreed to build a firewall between the religious and academic dimensions of the school. Academically they operate for all practical purposes as secular institutions, confining their institutional distinctiveness to the religious context they provide. But Jerald Brauer has argued that in making such a move, Christian institutions give up the only valid rationale for their existence:

---

18. See C. Stephen Evans's discussion of what he calls a "relevance continuum," from mathematics, to the natural sciences, human sciences, history, literature and the arts, philosophy, and theology, in Evans, "The Calling of the Christian Scholar-Teacher," in *Faithful Learning and the Christian Scholarly Vocation,* ed. Douglas V. Henry and Bob R. Agee (Grand Rapids: Eerdmans, 2003), pp. 40-43.

One ground of defense must be denied the Christian college. It cannot be allowed to argue that the inclusion of courses in religion and the presence of chapel, voluntary or compulsory, create an ethos that produces a "Christian" education through osmosis. Worship emerges out of a living religious experience and in turn nurtures and sustains such experience. If the Christian college is identified by a singleness of purpose expressed through its teaching, its academic and its communal life, then the worship service can play its role. It can never be a substitute for the content and method of the educational process as it is pursued within the context of the Christian faith. Nor can the academic quest completely dispense with worship in a Christian college. . . . The Christian college in America must be honest and admit that its failure has not been in upholding the necessity of worship service. Its sin has been and is the failure to provide a relevant enough academic life to offer the proper setting for worship in a Christian college.[19]

Providing "a relevant enough academic life" is precisely what, from a Christian perspective, the dichotomist model prohibits. Thus its take on the natural sciences will not do. Leaving aside the important question of what the dichotomist's scheme says about such things as the incarnation, miracles, and resurrection of Christ, at a different level this approach ignores the many ways theology and science may interact.[20] Perhaps most importantly, it undermines the most elevated Christian motive for engaging in the natural sciences in the first place: praise and worship. According to Arnold Nash,

The Protestant doctrine of justification by faith, as it originated in Luther, meant that man was to be reconciled to God in this world and not merely in heaven. Thus religion was secularized so that, as Luther put it, the shoemaker should shoe the sole of the Pope as religiously as the Pope should pray for the soul of the shoemaker. This attitude of mind is well expressed by Kepler in a prayer which

19. "The Christian College and American Higher Education," *The Christian Scholar* 41, no. 1 (March 1958): 244.
20. For example, see Part IV, "Philosophy of Science," in J. P. Moreland and William Lane Craig, *Philosophical Foundations for a Christian Worldview* (Downers Grove: InterVarsity Press, 2003).

he used in concluding one of his astronomical works: "Behold I have here completed a work of my calling with as much of intellectual strength as Thou has granted me. I have declared the praise of Thy works to the men who will read the evidence of it, so far as my finite spirit can comprehend them in their infinity."[21]

In an earlier chapter I raised the example of chemistry and offered the obvious point that chemical elements behave the same for Christians as they do for non-Christians. Yet theistic causal explanations do enter into our thinking — in fact, are *crucial* to our thinking — about chemical behavior if we're trying to think not simply scientifically, but holistically *as Christians* about chemistry. According to what God has revealed, we know that Jesus Christ is both the Creator and Sustainer of all things; that is, he is the One who "holds all things together" (Col. 1:15-20). Only God is truly independent; all created things, including the chemical elements chemists study, are utterly contingent upon him. They depend for their existence and their properties upon him in every instance, at all points and at every moment. Thus the very chemicals we study are Christ's handiwork and, if we allow them, they will declare to us his glory (Psalm 19:1). As Christians we do our chemistry with a deep reverence for what we study, not merely because it is fascinating and important in its own right, which it is, but because it is the craftwork of our Savior and Master. William Dyrness says, "Observation and analysis will remain essential because scientific knowledge has intrinsic value, but they alone will not be enough. The student will be called to *respond* to nature as well as understand it; indeed, the one will not finally be possible without the other."[22] Otherwise there would be nothing distinctively Christian about our study at all. It would be indistinguishable from that of the secularists or the pagan religionists whose focus never rises above the horizon of the created order.

When the disciples in Mark 4 watched Jesus still the storm, why were they so astonished? It was because they saw the wind and the

21. *The University and the Modern World: An Essay in the Social Philosophy of University Education* (London: S.C.M. Press, 1945), p. 64.

22. William A. Dyrness, "The Contribution of Theological Studies to the Christian Liberal Arts," in *Making Higher Education Christian: The History and Mission of Evangelical Colleges in America*, ed. Joel A. Carpenter and Kenneth W. Shipps (Grand Rapids: Christian University Press, 1987), p. 178.

waves obey his word. These men were knowledgeable observers of these natural phenomena; they had studied them all their lives. But now they saw something new. They came to see these phenomena in relationship to Jesus Christ. This meant that they not only came to view the phenomena differently; they came to view Jesus differently. They gained a new "Christ-centered" understanding of these natural phenomena, which no doubt made it impossible ever to experience a storm in the old way again. But even more importantly, they gained deeper insight into the glory and power of this One they claimed as their Lord. Similarly, when we gain any added insight into the Christ-centeredness of this or that dimension of the created order, it offers this same twofold prospect. We see not so much different things, but the same things differently, in a new light. And in doing so, we gain added insight into the person of Christ. The result is an enhanced sense of awe both toward his handiwork and toward the One whose handiwork it is.

Are the two statements, "$e = mc^2$" and "Jesus Christ has decreed that e shall equal mc^2," coterminous? At the level of what they affirm about e and m and c and the relationships between them, perhaps they are; at that level what a Christian holds will not differ from what a non-Christian holds. But at a deeper level — the level, as we have said, of Christian *thinking*, not merely Christian *communication* with secular colleagues — the two statements differ profoundly. The second not only affirms far more than the first; in the light of eternity — which is where all Christians must live their lives, including their scholarly lives, in the searching light of eternity — what it adds is by far the most important thing to be said about e and m and c. For "we look not at the things which are seen, but at the things which are not seen; for the things which are seen are temporal, but the things which are not seen are eternal" (2 Cor. 4:18). The Christ-centeredness of our focus does not — indeed, *must* not — deflect us from searching out all we can know about energy, mass, and the speed of light and the fascinating relationships between and among them; but taken seriously, such a focus does the opposite: It provides the motivation to delve more deeply.

The Christian scholar shares with the non-Christian all of his fascination with the things in themselves, but she is moved in addition by the impetus of her deepest Christ-centered convictions and loyalties. She wants not only to measure the creation; she wants to celebrate it for what it is and what it does: it is Christ's artistry and it tells us of him. Instead of a compartmentalized life — science during the week in the lab, faith and worship on Sunday at church — the Christian scholar experiences a profound unity, an integrated wholeness where the business of science and the practice of worship come together, each enhancing the other. Physicist Stephen Hawking has commented that if we were to discover a Grand Unified Theory, we would then know the mind of God. But for the Christian, *everything* we discover — whether about chemical compounds, or our own DNA, or the human mind, or the universe itself — is an insight into the mind of Christ. He is the One who has designed the created order to work in the way it does and it is his word that sustains it at every moment in this way. To study this created order is thus to learn of him.

One will sometimes — not often enough, I fear — discover this sort of thinking in the pulpit. I recall hearing a sermon based on the Apostle's exhortations to humility in Philippians 2:3-4, a humility grounded in Christ's own model. To deepen our appreciation of Christ's humility, the humility we are to emulate, the speaker drew our attention to the incident of Jesus washing the disciples' feet in John 13:

> The evening meal was being served, and Jesus, knowing he had come from God, that everything was in his power and that he was returning to God, stood up and provided a visible parable of humility. He removed his outer clothing, wrapped a towel around his waist, and took the position of a servant. He poured water into a basin and began to wash his disciples' feet, drying them with the towel. Remember, there is nothing made except what was made by him; he who created the water now dipped his hands into the basin. Unlike other substances, which become more dense in their solid state, water becomes less dense. That's why ice cubes float rather than sink. Otherwise the oceans would freeze from the bottom up rather than from the top down, killing all aquatic life, destroying the oxygen supply and making earth uninhabitable. He who had fashioned the earth by his wisdom, now dips his hands into a basin of the life-giving substance he had so wisely created — so as to wash the feet of humanity.

Here is a simple example of faith and learning working together to enhance our appreciation of both Christ's handiwork and the One whose handiwork it is. As I say, one sometimes hears this sort of thinking in the pulpit. But in the classrooms of a Christian college one can hear it every day, in an infinite variety of forms, drawn from every dimension of the created order. This sort of thinking does not displace serious academic work; it draws upon it, and then enriches and deepens it.

Christian Motives

Rightly understood, this motive supplies the answer to the appeal of historian Michael Hamilton. In an article in the *Christian Scholar's Review,* Hamilton argued that Christians doing technical, seemingly non-religious research sometimes find their work unappreciated in Christian circles. Instead, says Hamilton, "We need to encourage Christians to study things that have no apparent connection to Christianity. We need to give them Christian reasons for studying the chemical processes of algae growth, or methodology of interpreting Babylonian pottery shards, or hunter-gatherer kinship patterns. Why? Because it just may be that God has called them to the task, for reasons only he knows, and for outcomes only he can foresee."[23]

Hamilton supplies one explicitly "Christian reason" for pursuing technical, disciplinary research: namely, obedience. For who can say what God may purpose for such an endeavor? This is an important insight for Christian scholars, but is it enough? Left to itself such a motive might result in a faithful Christian researcher pursuing his calling with gritted teeth, determined to do his duty in completing his esoteric studies but without much enjoyment, meaning, or inspiration. But add to obedience a delight in studying Christ's handiwork as a way of growing not only in our exultation in what he has made, but also in our exaltation of the One who made it, and everything changes. Here we discover the most profound of motivations for Christian scholarship. It is the motivation Arthur Holmes traces through the history of Christian thinking, that of "doxological learning."[24]

23. "Reflection and Response: The Elusive Idea of Christian Scholarship," *Christian Scholar's Review* 31, no. 1 (Fall 2001): 21.

24. *Building the Christian Academy* (Grand Rapids: Eerdmans, 2001), p. 2.

If we will allow them, the sheer privilege of such a calling and the passion for such a goal can provide all the Christian reasons believing scholars need to pursue even the most technical and seemingly arcane of scholarly projects. For the Christian there can be no such thing as subject matter that lacks a connection to Jesus Christ. As Hamilton suggests, this connection may not be immediately apparent, but that surely makes the quest all the more intriguing. The Creator and Sustainer and Goal of all things is inherently relevant to all that exists, and all that exists is relevant to him. There is no dimension of the created order, nor can there be, in which he is not interested, or which does not in some way speak of him. The Lordship of Jesus Christ is so profoundly significant in the universe that it is related, if only we can see it, to all that exists, including the chemical processes of algae growth, the methodology of interpreting Babylonian pottery shards, and hunter-gatherer kinship patterns. To explore that relationship, whatever it might be, is to move beyond the study of the things in themselves and to begin to discern, however dimly, their true meaning and significance in the universe. What higher motivation for studying even the most obscure subjects could a Christian scholar desire?

Several decades ago Richard Weaver wrote an academic bestseller entitled *Ideas Have Consequences*. Weaver later described his book as "an intuition of a situation." It was a situation "of a world which has lost its center, which desires to believe again in value and obligation" but is not willing to "face what it must accept" in order to regain that faith. As part of his analysis Weaver observed that in our modern world "a former distrust of specialization has been supplanted by its opposite, a distrust of generalization":

> Obsession, according to the canons of psychology, occurs when an innocuous idea is substituted for a painful one. The victim simply avoids recognizing the thing which will hurt. . . . [T]he most painful confession for the modern egotist to make is that there is a center of responsibility. He has escaped it by taking his direction with reference to the smallest points. The theory of empiricism is plausible because it assumes that accuracy about small matters prepares the way for valid judgment about large ones. What happens, however, is that the judgments are never made. The pedantic empiricist, buried in his little province of phenomena, imagines that fidelity

to it exempts him from concern with larger aspects of reality — in the case of science, from consideration of whether there is reality other than matter.[25]

The tendencies described by Weaver have only intensified since his writing. But for the Christian, there can be no "little province of phenomena." Jesus Christ integrates all the "larger aspects of reality." He is the One through whom and to whom and for whom are all things. Because of him, Christians need not flee the general for the refuge of the particular. Christians can still speak in terms of an integrated worldview, the big picture, an overarching meta-narrative that — to the extent we can discern it, and we can indeed discern it only to a limited extent — subsumes and helps makes sense of the many particulars.

An Abstract Example

Even so abstract a subject as mathematics is capable of being handled integratively. In their *Mathematics in a Postmodern Age: A Christian Perspective,* Russell Howell and James Bradley begin apologetically: "We can almost hear the hallway whispers in response to the title of this book 'We certainly see the importance of discussing mathematics in a postmodern age, but, come on, what possible relevance could a Christian perspective bring to the issue? Is the Pythagorean Theorem different for Christians?'" Howell and Russell's response? Of course the Pythagorean Theorem is not different for Christians. "Even so," they say, "we believe there are a number of ways in which a Christian perspective can enrich our understanding of mathematics. Conversely, we think that many ideas in mathematics can enhance our understanding of the Christian faith."[26] In an effort at candor, the authors then summarize the sorts of ideas one finds throughout their book; that is, they spell out "the main features of our presuppositions" which serve as the "general overarching framework that shapes even the way we ask the ques-

25. *Ideas Have Consequences* (Chicago: University of Chicago Press, 1984), pp. 59-60.
26. *Mathematics in a Postmodern Age: A Christian Perspective* (Grand Rapids: Eerdmans, 2001), p. 1.

tions we seek to address." Here is an instructive sample of how they see their Christian presuppositions shaping their understanding of mathematics:

> First, we believe in the God of the Old and New Testaments, and believe that he is the creator of the universe. In particular, he is our creator, and for reasons we don't fully understand he has created us with the capacity to engage in mathematical inquiry. Thus, we reject the notion that this capacity is neutral, a tool to be used for good or ill. Rather we affirm that such capacity is inherently good and hence has intrinsic value. Second, we believe that humans are made in God's image, but they are "fallen" — that is, they have rejected God's authority over them and have replaced it with a claim of autonomy. This attempt at autonomy is a source of human evil. Hence, although mathematical capacity is good, humans can engage in mathematical exploration for evil ends. Third, we believe it is the responsibility of human beings to work for "redemption" — that is, to work to overcome the consequences of the fall. In a fundamental sense, of course, true redemption is possible only by the work that Christ did on the cross for us. But out of gratitude for this gift of God, we as believers desire to help fulfill God's purposes for creation, and that is the sense in which we work for redemption. For Christians interested in mathematics, this entails endeavoring to discern God's purposes in giving human beings the capacity to engage in mathematical activity, and seeking to help the mathematics community fulfill those intentions.

> What exactly were God's intentions in giving us the capacity to engage in mathematical inquiry? Scripture does not provide a direct answer to this question, so the answer must be inferred from broader purposes that have been revealed. If we go back to Genesis 1 and 2, we see that God's original purpose was that we be co-creators with him in two ways: that we be stewards of this world, walking closely with him in using his creation to build cultures and to care for this world, and that we ourselves would be built into "sons of God." But carefully studying anything in this world often involves forming precise definitions, measuring, and thinking deductively about the way things are and the way they might be. Thus mathematics is an essential component of co-creating. While such a vision does not give precise answers to every value question we might

ask, it gives us a framework from which to start. If, as we affirm, the capacity to do mathematics is a good gift of God, it reveals something about his nature, for example, his subtlety, order, beauty, and variety. When people respond to these qualities of mathematics with awe and joy and turn to God with reverence and thankfulness, they are fulfilling this purpose. Thus, we immediately see one consequence of a Christian perspective — mathematics does not need to be "applicable" to be of value. However, applicability is also important, as a second purpose of mathematics is its use in helping to build human cultures, to serve people, and to care for the earth. Thus a second consequence of a Christian perspective is that the mathematics community cannot stop at considering the abstract, formal aspects of mathematics, but must consider the consequences of these abstractions when they are reintroduced into the human community.[27]

Here are two Christian scholars attempting to think Christianly about even such an abstract subject as mathematics, and their book makes for a lively and informative read even to non-mathematicians. I can only commend the authors for their effort. On the other hand, were I to criticize their book, I would want to inquire as to why its exploration of mathematics is not more profoundly *Christ*-centered. It is worth noting that in the above statement of presuppositions, the Son, the Second Person of the Godhead, plays no central role; he appears only in a rather passing reference to the cross.[28] For the most part the book's argument is merely theocentric, so much so that, say, a non-Christian theist could echo most of its argument. But if that is the case, in what sense can we claim this represents distinctively *Christian* thinking? In offering this critique, I do not mean to suggest that I have thought through the issues and know what truly Christocentric things need to be said in a book whose title promises a distinctively Christian perspective on the subject of mathematics. I only know that until we

27. Howell and Bradley, *Mathematics in a Postmodern Age,* pp. 4-5.
28. Note the same pattern in Stephen Monsma's "five basic Christian beliefs" that form "the heart or core of a Christian worldview" ("Christian Worldview in Academia," *Faculty Dialogue* 21 [Spring-Summer 1994]: 140-41); or Michael Peterson's eight characteristics of "the Christian mind" (*With All Your Mind: A Christian Philosophy of Education* [Notre Dame: University of Notre Dame Press, 2001], pp. 208-12).

have made such an inquiry and delved specifically into the unique Son-centeredness of the subject, we have not fully risen to our integrative task.

A Question of Definition

But, one may ask, can any such integrative thinking truly be called scientific? The answer is surely a definitional one. If we begin by defining science so as to limit its focus to the created, so-called natural order — which today is probably necessary, and therefore wise, and not, it seems to me, inherently problematic for Christians — then by definition the answer must be no. But then, we must also say that if one defines science thusly, no Christian thinker can ever be satisfied with *merely* scientific thought. Integrative Christian thinking by definition constitutes an attempt to pull into a unified whole all we can know from whatever source. It neither can nor will, in the end, ever tolerate bracketing Jesus Christ out.

For the Christian scholar, the difficulty with scientific thinking is not its limited focus on the created order. Properly understood, this limitation can be conceived as a useful one.[29] It enables science to specialize — to become, so to speak, an instrument constantly honed to do an ever better job of the focused task for which it is designed. The difficulty for the Christian begins when this self-limitation — science as useful for the study of the created order — metastasizes into something quite different, an all-embracing philosophical presupposition that blusters, "If science cannot study it, it does not exist." This is merely a backdoor way of saying the natural world is all that exists. At this point the humility of science as a powerful but limited tool disappears and is replaced by a hubris that proclaims science as the arbiter of all things. The former vision of science Christians can embrace and applaud; it contributes wonderfully to integrated Christian thinking. But the latter, which masquerades as science but is in reality only another face of philosophical materialism, we must resist. For if we begin by defining

29. For a debate on how Christians may best understand this limitation, see *Perspectives on Science and Christian Faith: Journal of the American Scientific Affiliation* 54, no. 1 (March 2002).

Jesus Christ permanently out of the picture, as this sort of philosophical materialism surely does, how could any Christian concur?

Or consider the humanities. The dichotomist tends to limit these to the value side of the fact/value dichotomy. They are relegated to making subjective, interpretative, or moralizing contributions. Yet for the Christian, the humanities should be viewed as only a different way of exploring God's complex world. They are indeed highly value-laden, but not entirely so. Thus it is overstatement, it seems to me, to declare that "truth claims involving statements about how the world *is* play little or no role in art, literary criticism, musicology and so on."[30] As artists will sometimes say, newspapers and history books try to tell us what happened, but great art and literature tell us what happens. They merely address a different dimension of God's reality, in Leland Ryken's words, "the reality that never goes out of date because it is universal in human experience."[31] If the social sciences are ways of examining human experience, in their own manner so are the humanities. If the humanities tend to be value-laden, the social sciences are as well, if typically less so. Thus it is misleading to consign the humanities to the subjective side of a fact/value divide, as if they had nothing to add about the objects of their attention. As Ryken argues, while the humanities and the arts commonly address issues of morality and values, they also address the question of "reality," asking among other things, "What really exists, and what is its nature?"[32]

Or consider the social sciences. According to a dichotomist model the facts of social science will be the same for theists as for non-theists — because they are, after all, just facts. As such they may be combined with Christian interpretations as desired, so long as we keep the two distinct. The two may coexist, but they do not impinge. When talking among ourselves we may add in our theistic values as desired, but these can have no effect on the facts already present, for values and facts, we must remember, are immiscible.

---

30. Francis Oakley, "Concluding Reflections on the Lilly Seminar," in *Religion, Scholarship and Higher Education,* ed. Andrea Sterk (Notre Dame: University of Notre Dame Press, 2002), p. 234.

31. Leland Ryken, "The Creative Arts," in *The Making of a Christian Mind: A Christian World View and the Academic Enterprise,* ed. Arthur F. Holmes (Downers Grove: InterVarsity Press, 1985), p. 108.

32. Ryken, "The Creative Arts," p. 122.

From a Christian viewpoint this is surely a short-sighted view of the social sciences. The notion of the social sciences providing value-free facts to which we can simply add in our own Christian thinking is woefully inadequate. If even the natural sciences are not these days considered value-free, the social sciences, second only to the humanities, manifest evaluative tendencies from top to bottom. As anthropologist Eloise Meneses says, "conflict [between Christian and secular presuppositions] at the foundational level is more severe in the social sciences than in the natural ones."[33] Meneses cites Emil Brunner by way of explanation: "The nearer anything lies to that center of existence where we are concerned with the whole, that is, with man's relation to God and the being of the person, the greater is the disturbance of rational knowledge by sin; the farther away anything lies from this center, the less is the disturbance felt, and the less difference is there between knowing as a believer or as an unbeliever."[34]

For this reason the factual claims of any of the social sciences — and the natural sciences, too — must be themselves submitted to a rigorous examination. In doing so we will find much that comports with and enriches what we know as Christians.[35] But we may also find much that is the product of faulty assumptions and theories and is therefore inadequate, at least as is, from a Christian point of view. The presuppositions, the paradigm, the perspective from which one engages in the task will often color even what passes for facts, and of course the conclusions drawn from them.

Curiously for a Reformed thinker serving in a strongly Reformed community, this is the point seemingly missed by D. G. Hart in his attempt to play down the antitheses between Christian and secular scholarship. In arguing, *contra* the Kuyperian Calvinists, that there need be no inherent antagonism between believing and unbelieving minds, minds that "share a world of inquiry in common," Hart swings to the opposite extreme of embracing a quasi-Lutheran two-kingdom model

---

33. "No Other Foundation: Establishing a Christian Anthropology," *Christian Scholar's Review* 29, no. 3 (Spring 2000): 534-35.

34. *Revelation and Reason* (Philadelphia: Westminster, 1946), p. 383.

35. Cf. John Paul II on the Church Fathers: "Faced with the various philosophies, the Fathers were not afraid to acknowledge those elements in them that were consonant with Revelation and those that were not. Recognition of the points of convergence did not blind them to the points of divergence" (*Fides et Ratio*, 41).

that appears content to take the work of unbelieving thinkers as automatically unproblematic. Says Hart, "The norms and procedures of the university are not inherently in rebellion against God if they do not take into account special revelation or faith-based perspectives. Instead, the work performed by non-Christian scholars may simply be a God-ordained way of reflecting on creation, whether or not such academics recognize that their power of observation and analysis actually come from God."[36] Hart's language here is significant. He is surely right that the conflict may not be "inherent," and that the work of secular scholars "may" be unproblematic from a Christian point of view. But this cannot be merely assumed. An absence of conflict may emerge as the conclusion of the Christian scholar's integrative efforts, but it cannot serve as a presupposition.

Hart's well-intentioned effort to play down unnecessary tensions appears to fall into the trap of obliviousness toward genuine tensions that may well exist. It also leads him to this surprising conclusion: "Scholars at Christian institutions will not feel the need to introduce questions of faith in literature or chemistry classes, or to require theological precision from every new hire in sociology. Indeed, only in the Bible and theology departments, where faith and theological convictions make the most difference, is close scrutiny of a professor's profession of faith immediately relevant to academic work."[37]

It seems to me a profound mistake to concede so much to a dichotomist, compartmentalized model. Here now is not the question of how a Christian scholar is to communicate with her non-Christian colleagues; the focus of Hart's comments is the Christian institution where the assignment is intentional Christian thinking. Yet, strangely, here is Hart foisting a dichotomist model onto such institutions. Vast segments of the curriculum are cordoned off from explicitly Christian thought, as if distinctive Christian thinking has no place in the realms of literature or chemistry or sociology. Can it be that the expansive claims of the Lordship of Jesus Christ have no relevance to these and other such disciplines, that what we know from special revelation will have no impact on how we understand these dimensions of general revelation, that the faith

---

36. "Christian Scholars, Secular Universities, and the Problem with the Antithesis," *Christian Scholar's Review* 30, no. 4 (Summer 2001): 400.

37. Hart, "Christian Scholars, Secular Universities," p. 401.

commitments of professors matter only in the Bible and theology departments? This is a disastrous prescription for Christian schools.

Worst of all, however, is what a dichotomist model does to the role of special revelation. As an instance of God interfering in the material world,[38] it becomes the first victim of Gould's dictum: "Thou shalt not mix the magisteria." Or if, inconsistently, it is not denied altogether, it winds up relegated, along with the humanities, to the realm of the subjective. As such it can have nothing to say about the so-called factual dimension. To the extent special revelation may be allowed to exist, much less to inform us in any way, it will only be permitted to address the realm of values. Such a proposal might be well received by classical theological liberals, and is in fact advocated by many secular scientists, not to mention assorted other religious groups. But it will hardly do for those who stand with historic Christianity and who believe in a God who is so intimately involved with time/space history that he became part of it — and provided us an inscripturated account of his actions and purposes in the bargain. As Harry Blamires argues in *The Christian Mind*,

> To think christianly is to think in terms of Revelation. For the secularist, God and theology are the playthings of the mind. For the Christian, God is real, and Christian theology describes his truth revealed to us. For the secular mind, religion is essentially a matter of theory: for the Christian mind, Christianity is a matter of acts and facts. The acts and facts which are the basis of our faith are recorded in the Bible. They have been interpreted and illuminated in the long history of the Church. The Christian mind is inescapably and unbrokenly conscious of the hard, factual quality of the Christian Faith. The Christian mind is alert to the solid, God-given, authoritative factualness of the Christian Faith and the Christian Church.[39]

---

38. These two things — God's speaking and his involvement in human history — are inherently related. Says Nicholas Wolterstorff, "Divine discourse of anything like the range and diversity claimed in the scriptures and traditions of Judaism, Christianity, and Islam, almost certainly requires direct intervention by God in the affairs of human history; and contemporary science provides us no good reason for thinking that such intervention does not occur." *Divine Discourse: Philosophical Reflections on the Claim That God Speaks* (Cambridge: Cambridge University Press, 1995), p. 129.

39. Harry Blamires, *The Christian Mind* (London: SPCK, 1963), p. 111.

A Different Scenario

These are the kinds of things that from a Christian point of view render a fact/value dichotomy inappropriate as a starting point for our thinking. Its bifurcations make for a superficial analysis that owes more to modernity than to a historic Christian understanding of the obligations of Christian thinkers. It is disintegrative rather than integrative, and therefore leads Christians away from their intellectual task rather than toward it.

A Christian worldview, by contrast, makes genuinely integrative thinking possible. As we have seen, it posits the existence of an infinite God who has created all that is. This God knows his created order intimately and exhaustively; hence the possibility of a crucial intellectual construct: reality, or "things as God knows them to be."

We humans exist as part of God's created order. In fact God made us his image-bearers. As such he has given us minds capable, in finite and proximate ways, of apprehending both God himself and the reality he created, through both the special revelation he has provided and through an exploration of the world around us. The Christian's intellectual task therefore consists of glorifying God by, among other things, utilizing our God-given capacities to discover and correlate truth — truth about God and truth about the spiritual, moral, and material dimensions of the world he created. This process of apprehension and correlation is what we mean by the phrase "the integration of faith and learning."[40]

But suppose we were to happen upon a Christian scholar who has made the initial mistake of founding her analytical system on a fact/value dichotomy. Then she works out her analysis accordingly. Of course as a Christian she stops short of facing the full implications of what she has embraced, but one result of the dichotomy she does celebrate: the absence of conflict between science and religion, fact and value. They need never come into conflict, she argues with Gould; they can remain peacefully coexistent. But here's the kicker: The Christian community our scholar works in talks incessantly of "the integration

40. For a fuller and more technical discussion of the nuances of the term "integration," see Ken Badley, "Two 'Cop-Outs' in Faith-Learning Integration: Incarnational Integration and Worldviewish Integration," *Spectrum* 28, no. 2 (1996): 105-18.

of faith and learning." So our scholar adopts this language to refer to the coexistence she has achieved. Never mind that she does not — indeed, cannot — mean by it anything that is truly integrative. Her dichotomist premises allow no such thing. What she aspires to is not a unified whole but only a peaceful coexistence between dissimilar things. Yet for her the language of integration will do. Our scholar uses the right jargon, so all is well.

But all is not well. As Ralph McInerny remarks, "Inconsistency is the tribute that confusion pays to reality."[41] However well-meaning she may be, our hypothetical scholar has been drinking seawater. Since she is a Christian she will be unlikely to follow her starting point through to its logical conclusions, as Gould does. But the relation between her position and Gould's will nonetheless be one of common descent. They are both in hock to the object/subject divide — Gould thoroughly and consistently, our hypothetical scholar less thoroughly and less consistently.

Gould serves us well in this comparison because he demonstrates the full implications of what happens when we ground our intellectual enterprise in a fact/value dichotomy. In Gould we can see that such a dichotomy need not lead to a repudiation of religion — only its evisceration. No divine intervention in time/space history, no special revelation — for revelation is by definition an instance of such intervention — religion as pure subjectivity, and most relevant to our present discussion, certainly no possibility of any unity of knowledge. Yet Gould portrays himself as a friend of religion; it may well have some genuine value, he concedes. What's more, it will never — indeed, *can* never — come into conflict with science. All such conflict arises only when religion unreasonably attempts to address something on the factual side, or vice versa. But it's all so unnecessary. Prevent the two sides from crossing over and we can easily maintain a harmonious coexistence.

If we embrace a fact/value dichotomy for our starting point, this is the package we have purchased. We may insist upon weeding out the conclusions we do not like, but we can have no intellectually consistent grounds for doing so. If we are honest enough to follow it through, Gould's position is where the fact/value divide takes us.

So what should we make of our hypothetical Christian scholar's

41. McInerny, *Characters in Search of Their Author*, p. 111.

analysis? Are we to be impressed by it? Should we not consider her analysis fundamentally flawed, a house divided? The business of integrated thinking is surely difficult, complex, and resistant to simple definition, but does that mean anything will suffice so long as we use the right terminology? Does *calling* one's work integrative, in some almost Orwellian sense, *make* it integrative, despite the fact that one has embraced one of the fundamental divorces the effort toward integration was designed to offset? "Tell me," says Socrates in Thomas Schmidt's fanciful dialogue with a Christian college professor, "if one were to place side-by-side a sculpture of tin and a sculpture of copper, would the resulting display rightly be called a sculpture of bronze?"[42] Surely we must be more discerning. As Mark Noll reminds us, "Christian world views cannot be simply veneered versions of current intellectual fashions."[43] History records the dangers of what Harry Blamires rightly referred to as "slovenly thinking."[44] Certain intellectual approaches are inimical to the integrative task, and we should not shy away from saying so.

It is possible for even the most well-meaning Christian to adopt a faulty starting point or take some intellectual wrong turns, and such mistakes can have profound significance. In his study of the origins of unbelief in America, James Turner argues that "it was not the inexorable juggernaut of history that crushed belief. It was, rather, the specific responses to modernity chosen by thousands of specific believers which made belief vulnerable."[45] Given such high stakes, it does not seem to me that such issues should be left to the *adiaphora* of the Christian's intellectual task. They appear to be of primary significance, in our present case having to do with the fundamental conception of what we mean in the first place when we speak of integrative thinking. They have to do not with the various ways different disciplines seek to implement a common integrative goal, but with the very nature of the task itself — that is, with the fundamental assumptions that prompt us to seek to integrate our thought to begin with.

42. "Should Jerusalem Honor Athens?" *Christian Scholar's Review* 21, no. 3 (March 1992): 251.

43. "Christian World Views and Some Lessons of History," in *The Making of a Christian Mind*, p. 51.

44. *The Post-Christian Mind: Exposing Its Destructive Agenda* (Ann Arbor: Servant Publications, 1999), p. 123.

45. *Without God, Without Creed,* p. 268.

Starting with the Right Question

Before we are too hard on our hypothetical scholar, however, let us confess what is not hypothetical at all. We are all susceptible to slipping into such thinking — that is, of allowing dichotomist categories to set the terms for our conversation. It is in the intellectual air we breathe, the cultural water we drink. These are the categories most people around us use, and we can unwittingly embrace them if we're not careful. For example, suppose we heard someone refer to murder being wrong as one of our "values." Would our ears perk up? Would we recognize this as dichotomist language?

If we begin by dividing everything along a fact/value fault line, we must of course put the wrongness of murder on the value side. But notice what this does to the discussion. The fact/value divide is the product of the object/subject divide; by adopting this way of analyzing the issue we mandate from the beginning that our discussion will be a purely human-centered affair. Why? Because to speak of "subjects" and "values" is to think only on a horizontal plane.

A value, at least in our contemporary way of speaking,[46] is the product of some perceiving subject valuing something. This is what renders all values inherently "subjective." Only humans can in this sense be subjects, and only humans can have such values. How could it be otherwise? We cannot imagine stones or cows or mosquitoes as perceiving subjects having values. And the language is equally inappropriate when we try to apply it to God. Quite apart from the theological blunder of thinking of God as what we mean by a perceiving subject, for God to "value" something renders it far more than what we mean by a human value. God is good, the ultimate source of all goodness. For God to "value" something is to say, in effect, that it is good with refer-

---

46. But see Owen Barfield, "Language, Evolution of Consciousness, and the Recovery of Human Meaning," *Teachers College Record* 82, no. 3 (Spring 1981): 427-33. Barfield asks, "Do we value a thing because it has value, or is it valuable because we value it?" (p. 128) The latter is almost exclusively our contemporary meaning of the term, mainly by default. Once God is removed from the frame it can scarcely be otherwise. Only by recovering a theocentric perspective could we recover the ability to think of something as intrinsically valuable, along the lines of C. S. Lewis's observation that "The human mind has no more power of inventing a new value than of imagining a new primary colour" (*The Abolition of Man* [New York: Simon and Schuster, 1996], p. 56).

ence to himself, for he and no other measure is the standard by which he deems something good. The fact that God has constituted something as good signifies that its goodness is an intrinsic thing. It does not depend, as do "values," on the valuing of some perceiving subject. Which of course indicates that it is a category error even to try to use this language of God. Humans may *subject*-ively value something, but when we try to apply the same categories to God the language fails. It cannot bear the weight. In the end the language of "subjects" and "values" is purely horizontal, anthropocentric language.

Which is exactly the problem. Object/subject, fact/value — this is language designed to speak only of humans. It describes us and our relation to the world, and only that. It furnishes no capacity to take God into consideration. In fact it quite intentionally leaves God out. Thus, to consider the wrongness of murder as a value is no error; we human subjects do so consider it. So far as it goes this language will do. But such language can only go so far. Our complaint is not that what it says is false; it is that all it is capable of talking about is us. It offers no capacity to bring God into the frame. He is ruled out from the moment these purely horizontal categories are adopted as our starting point.

What, then, are the categories we require if God is to be part of the discussion — in fact, at its center? Not the question of what is fact and what is value. Christian thought starts with the question we can almost know is the right one by the way moderns (and even more so postmoderns) fight it off. It is the question that instead of cutting God out builds him into the very stuff of the question, rendering it impossible to answer without considering him. It is the question *What is true?* That question — which Alister McGrath calls "the first, and most fundamental of all questions"[47] — puts God where in any Christian worldview he belongs: at the beginning.

God exists. He has created. There is therefore such a thing as reality, which encompasses moral, physical, and spiritual dimensions. Humans can to some degree apprehend that reality. To the extent we do so accurately, our apprehensions are true; to the extent our apprehensions do not accord with that reality, they are false.

Against this background the matter of the wrongness of murder

47. *A Passion for Truth: The Intellectual Coherence of Evangelicalism* (Downers Grove: InterVarsity Press, 1996), p. 191.

takes on a very different cast, making it grossly inadequate to speak of it as merely a value judgment. To speak of it as a value is to say no more than what you or I may think. It is to relegate the issue to mere human evaluation, with no more moral weight, in the end, than "I prefer chocolate." Perhaps the fact that so many agree that murder is wrong seems to add the requisite *gravitas,* but not so; it is still only as if, say, *everyone* thought chocolate best. We would then have the accumulated force of numbers, and this would feel to us like a weighty judgment. We would probably then be astonished than anyone could be so mistaken as to prefer vanilla. But the judgment would remain a human value.

But the statement "It is *true* that murder is wrong"[48] is of a different order. It says, in effect, that the claim "Murder is wrong" accords with a moral reality in the universe, one that is just as real as any star, or your hand, or for that matter, your existence. Why? Because each of these things is anchored in what God has designed and knows to be the case. Thus the statement "Murder is wrong" is just as true as any scientific fact. Murder is wrong precisely because God knows it to be wrong. Its wrongness is an inherent thing, intrinsic to its nature, built there by God himself. As philosopher Stephen Evans says, "In addition to the physical order that provokes the experience of purposive order, there is another kind of order in the universe: a moral order. It is right to be kind, generous, honest, courageous, and just. It is wrong to be selfish, cruel, deceptive, and cowardly. It is wrong to be abusive, unfriendly, and ungrateful. These are truths that human beings discover. We do not invent them; in their own way they are as objective as the laws of science or mathematics."[49]

What a sad comedown to think of murder's wrongness as merely one of our subjective values. It is that, but saying so says so little. We need language that will not blinker us and shackle us to the ground. We need categories that give us full permission — in fact, require us — to think not just about ourselves but about God. Those who hold that

48. In his Encyclical *Fides et Ratio,* John Paul II speaks of ethical values as "a question of truth" (25). What genuine Christian thought requires, he argues, is "a philosophy which does not disavow the possibility of a knowledge which is objectively true, even if not perfect. This applies equally to the judgment of moral conscience, which Sacred Scripture considers capable of being objectively true" (82).

49. C. Stephen Evans, *Why Believe? Reason and Mystery as Pointers to God* (Grand Rapids: Eerdmans, 1986), p. 41.

nothing exists but humans and the rest of the universe, subjects and objects, values and facts, will, if allowed, be pleased to set the terms of the conversation so as to design their philosophical materialism into the dialog before it begins. But we should not permit them to do so.

That is why, it seems to me, these issues are so important. As Richard Weaver's title reminds us, *Ideas Have Consequences*. If we genuinely believe in the integration of faith and learning, we must recognize that probably its single greatest competitor is the language of dichotomy. Once we become alert to it we hear it everywhere. The media trumpets it, documentaries and textbooks assume it, secular voices appear to have come to one accord on it. For many it seems the best way to resolve all tensions between faith and reason, religion and science. But from the point of view of historic Christianity this dichotomy exacts a fearful price. Religion is relegated to the realm of merely human values and God effectively disappears, or at most is granted an empty ceremonial role. How could Christians possibly relax about such a thing? Says the Apostle Paul, "For though we live in the world we are not carrying on a worldly war, for the weapons of our warfare are not worldly but have divine power to destroy strongholds. We destroy arguments and every proud obstacle to the knowledge of God, and take every thought captive to obey Christ" (2 Cor. 10:4-5).

Conclusion

Whether a positivist, fact/value starting point can be conclusively refuted in some abstract philosophical sense I do not claim to know. It would seem not, since it remains so widely held throughout both the academic and popular cultures. But if we begin with a clear, well thought out, historically Christian worldview in place, there are a dozen points at which such an analysis must be called into question. Or more to the point, a dozen points at which this fact/value analysis cuts against crucial aspects of a Christian worldview. If there are only two utterly immiscible realms, facts and values, as the dichotomist argues, then there can be no revelation, no incarnation, no miracles, and no illusions of any integration of faith and learning.

But Christians need not capitulate to a dichotomist model. We do not question the existence of an objective reality that is observed by perceiving subjects, or even that this may lead to what we can define as facts and values. We just don't believe this is the place to begin our thinking. A better starting point is the question *What is true?* This starting point not only does not rule God out from the beginning; it points us toward him, and toward the integrated, Christ-centered reality he has created.

9 Faith and Learning

CHALLENGE *To Reinforce Our Commitment to Revealed Truth*

To speak of the integration of faith and learning is to speak of three things. We have scrutinized the first, the notion of integrative thinking. Now we must turn to the remaining two, faith and learning. Our goal will be to provide these familiar terms definition and explore their relationship.

But if faith and learning are already familiar, one may ask, why should this be necessary? Precisely because they are so commonplace. We use these tags so often and so casually that their very familiarity may have bred within us not contempt, we hope, but a certain emptiness of meaning, a sense that such old friends scarcely need thinking about anymore. In short, we take them for granted. Or worse, we may sometimes reduce them to code words or even euphemisms whose blandness enables us to speak safely of things that would startle or even offend if we described them more explicitly. Vague references to faith and learning, we have discovered, raise few hackles.

Yet there is always a price to pay for such a loss of meaning. Just as inflation robs us of spending power, when we resort to the inflated currency of empty language we should not be surprised to find our discourse impoverished. The concepts behind these two terms are too important, too central to what we in Christian higher education do, to allow that to happen. Christian scholars must think hard about what they mean by faith and learning so that they can remain clear on the matter even among themselves — perhaps *especially* among themselves. So let us remind ourselves of the biblical ideas these two terms were designed to conjure up in the slogan "integration of faith and learning."

The Seen and Unseen

In 2 Corinthians 4:16-18 the Apostle Paul says, "Though outwardly we are wasting away, inwardly we are being renewed day by day. For our light and momentary troubles are achieving for us an eternal glory that far outweighs them all. So we fix our eyes not on what is seen but on what is unseen. For what is seen is temporary, but what is unseen is eternal." The Apostle here cites a distinction we find throughout the Bible. It is the distinction between the world of the *unseen* and the world of the *seen*. This is essentially the distinction we are after when we speak of faith and learning.

Let us not take the Apostle's language here too literally. By "seen" he does not necessarily mean seen with the eye, though he certainly includes that. Paul is speaking metaphorically. By the seen he means all that is for humans independently discoverable, all that we can learn on our own through the application of our own faculties. The seen for Paul is the world of the ascertainable, the accessible, what we can establish for ourselves. It is the way things seem to us, how they appear from our efforts of investigation, examination, and analysis.

What, then, is the unseen? If it is not for us discoverable, how can we know it at all? Paul's answer: through special revelation, the testimony of God. The world of the unseen represents all we know is the case because God has told us it is so; otherwise we might not know it. And this is just as we should expect. "If God were going to give humans a special revelation, it should contain some truth that humans would be unable to discover on their own. Otherwise, why would he bother? In other words, we would expect a genuine revelation from God to contain mysteries."[1]

Central to this revealed knowledge, knowledge of the unseen, is insight about how we are to construe the seen. Through revelation we discover what things look like from the perspective of heaven. We learn

1. C. Stephen Evans, *Why Believe? Reason and Mystery as Pointers to God* (Grand Rapids: Eerdmans, 1986), p. 125.

what otherwise would be unavailable to us; namely, how things appear to God. From revelation we gain access to a God's-eye view of things, "'a view from above' expressed in language from below."[2]

In penning these last few sentences I realize, of course, how outrageous such an idea sounds to our contemporaries. For some, their objections would focus on any such notion of revelation. To the extent they are willing to speak of revelation at all they certainly do not mean anything like the above.[3] For others the difficulty would be an epistemological one. In our radically anti-foundationalist, perspectivist world, the notion of breaking free from our own situatedness is folly. Even if revelation could offer a God's-eye view of things, we would still have to perceive it from our own particular social and political location. There is no such thing as a view from nowhere. We humans are not free and independent selves facing a similarly independent world to which we are linked by the rules of a universal language, says the critic; rather, we live in a world "no more stable than the historical and conventional forms of thought that bring it into being."[4] How could we ever speak, then, of achieving heaven's view of anything? Nonsense, says the critic.

But note well: it is nonsense only if we embrace the critic's views of revelation, or his radically perspectivist presuppositions, neither of which any Christian need do. As Ralph McInerny observes, in our day "the search for truth has given way to pragmatic compromises based on the epistemological assumption that the mind is incapable of grasping a reality which would render its judgments true. But a mind incapable of the truth is not an apt subject for Christian faith."[5] If a critic's worldview rules out the possibility of gaining in any way any dimension of heaven's view of anything, the Christian's response may

2. Darrell L. Bock, *Purpose-Directed Theology: Getting Our Priorities Right in Evangelical Controversies* (Downers Grove: InterVarsity Press, 2002), p. 31.

3. But for a detailed defense of this view of revelation, see Kevin Vanhoozer, *Is There a Meaning in This Text?: The Bible, the Reader, and the Morality of Literary Knowledge* (Grand Rapids: Zondervan, 1998).

4. Stanley Fish, "Anti-Foundationalism, Theory Hope, and the Teaching of Composition," in *Doing What Comes Naturally: Change, Rhetoric, and the Practice of Theory in Literary and Legal Studies* (Durham: Duke University Press, 1989), p. 45.

5. *Characters in Search of Their Author,* The Gifford Lectures, 1999-2000 (Notre Dame: University of Notre Dame Press, 2001), p. 132.

well be to call into question any worldview that would do such a thing. For gaining a God's-eye view of things is precisely what a historically Christian concept of revelation promises. It certainly is what the Apostle Paul believed it offered.

This point is so controversial these days, and yet so important to Christian higher education, that we should perhaps pause with it for a while. We cannot attempt a historical survey of the Church's view of revelation through the centuries; in fact, it would take us too far afield even to explore the full Apostolic witness on the matter. So let us settle for a quick sweep of just two prominent books of the Bible, the Apostle Paul's epistles to the Corinthians.

A Pauline Contrast

Throughout Paul's writings one discovers a fundamental contrast or antithesis at work.[6] This antithesis constitutes one of the pillars of the Apostle's thought and provides the conceptual framework for his analysis. It is a contrast Paul emphasizes repeatedly in the Corinthian correspondence, which indicates that understanding it may have been as difficult for the worldly Corinthians as it was important for Paul. The Apostle captures this contrast with a variety of language, so that choosing a particular set of terms to describe it runs the risk of oversimplification. For our purposes it will be enough simply to cite the Apostle's own language, allowing his terminology to speak for itself. On page 185 is a selected list of some of the Apostle's most explicit references to this contrast in the Corinthian epistles. In some instances he leaves the opposite member of the antithesis implicit.

The antithesis highlighted in these references is one of realm (cosmos — heaven), of time (this age — the age to come), but most of all, of persons (humans — God). Paul portrays here a basic two-sidedness of things, a fundamental dualism, not of ontology but of viewpoint.[7] There

6. This section is adapted from my *St Paul's Theology of Proclamation: 1 Corinthians 1-4 and Greco-Roman Rhetoric,* Society for New Testament Studies 79 (Cambridge: Cambridge University Press, 1994), pp. 174-78. For further exploration of this contrast, set against a perspectivist, postmodern background, see Brian D. Ingraffia, *Postmodern Theory and Biblical Theology* (Cambridge: Cambridge University Press, 1995), pp. 62-87.

7. On this two-sided perspective, see T. W. Manson, *On Jesus and Paul* (London:

1 Corinthians

1:20	. . .	of this age
1:20	God	the world
1:21	of God	the world
1:26	. . .	by human standards
1:27-28	God	of the world
2:5	of God	of humans
2:6-8	of God	of the rulers of this age
2:12	from God	of the world
3:18	. . .	of this age
3:19	before God	of this world
7:31	. . .	of this world
7:33-34	of the Lord	of the world
9:8	. . .	according to human judgment
10:18	. . .	according to the flesh
13:12	then	now
15:19	. . .	this life only
15:32	. . .	from a human perspective
15:40-49	heavenly	earthly — of the earth

2 Corinthians

4:7	of God	from us
4:17	eternal	for the moment
4:18	the things not seen	the things seen
4:18	eternal	temporal
5:1	from God . . . in heaven	earthly
5:16	. . .	by human standards
10:2-3	. . .	by human standards
11:18	. . .	by human standards

SCM Press, 1963), pp. 38ff.; R. S. Barbour, "Wisdom and the Cross in 1 Corinthians 1 and 2," in *Theologia Crucis — Signum Crucis: Festschrift für Erich Dinkler,* ed. C. Andresen and G. Klein (Tübingen: J. C. B. Mohr, 1979), pp. 58-59, 64; C. H. Giblin, *In Hope of God's Glory: Pauline Theological Perspectives* (New York: Herder and Herder, 1970), p. 128.

is God's perspective, and over against it there is another perspective comprising all the rest, the perspective *tou kosmou,* "of the world." The nature of the constructions in both columns varies, yet each holds in common — in fact, each depends upon — the same general presupposition: the existence of a dichotomy of viewpoint, a "this side" — "that side" sort of antithesis. Furthermore, despite the obvious diversity within the *tou kosmou* side of the contrast, Paul seems to treat it monolithically, as if any diversity here is ultimately less important than its basic coherence.[8] The complexity inherent in such descriptions as "of the world" or "from a human point of view" does not seem to trouble Paul. He is apparently dealing with his subject at a level of abstraction that transcends such diversity.

Paul's treatment of these twin perspectives prompts several important observations:

(1) The Apostle's constant repetition of the antithesis suggests a fundamental opposition of the two perspectives. God's perspective is that of deity, of heaven, of eternity, while from this side the perspective is that of mortal flesh, the world, this age. The two represent divergent ways of perceiving reality, and according to Paul, they often clashed. From out of the constricted viewpoint of the world grow distorted conceptions of God and ultimate things that compete with God's conception (2 Cor. 10:5). According to Paul, God is determined to set aside these false conceptions, and by such means moreover as to demonstrate in the end their utter futility (1 Cor. 1:19-21, 27-29; 3:19-21).

(2) There can be little question which of the two perspectives Paul espoused. Having been granted his own special glimpse into the other side (1 Cor. 15:8; 2 Cor. 3:6, 4:1ff., 5:16, 12:1ff.; cf. Gal. 1:1-12), Paul now saw himself as a champion of God's perspective (2 Cor. 5:20), engaged in open warfare with its alternative (2 Cor. 10:3-5; cf. 1 Cor. 15:34). He perceived temporal things as so partial as to be, given the sinfulness of the race, intrinsically misleading. From humanity's congenitally truncated viewpoint — limited as it is to the seen, the merely apparent — reality is bound to be misunderstood. Only from God's perspective can one see ultimate things as they must be seen to be understood.[9] Hence Paul

8. Hans Conzelmann: "The cosmos appears as a collective subject, the bearer of 'its' wisdom." *1 Corinthians,* Hermeneia Series, trans. J. W. Leitch (Philadelphia: Fortress Press, 1975), p. 43.

9. For the Old Testament roots of such ideas, see G. von Rad, *Wisdom in Israel,* trans. J. D. Martin (London: SCM Press, 1975), pp. 96-110.

counsels the Corinthians against understanding life merely as it appears from the vantage point *tou kosmou*. The Christian must not operate "by sight" (2 Cor. 5:7; cf. 5:12). To live on the level of "this life only" meant for Paul only vanity and emptiness, a life devoid of ultimate significance (1 Cor. 15:19, 32). The "things seen" are merely the temporal, the transient things; the "things not seen" constitute the eternal (2 Cor. 4:18). By the yardstick of eternity the particulars we can discover for ourselves are not the truly important things. They are merely facets of the "form of this world," which is passing away (1 Cor. 7:31). Only from God's perspective can the true nature of ultimate things be grasped.

(3) Paul maintained that it is impossible for humans to gain access to the other side, God's side, apart from revelation.[10] Despite our best efforts, the limitedness of our worldly perspective is, in so far as we struggle on our own, without remedy. Ultimate things are hidden from us quite by design, says Paul (1 Cor. 1:21, 27-29; Rom. 11:33-36; cf. 2 Cor. 4:3-4). In the end all of our speculations leave us short, with a one-dimensional and merely this-sided view that can never suffice. Only the Spirit of God knows fully the truth about God, and he is the only source from which an understanding of this truth can come (1 Cor. 2:10-12). The world cannot construct this divine conception of things for itself (1 Cor. 1:6-9); it must be willing simply to embrace the truth revealed by the Spirit (1 Cor. 1:21-25; 2 Cor. 3:14-18). Viewed strictly from the world's perspective, of course, this appears a foolish thing to do, an act of abdication or capitulation (1 Cor. 2:14). But viewed in the full light of the other, divine perspective, such a capitulation becomes for Paul the ultimate act of wisdom for one who genuinely desires to find the truth (1 Cor. 2:6-8; 3:18).

(4) Yet Paul did not maintain that any mortal could fully understand as God understands, even with the benefit of revelation. If the veil is lifted for one who turns to the Lord (2 Cor. 3:16), it is by no means lifted entirely. The believer is given by the Spirit enough of a glimpse of God's perspective to know wherein the truth consists (1 Cor. 1:23-24, 30), enough to provide a plumb line against which to order her own re-

10. For an insightful discussion by a philosopher of this point, contrasted with the general position of ancient Greek philosophy, see S. R. Letwin, "Hobbes and Christianity," *Daedalus* 105 (Winter 1976): 3-5. Cf. also O. Cullmann, *Salvation in History*, trans. S. G. Sowers et al. (London: SCM Press, 1967), pp. 118, 252; E. Best, "The Power and the Wisdom of God: i Corinthians 1.18-25," in *Paolo a una Chiesa Divisa (1 Cor. 1-4)*, Serie Monografica di "Benedictina," 5, ed. L. DeLorenzi (Rome: S. Paolo, 1980), p. 25.

sponses, but only just so. At best we still understand only "in part," says Paul, as if peering "through a glass dimly." But there will come a time in the future when the believer will discover a final knowledge of the truth, a time, says the Apostle, when "I shall know fully, just as I have been known" (1 Cor. 13:12). It is in this same future, in fact, that all things will be made manifest, including "the hidden things of darkness" and "the counsels of the heart" (1 Cor. 4:5). Then will the ones who have operated in the light of "the things not seen" — and been ridiculed as foolish for it by those whose vision is limited to "the things that are seen" — then will the full truth emerge and the ones who were truly wise be vindicated (1 Cor. 3:13; 4:5; cf. 2 Cor. 10:18).

This contrast is a theme that runs like a thread through the Apostle's writings. For every place we see it lying on the surface there are many more where it has slipped out of sight but is working nonetheless to hold the fabric of his thought together. It is a contrast, in fact, we find throughout the Bible.

If we Christians are to think biblically, we shall have to follow the Apostle's lead. Others may reject any such antithesis; their radical perspectivalism eliminates one whole side of the contrast, and the most important side at that. But as Christians we are under no obligation to embrace this perspectivist epistemology and then tailor everything else to fit. Our starting point is special revelation, and in particular, the inscripturated Word of God, the Bible, for it is here that we learn of the Living Word, the Lord Jesus Christ. With Christians of earlier ages we take our stand with the Scriptures, our ever-trustworthy "rule of faith and practice." Thus for us it is the radical perspectivalism that must go.

Faith and Revelation

The biblical notion of faith, in fact, *requires* revelation. It involves "taking a claim to be true on the word of another."[11] And in this instance, the word taken as true is from God.

Other popular notions of faith typically involve no such implica-

---

11. McInerny, *Characters in Search of Their Author,* p. 123. For an extended exploration of how testimony may lead to knowledge, see C. A. J. Coady, *Testimony: A Philosophical Study* (Oxford: Clarendon Press, 1992).

tion. For example, some appear to conceive of faith as a "blind leap" into the unknown. The leap is blind precisely because by it we are casting ourselves into *terra incognita,* groping our way toward something about which we have no knowledge. But, the argument goes, life sometimes requires such a leap. To take that leap, and then see what happens, is to exercise faith.

Others would argue for a conception of faith only marginally less blind. In his ode to "Faith," for example, George Santayana warned that:

> Our knowledge is a torch of smoky pine
> That lights the pathway but one step ahead
> Across a void of mystery and dread.

Thus we require something more, "the inward vision." We must "believe the heart." For after all,

> Columbus found a world, and had no chart
> Save one that faith deciphered in the skies.

Faith conceived along these lines is thus something akin to a trust in our intuition or imagination, the soul's "invincible surmise." Santayana usefully labeled this experience "animal faith."[12]

At the popular level these notions of faith approximate what many of our contemporaries mean when they use the term. Yet, while we may agree that life sometimes requires this sort of stepping into the unknown, such exercises are a far cry from what the Bible means by faith. And still less satisfactory is another common variant, what we may call a Peter Pan version of faith. It works like this: if you really *believe* that Tinkerbell exists — that is, if you squint your eyes very hard and really, really *believe* it — then she will exist. Your belief will make it so. You just have to "have *faith.*" William James long ago dissected this "will to believe" and the "faith ladder" by which it is achieved:

> A conception of the world arises in you somehow, no matter how.
> Is it true or not? you ask.

---

12. For example, see George Santayana, *Scepticism and Animal Faith: Introduction to a System of Philosophy* (New York: Dover Publications, 1955).

It *might* be true somewhere, you say, for it is not self-contradictory.

It *may* be true, you continue, even here and now.

It is *fit* to be true, it would be *well if it were* true, it *ought* to be true, you presently feel.

It *must* be true, something persuasive in you whispers next; and then — as a final result —

It shall be *held for true,* you decide; it *shall be* as if true, for *you.*[13]

Despite the fact that, as James argues, no step in this process bears weight, this is nonetheless the way many conceive of faith. At the popular level this conception may be the most common of all. Yet it represents a serious departure from what the Bible means by the term. C. S. Lewis said, "The state of mind which desperate desire working on a strong imagination can manufacture is not faith in the Christian sense. It is a feat of psychological gymnastics."[14] For the Christian, the efficacy of one's faith lies not in faith itself but in the faithfulness of the One who is the object of that faith. In other words, our faith is only as good as the One we're trusting. If God is not faithful to his Word, then our faith can accomplish nothing at all.

In the Bible, faith always requires taking God at his word, so much so that if God has not spoken, it would not be possible to exercise faith in the biblical sense at all.[15] For Christians, faith has traditionally been understood to include *notitia* (knowledge), *assensus* (assent) and *fiducia* (trust), and these remain helpful distinctions. By "taking God at his word" I mean giving assent to its truthfulness *(assensus)* and therefore entrusting oneself to *(fiducia)* what God has revealed *(notitia)*. As Paul Helm says, in so doing, we are inherently trusting God himself:

> If my friend Jones says that he will lend me his ladders and I believe what he says, then my reliance upon him — my faith — must have both a propositional and a personal aspect to it. I believe Jones. I

13. *A Pluralistic Universe* (London: Longmans, Green, and Co., 1920), pp. 328-29.

14. *Letters to Malcolm* (San Diego: Harvest Book, Harcourt, Inc., 1964), p. 60.

15. For a technical defense of the idea that God can and does speak — that is, that there can be what we are loosely calling here "a word from God" — see Nicholas Wolterstorff, *Divine Discourse: Philosophical Reflections on the Claim that God Speaks* (Cambridge: Cambridge University Press, 1995).

may or may not give him unconditional belief, believe him whatever he may say. But what is undeniable is that I believe him in respect of the ladders. The proposition expressed by the sentence "Jones will lend Helm his ladders" is believed by Helm because it is taken to be a trustworthy assertion of Jones. In believing the proposition, I believe — trust — the person, and in believing the person on this occasion I believe what he says, his utterance about the ladders. So the two senses of faith, the personal and the propositional, are interconnected, and highlight two aspects of one situation.[16]

This is why we may say that if God has not spoken, it is not possible to exercise faith in the biblical sense of the term. What would we be trusting? In God himself, apart from his word? Perhaps so, we might say; we face many situations in life where we do not have a specific word from God. Yet we are called to respond in faith. But a closer look shows that even here, what the Bible means by faith is impossible without some word from God.

Suppose, for instance, a Christian receives from her doctor a terminal diagnosis. What would it mean for her to respond to such news in faith? Believing that God is going to heal her? We know that sometimes God brings healing, and often he does not. Has he somehow in this instance informed our Christian that he will heal her? If so, then trusting that word and believing he will heal her constitutes a classic instance of biblical faith.[17]

But suppose she has received no such word. Does that mean her illness presents no opportunity to respond in faith? Clearly not. It would surely preclude her from saying things like, "I have *faith* God is going to heal me," for if God has told her no such thing, what is she trusting? Suppose God does not will her healing; suppose he wishes to use her illness, as he did the Apostle Paul's "thorn in the flesh," for his own purposes, purposes she does not know or understand. If this were

---

16. Paul Helm, *Faith and Understanding* (Grand Rapids: Eerdmans, 1997), p. 10.

17. I will bypass the debate among evangelical Christians over how God may speak to us today, not because the subject is unimportant but because it is another subject, one that would take us too far afield from our present focus. When I speak here of God's word I obviously have in mind, first and foremost, the living Word of God, Jesus Christ, and the inscripturated Word of God, the Bible. Others may wish to add further sources, but doing so will not in principle affect our present discussion.

the case, then making such a claim — "I have *faith* God is going to heal me" — reduces to presumption, an attempt to obligate God to perform to her command.

Even without a promise of healing, however, as a Christian our patient still has challenging opportunities for exercising biblical faith. If God has not said he will heal her, what has he said? He has told her that he is loving, and that he loves her with an everlasting love; that he is trustworthy and that she can depend on him even when her world is dark and she does not understand; that he is working all these things, including her illness, together for good according to his own purposes; that his grace will be sufficient for her whatever she may face; that he will never leave her nor forsake her, but will stick closer to her than a brother; and so on through scores of divine promises. Exercising faith in such situations does not involve claiming promises God never made; it means trusting fully the promises he has made. In short, it means "taking God at his word." "Blessed is the womb that bore you, and the breasts that you suckled," said the woman to Jesus; to which he replied, rather abruptly, "On the contrary, blessed are those who hear the word of God and keep it!" (Luke 11:27-28; cf. Luke 8:21).

This is the concept of faith we find from cover to cover in the Bible, but it is nicely summarized in the classic passage on the subject, Hebrews 11. The writer to the Hebrews prepares us a few verses earlier when he enjoins us to "hold fast the confession of our hope without wavering, for he who promised is faithful" (10:23). Here we have the key to understanding the great gallery of saints described in the following chapter. They built their lives on the promises of God because of their confidence in the One who made the promises. If we are speaking biblically, faith is trusting God's word precisely because we trust God himself. Or to express it the other way around, the Christian's faith is precisely a faith in God, which requires trusting what he says. The Apostle Paul asks: How then shall they call on him "in whom" they have not believed? And how shall they believe in him "about whom" they have not heard? (10:14) The Christian faith inherently involves both: it is a "believing in" that inherently involves a "believing that" (Rom. 10:9).

The relationship between trusting God and trusting his word is perhaps analogous to the relationship between loving Christ and obeying him. Jesus said, "If you love me, you will keep my commandments" (John 14:15); or reversing the thought, "If you keep my commandments, you will abide in my love" (John 15:10). In short, we love Christ by doing what he says. In the same way, we trust God by trusting his word. The two must never be separated, much less set in opposition to one another. "Revelation is not *either* personal *or* propositional, but both," as John Paul II reminds us in his Encyclical, *Fides et Ratio*. "By faith, men and women give their assent to [the] divine testimony. This means that they acknowledge fully and integrally the truth of what is revealed because it is God himself who is the guarantor of that truth" (13).

"Faith," says the writer of Hebrews as he begins his account of the great heroes of redemptive history, "is the assurance of things hoped for, the conviction of things not seen" (11:1). What is the basis for such a hope, for such a conviction? By definition, it is not the seen. As the Apostle Paul says, "we walk by faith, not by sight" (2 Cor. 5:7; cf. Rom. 8:24-25). Biblical faith is always dependent on a word from God, not seldom in contradiction to the seen, that is, against our experience or our own understanding of things: "Against all hope, Abraham in hope believed and so became the father of many nations, just as it had been said to him" (Rom. 4:18). And this is what these champions of faith held in common: they lived their lives on the basis of God's word, not their experience. Thus: "By faith Noah, being warned by God concerning events as yet unseen, took heed" (11:7); "By faith Abraham obeyed when he was called, . . . not knowing where he was to go" (11:8; cf. Rom. 4:18); and so on through the list: "These all died in faith, not having received what was promised" (11:13; cf. v. 39). Yet they continued to trust the One who promised. They took God at his word and lived their lives accordingly, which is why they are recorded in the Hall of Fame of the Faithful. They are each models of what the Bible means by faith.

This biblical concept of faith is painted in the Scriptures as one of the great Christian virtues. Thus from a Christian point of view it seems unfortunate to speak of the "epistemic deficiency" of faith, as does Paul Helm when he says, "Faith, though it involves belief, is necessarily unjustified true belief, for it falls short of knowledge. Understanding aims at remedying this epistemic deficiency. There is a progression from belief, in which propositions are accepted upon authority, the authority of God in revelation, to knowledge."[18]

We should be careful about how we think of any such progres-

---

18. Helm, *Faith and Understanding,* p. 39.

sion. In this age we should not portray accepting something on the basis of God's word as epistemologically inferior to knowledge. As Emil Brunner reminds us, "Until the period of the Reformation the Church suffered badly from the devastating error derived from the Gnostics of the Early Church, who, under the influence of Platonism, regarded faith as a lower stage in the realm of knowledge."[19] It would be unfortunate to lapse into this same error now.

One day knowledge will indeed supplant faith (1 Cor. 13:12-13), and perhaps in this sense faith may be considered inferior. The Apostle intimates as much when he says of the three great Christian virtues, faith, hope, and love, that love is superior because we will never outgrow it. By contrast, once we come to know as we are presently known — that is, fully — we will no longer require faith, or hope either for that matter, for when we are in possession of that in which we believed and for which we hoped, faith and hope become passé. But all that is for the age to come. For the present, while we still see only through a darkling glass, we are called to live on the basis of God's word, to walk by faith, so much so that if we are unwilling to do so it is impossible to please God (Heb. 11:6).

In the present age, therefore, faith should not be considered as something deficient, something inferior to knowledge. Thomas apparently preferred knowledge to faith and was rebuked for it: "Have you believed because you have seen me? Blessed are those who have not seen and yet believe," said Jesus (John 20:29). The blessed are not those who insist on sight, but those who take God at his word and trust him, for this pleases him. The Scriptures thus valorize faith as a grand Christian virtue, a willingness to trust God's word even when we are without sight. The aim of knowledge in this age should therefore be viewed not as supplanting or replacing what we can know from revelation, but as enhancing, complementing, or deepening it.

In any case, our point here is that biblical faith inherently requires some sort of word from God, the presence of revelation of some sort. If there is no revelation, no word from God, there can be no faith, no taking God at his word. Hence revelation is critical to Christianity. In his little book, *Religion Without Revelation,* Julian Huxley argues for

---

19. *Revelation and Reason: The Christian Doctrine of Faith and Knowledge,* trans. Olive Wyon (London: Student Christian Movement Press, 1947), p. 115.

precisely what its title suggests, but what he comes up with is a far cry from historic Christianity. There can be no such thing as Christianity without revelation. A faith-based Christian worldview requires it. Without faith it is impossible to please God, and there is no faith, at least on the Bible's terms, without revelation. Thus the idea of revelation is a *sine qua non* of truly Christian thinking. We cannot dispense with it.

The language of faith and learning is simply another way of speaking of what the Apostle calls the worlds of the unseen and the seen. The Enlightenment sought to drive a wedge between these ways of knowing by dismissing revelation from the table. Hence these many generations later we live in a this-worldly culture obsessed with the realms of the seen and confused about the rest. Which is why the enterprise of Christian thinking is at once today so important and so controversial. What Christians seek is nothing less than the unification of knowledge, bringing together into one Christ-centered, re-integrated whole all we can know from God's revelation and all we can discover through the exercise of our own faculties. This is what we mean by "the integration of faith and learning."

Our Conceptual Lens

As if explaining such an ambitious integrative vision were not difficult enough, the problem is exacerbated by insisting that Christian thinking must start — meaning, of course, a conceptual starting point, not necessarily a chronological one — with what we know from revelation. Nothing less is required by what Lesslie Newbigin calls the "radical conversion" of becoming a Christian. "This will be not only a conversion of the will and of the feelings," says Newbigin, "but a conversion of the mind — a 'paradigm shift' that leads to a new version of how things are and, not at once but gradually, to the development of a new plausibility structure in which the most real of all realities is the living God whose character is 'rendered' for us in the pages of Scripture."[20]

The generation of this new version of how things are, this new plausibility structure, is the result of giving priority, in the Apostle's

---

20. *Foolishness to the Greeks: The Gospel and Western Culture* (Grand Rapids: Eerdmans, 1986), p. 64.

words, "not to the seen but to the unseen," of walking by faith — that is, taking God at his word — and not by sight. In this way, what we know from revelation becomes our beacon, our yardstick, our plumb line, our entry point into everything else we can know. These unseen realities form our initial reference point, the "lodestar"[21] of our learning. They become the lens through which we view everything else. "In God's light, we see light," says the old adage. It is to proceed, says Mark Noll, "as any Christian exploration of anything surely ought to proceed — namely, by trying to see first what the Bible says and then using those conclusions to shape our investigation of what we are concerned about."[22] "Trust in the Lord with all your heart and do not rely on your own insight," says the ancient wisdom of the Scriptures. "In all your ways acknowledge him and he will make straight your paths" (Prov. 3:5-6).

Why must we insist on the priority (though not, of course, the exclusivity) of what we can know from revelation? Why is starting with God "the beginning of wisdom" (Ps. 111:10)? Edward Curtis says, "Since we accept special revelation as coming to us from the all wise and omniscient God who is not limited in time or perspective, there is a clear sense in which the priority of special revelation must be recognized in our integrative pursuits."[23] Intellectuals in particular, says Nathan Hatch, "very easily cross the fine line and begin affirming their own intellectual self-sufficiency, trusting in their own wisdom rather than submitting the mind humbly to the truths of holy Scripture. Given their well-honed intellectual skills, academics are always prone to move in the direction of an unwarrantably high opinion of human natural powers."[24]

A proper creaturely humility requires us to acknowledge Hatch's point and to admit that what we can discover on our own is inherently deficient for our ultimate needs. It can, to be sure, tell us a great deal about the creation, but how far will that take us? Hebrews speaks of the

21. John Paul II, *Fides et Ratio*, 15.

22. *The Scandal of the Evangelical Mind* (Grand Rapids: Eerdmans, 1994), p. 200.

23. Edward M. Curtis, "Some Biblical Contributions to a Philosophy of Education," *Faculty Dialogue* 21 (Spring-Summer 1994): 98.

24. Nathan O. Hatch, "Evangelical Colleges and the Challenge of Christian Thinking," in *Making Higher Education Christian: The History and Mission of Evangelical Colleges in America*, ed. Joel A. Carpenter and Kenneth W. Shipps (Grand Rapids: Eerdmans, 1987), p. 167.

fragility of this created order, and of its temporal, and therefore temporary, nature: "This expression, 'Yet once more,' denotes the removing of those things which can be shaken, as of created things, so that those things which cannot be shaken may remain" (12:27-29). To learn of the created order is crucial, but in the end even the most extensive knowledge of the seen will leave us short. "The form of this world is passing away," says the Apostle (1 Cor. 7:31). One day it will be shaken and sifted and transformed altogether. What we require in the meantime is knowledge of that realm which cannot be shaken; in other words, what we need is God. But therein lies our dilemma: "Can you by searching find out God? Can you discover the limits of the Almighty?" (Job 11:7).

Truth be told, the answer to Zophar's questions to Job is yes. To a limited extent humans can "find out God." "For what can be known about God is plain to them, because God has shown it to them. Ever since the creation of the world his invisible nature, namely, his eternal power and deity, has been clearly perceived in the things that have been made" (Rom. 1:19-20). By searching out the created order, the world of the seen, we can learn that there is a Creative Orderer, a God who made the world, and that this God is mighty. But not much more. Thus what we can learn about God from our own unaided discovery is very limited. In the end it will prove deficient in the very realm we need most, the truth of the gospel of Jesus Christ. For that we require an unshakable word from God, which is to say, special revelation. "Heaven and earth shall pass away," Jesus said, "but my words shall not pass away" (Mark 13:31). That's why "a genuine Christian *Weltanschauung* must always be formed and reformed by the Bible as the Word of God."[25]

If we begin with our own unaided discovery, rather than revelation, we will likely wind up losing both. This is, so to speak, what occurred when the Enlightenment took the so-called Cartesian turn, the turn to the subject. Excluding any possibility of revelation, Enlightenment rationalism attempted to limit itself to what human reason — autonomous, ahistorical, detached, value free   could discover on its own. In fact it set the two, learning and faith, against one another; revelation was attacked from the viewpoint of learning. This led to an unseemly struggle from which we have not yet recovered.

---

25. David Naugle, *Worldview: The History of a Concept* (Grand Rapids: Eerdmans, 2002), p. 336.

Taking this tack leads to both philosophical and theological dead ends. If we begin philosophically with the world of the seen, with any hope of moving to the world of the unseen, we will have set ourselves a sisyphean task. As the saying has it, you can't get there from here. What may be known about God through the created order can provide us with some rudiments of knowledge; it provides mute testimony to the fact that he exists and that he is powerful. But even that limited light proves of value only insofar as it propels us toward further light, the light of special revelation. If we take that direction, then we are back to our point about the importance of special revelation. But if we do not, then the knowledge of God available in nature serves only the negative purpose of rendering us excuseless before God (Rom. 1:20). At best, we remain Deists who will one day give an account for why on the basis of the light God gave us in nature we did not seek the further light of special revelation.

But there are not many Deists around these days. That's because the much more common response to the created order is to reject or suppress what it tells us about God altogether, and to venerate instead the creature and the created order itself (Rom. 1:21-32). This response leads to a philosophical naturalism, which in turn leaves us, if we are honest and courageous enough to follow it through, with skepticism and nihilism. This is plain enough in the metaphysical naturalism of our own day. We are told that the universe is all that exists, all that can exist, all that ever will exist, and that it is utterly without design, purpose, or meaning. But if that is so, how could it be otherwise that humans should find their lives devoid of design, purpose, or meaning? So why not a Nietzchean nihilism wherein the will to power becomes all? When we begin with the created order, the world of the seen, we not only do not wind up with God; we lose the wondrous meaning and significance of the created order in the bargain.[26]

---

26. Cf. Stanley Rosen's parallel point on the subject of hermeneutics: "In the nineteenth century we learned, first from Hegel and then more effectively from Nietzsche, that God is dead. In the twentieth century, Kojève and his students, like Foucault, have informed us that man is dead, thereby as it were opening the gates into the abyss of postanthropological deconstruction. As the scope of hermeneutics has expanded, then, the two original sources of hermeneutical meaning, God and man, have vanished, taking with them the cosmos or world. . . . If nothing is real, the real is nothing; there is no difference between the written lines of a text and the blank spaces between them." *Hermeneutics as Politics* (New York: Oxford University Press, 1987), p. 161.

But this approach also leads to a theological dead end. If we determine to find God apart from special revelation we immediately lose the uniqueness of Christ. At most this strategy allows one to posit a sort of general religion. But such a religion is quickly embarrassed by the unique claims of Christ. The gospel winds up repudiated or redefined and the uniqueness of God's revelation in Christ denied. In such a transaction we thus lose not only the gospel; we also lose the key to grasping the meaning of creation, which is Christ. Both philosophically and theologically, starting with the seen rather than with special revelation may mean we wind up with neither. It is, as William James remarked, "to be in the universe as dogs and cats are in our libraries, seeing the books and hearing the conversation, but having no inkling of the meaning of it all."[27] We never arrive at the truths we can know only from special revelation, and we lose the ultimate meaningfulness of the created order to boot.

But notice how the opposite is also true. If we begin our thinking with revelation we wind up not only with the gospel but with the created order as well. We cannot begin with the created order and find out God; the bridge cannot be built from this side. God must build the bridge from his side through revelation. Then, on the basis of what we learn there we are able to make sense of the created order. This is, I think, C. S. Lewis's point in the introduction to *The Great Divorce* when he asks, "But what, you ask, of earth? Earth, I think, will not be found by anyone to be in the end a very distinct place. I think earth, if chosen instead of Heaven, will turn out to have been, all along, only a region in Hell: and earth, if put second to Heaven, to have been from the beginning a part of Heaven itself."[28] Lewis's point is that the things of the created order can only be truly grasped from the perspective of heaven. In his essay on *Transposition* he cogently argues that the heavenly (the higher, richer, more varied, more subtle) can be transposed to the lower (the earthly, less rich, less varied, less subtle), but if we begin with the lower we can never discover the higher. Special revelation enables us to look along the created order to see its meaning. Without it we not only do not find heaven; we do not fully comprehend the created order either.

27. James, *A Pluralistic Universe,* p. 309.
28. *The Great Divorce* (New York: Macmillan, 1946), p. 7.

Historical Stance

This stance, which gives conceptual priority to faith over learning, is the historic approach to the Christian's intellectual task we discover in some of the greatest thinkers throughout the history of the Church. It is the approach, for example, we find in St. Paul's first-century call to "bring every thought *(noēma)* into captivity to Christ"; or in Augustine's fourth-century instruction, "Believe, so that you might understand"; or in Anselm's eleventh-century phrase, "faith seeking understanding" *(Fides quaerens intellectum);* or in Pascal's seventeenth-century dictum, "Not only do we only know God through Jesus Christ, but we can only know ourselves through Jesus Christ."[29] It is the approach that views faith — a willingness to take God at his word — as the prerequisite for the right use of reason. "Because reason's light is darkened by sin, the redemption afforded by the incarnate Logos must . . . illumine learning."[30]

That is why the Scriptures are so important to Christian higher education. As God's special revelation, the Bible provides us our starting point: the Lordship of Jesus Christ. He is the central person of the Bible and of the universe, the key to understanding all of existence, the lodestar for all our learning. Virtually all we know about the Living Word we know from the Written Word, all of which speaks of him (John 5:39). One day, "when Jesus Christ is revealed," we will see him face to face; but for now, "though you have not seen him, you love him; and even though you do not see him now, you believe in him and are filled with an inexpressible and glorious joy, for you are receiving the goal of your faith, the salvation of your souls" (1 Peter 1:7-9). On what basis do we come to know and love the unseen Christ? Not by studying the world of the seen, but by believing in him on the basis of what God has revealed in the Scriptures.

St. Augustine said, "Unless we walk by faith, we shall not be able to come to that sight which does not fail but continues through a cleansed understanding uniting us with Truth."[31] Augustine's point

29. *Pensée* 417.

30. Arthur F. Holmes, *Building the Christian Academy* (Grand Rapids: Eerdmans, 2001), p. 68.

31. *On Christian Doctrine,* trans. D. W. Robertson, Jr. (Indianapolis: Bobbs-Merrill, 1958), p. 45.

has echoed through the centuries and continues to be heard today, as when Eloise Meneses says, citing both Lesslie Newbigin and Parker Palmer, "It is not by transcending ourselves that we are able to attain [objective, transcendent] truth. It is by *descending,* by penetrating, by 'standing somewhere' that we are able to perceive truth."[32] And the Christian's "somewhere" is the inscripturated Word of God, which tells us of the Living Word. This Christocentric key, available to us only through special revelation, opens up to us the world of the seen as well. Revelation is the glass through which we are again in a position to read the book of nature. It enables us to see the created order with new eyes, to understand it from God's point of view. Thus the world of the seen can come alive to us.

The created order is God's handiwork and at its best it is a pointer to the One we serve. Even its brokenness, if we look along it — that is, if we view it in the light of what the Scriptures say about it — can tell us of him: his grace, his mercy, his redemption. Revelation shows the created order to be fraught with meaning and purpose and significance. In this way the Bible becomes central to Christian higher education, primarily because it tells us of Jesus Christ.

To think Christianly thus means to think biblically. We do not merely abstract from the Bible a handful of theological themes and settle for reflecting on those; we actually study the text of Scripture, all of it, seeking out "the whole counsel of God" (Acts 20:27). We are looking for all the many ways those grand theological themes are adumbrated in the Bible, and for all that lies between them. This requires much more than a superficial, prooftexting approach to Scripture. It requires allowing a deep, Trinitarian, Christocentric reading of the entire Bible to permeate all of our thinking and every aspect of the curriculum. As Stephen Evans puts it, what Christian scholars "need to develop is the habit of continually looking to Scripture to provide the basic or foundational narrative in terms of which we understand the world."[33] This requires steeping ourselves in this grand account, the ultimate metanarrative of God's purposes — his creation, redemption, and restora-

32. Eloise Hiebert Meneses, "No Other Foundation: Establishing a Christian Anthropology," *Christian Scholar's Review* 29, no. 3 (Spring 2000): 538.

33. "The Calling of the Christian Scholar-Teacher," in *Faithful Learning and the Christian Scholarly Vocation,* ed. Douglas V. Henry and Bob R. Agee (Grand Rapids: Eerdmans, 2003), p. 37.

tion of the world through Christ — and then privileging this account by permitting it to function as the touchstone for everything else we study. This is indispensable for truly Christian thinking. As Pascal put it, "Without Scripture, whose only object is Christ, we know nothing, and can see nothing but obscurity and confusion in the nature of God and in nature itself."[34]

The Process

How does this work? It begins with our commitment to the priority of revelation. Chronologically, genuine Christian thinking may begin anywhere. But our logical starting point is the God's-eye view we gain from the Bible. As Lesslie Newbigin says, "The twin dogmas of Incarnation and Trinity . . . form the starting point for a way of understanding reality as a whole." It is only from this disclosed standpoint, he says, that we "can begin to understand and cope with a world that is both rational and contingent. For at the center of this disclosure, providing the clue to the whole, there stands the cross, on which the one whose purpose is the source and goal of all was slain in shame and dereliction, and the resurrection, in which that very death became the source of life."[35]

Because Jesus Christ is precisely this "clue to the whole," Christian thinkers seek to steep themselves in the Bible's Christ-centered understanding of the world. Why such rigor? Because as Richard Riesen says, "The most effective integration of biblical notions and academic content is done artfully rather than obviously."[36] Integrative thinking works well, says Riesen, "to the extent that it is woven into the warp and woof of our thinking. . . . Biblical notions permeate everything we say and think. Their force is lost when they are too self-conscious, their self-consciousness perhaps the evidence that the integration has not been thoroughly effected."[37] Thankfully, in this intricate project we do not start from scratch. We benefit from over two millennia of the work

34. *Pensée* 417.
35. Newbigin, *Foolishness to the Greeks,* p. 90.
36. Richard A. Riesen, *Piety and Philosophy: A Primer for Christian Schools* (Phoenix: ACW Press, 2002), p. 99.
37. Riesen, *Piety and Philosophy,* p. 99.

of others who have sought to love God with their minds. Our goal is a far-reaching specifically Christian way of viewing the world. For us, this worldview is the intellectual stepping-off point for all we can know as humans.

Then, working out from this revealed worldview — in fact *propelled* by it — this approach values supremely the broader intellectual task, the task of loving God with our minds. We understand, as John Henry Newman put it, that it "is the highest wisdom to accept truth of whatever kind, wherever it is clearly ascertained to be such."[38] The Christian stands committed to the revealed premise that God has made a universe that can be studied and understood, and us with minds capable of doing so. We recognize that there can be a unity to truth because all that is true has its source in the One who has revealed himself in Jesus Christ. In fact we become committed to the search for that unity precisely because of our love for and obedience to that One.

This is the finest motive for Christian scholarship. From our Christ-centered understanding of things we reach out to engage whatever can be discovered. Whether our own insights or the insights of others, our goal is to assess them in the light of the Lordship of Jesus Christ. In this process we celebrate and embrace all that measures up, and we carefully evaluate and, if need be, call into question whatever may not. This is what is understood in this historic Christian stance as "the integration of faith and learning."

Such an approach to learning requires a willingness to engage in thinking that is radically Christian. The task of the Christian scholar, says Nicholas Wolterstorff, requires nothing less, "for the connection does not always leap out. The belief-content of one's authentic Christian commitment is a wonderfully rich and complex structure, and ever again one discovers that some connection of commitment to theory has been missed by oneself as well as by one's predecessors."[39] Wolterstorff suggests two reasons why this happens. The first, he says, is that many of us "scarcely see the world as Christians" because our "patterns of thought are not those of Christianity" but those of our time and place in history. Second, and conversely, many Christians, in-

---

38. *The Idea of a University,* ed. Martin J. Svaglic (Notre Dame: University of Notre Dame Press, 1982), p. 348.

39. *Reason within the Bounds of Religion* (Grand Rapids: Eerdmans, 1976), p. 103.

cluding Christian scholars, also lack a deep understanding of their Christian faith. "We see only pieces and snatches and miss the full relevance of our Christian commitment."[40] Wolterstorff's indictment, if accurate, is a sobering one for our generation of Christian thinkers. If he's right, our condition is a textbook example of precisely what Christian scholarship aspires to avoid. According to the Apostle Paul, as an essential element in our service to God our thinking is not to be conformed to the world — that is, shaped merely by our cultural moment — but we are to be transformed by the renewing of our minds (Rom. 12:1-2).

Noetic Effects

Genuine Christian thinking can never settle for superficiality, and it is certainly never naive about its task. What it demands is thinking which brings all we can know into "an integral whole, into a complex, unified view of reality,"[41] all centered upon the person of Christ. And in this effort there can be no room for laxity or shallowness. Why? Because this biblical approach to learning appreciates fully the so-called "noetic" (from the Greek *nous*, mind; and hence *noein*, to perceive) effects of sin. As Lewis put it, "Though Reason is divine, human reasoners are not."[42] Sin can introduce systematic intellectual problems, problems which must be sorted out. We need not think of outright falsehood, although this on occasion occurs; difficulties more likely arise from such things as "unintentional mistakes, self-deception, faulty imagination, misleading language habits, . . . disorganized relationships with colleagues,"[43] and above all, false presuppositions.

Such intellectual wariness is based upon the simple fact that human intellectual efforts are never purely neutral. From a Christian perspective human ideas often show themselves to be, to one degree or another, expressions of the mutinous state of the human heart. Hence

---

40. Wolterstorff, *Reason within the Bounds of Religion,* p. 104.

41. David Wolfe and Harold Heie, *Slogans or Distinctives: Reforming Christian Higher Education* (Lanham, Md.: University Press of America, 1993), p. 4.

42. "Religion: Reality or Substitute?" in *Christian Reflections,* ed. Walter Hooper (Grand Rapids: Eerdmans, 1967), p. 43.

43. Holmes, *Building the Christian Academy,* p. 105.

philosopher Alvin Plantinga's reminder that "scholarship and science are not neutral with respect to [the] struggle for our souls." Says he, "It is not as if the main areas of scholarship are neutral with respect to this struggle, with religious or spiritual disagreement rearing its ugly head only when it comes, say, to religion itself. The facts are very different: the world of scholarship is intimately involved in the battle between [Christian theism and its alternatives]; contemporary scholarship is rife with projects, doctrines, and research programs that reflect one or another of these ways of thinking. At present, the sad fact is that very many of these projects reflect . . . fundamentally non-Christian ways of thinking."[44]

Truly Christian thought requires that we sift the products of human reason at every point. Presuppositions or reigning intellectual paradigms are not like marbles in a glass we can simply extract, leaving the water clear; they are more like drops of ink that intermingle and color the whole. That is why for the Christian thinker everything must be brought to the bar of an historically Christian, biblical, Christ-centered worldview, to discover what comports with revealed knowledge and enriches it and what must be modified or criticized or at times rejected outright. It is a rigorous process of exploration, discovery, and measurement against the yardstick of God's revealed truth in the search for a unified Christian understanding, bringing together all we can know from a study of both God's word and God's works. This, again, is what it means to integrate our faith and learning.

Double Effect

The noetic effects of sin, of course, cut both ways — that is, they affect our understanding of both revelation and the world. But they do not affect the two equally. In our attempts to understand both God's word and God's works it is revelation that takes precedence, for faith is the precondition for the right use of reason. This is why, to use the Church's ancient language, it is a committed faith in Jesus Christ that seeks understanding, not a committed understanding that seeks how it

44. "On Christian Scholarship," in *The Challenge and Promise of a Catholic University,* ed. Theodore Hesburgh (Notre Dame: University of Notre Dame Press, 1994), p. 280.

may somehow cut its faith to fit. As Augustine put it, "Do you wish to understand? You must believe. . . . For understanding is the reward of faith. Therefore do not seek to understand in order to believe, but believe that you may understand" (*Tracts* 29:6).

It would be a mistake, of course, to think of the interplay between faith and learning as invariably a one-way process. That is why this historic Christian stance speaks of the priority of revealed knowledge, not its exclusivity. Obviously, one cannot understand anything, including revelation, apart from the application of reason,[45] and Scripture too must be interpreted. Moreover, there are times when the products of human discovery can and must help us understand revelation more accurately.[46] But this interaction cannot for the Christian be a dialogue of equals. As the adage has it, "Faith informs reason; reason confirms faith." Thus Darrell Bock says, "Scripture as revelation has a primary and privileged claim on forming and shaping our understanding, even though we still must engage in the difficult task of reading and determining what Scripture affirms."[47] The Bible plays this "central and primary role" for Christians "because it has always been recognized by the believing community as the central and even defining means of understanding God and his creation through his core act in Christ. This disclosing quality and defining ability make the whole of Scripture special revelation. This role for Scripture is part of the claim of what it means

45. "Faith asks that its object be understood with the help of reason; and at the summit of its searching reason acknowledges that it cannot do without what faith presents" (*Fides et Ratio,* 42). Cf. David W. Diehl, "Evangelicalism and General Revelation: An Unfinished Agenda," *Journal of the Evangelical Theological Society* 30, no. 4 (1987): 441-55.

46. For example, Edward Curtis says, "Special revelation was given in a specific historical and cultural context . . . and thus in a sense derives its meaning from that general revelation. The meaning attached to 'covenant' in the special revelation was significantly influenced, if not entirely determined, by the cultural context (and thus general revelation). General revelation (i.e., our awareness of how poetic language works and our knowledge of procreation) allows us to determine the meaning of Job 2:21 ('naked I came from my mother's womb, and naked shall I return there'). General revelation was responsible for forcing us to more correctly understand verses once thought to teach that the earth was the center of the solar system. Even as we affirm a certain priority of special revelation we must take seriously the authority and legitimate necessity of general revelation in integration, and this will include the authority of general revelation in biblical interpretation and theology." "Some Biblical Contributions to a Philosophy of Education," p. 99.

47. Bock, *Purpose-Directed Theology,* p. 22.

to be Christian, because through the Spirit's work with both testaments of Scripture comes an understanding and affirmation of what Christian experience is and what God has done through Jesus, the Christ."[48]

Does such a stress on the Bible suggest for Christians some sort of bibliolatry? Nicholas Wolterstorff concludes his book on *Divine Discourse* by protesting that it does not. "The focus of the Christian scriptures is of course on Jesus Christ," says Wolterstorff. Yet we require the Bible in order to know of him, wherein lies its primary importance. "Why is it," asks Wolterstorff, "that if we interpret God as telling us, by way of the scriptures, about God's entrance into our history centrally and decisively in Jesus Christ, we have turned the Christian religion into a 'religion of the book' — worse yet, into *bibliolatry?*"[49] Wolterstorff's answer: We haven't. We are simply making ourselves available to hearing God speak to us through the "sacred writings" *(hieros gramma)*, the divinely-inspired *graphe* (2 Tim. 3:15-16) we know as the Bible.

Revelation as Plumb Line

All of this is why revelation is so crucial to the task of Christian thinking, and thus to the mission of Christian higher education. "There can be only one *ultimate* commitment," observes Eloise Meneses. "All other commitments must be subordinated."[50] Historically Christians have spoken of their ultimate epistemological commitment in terms of the "transcendence and precedence of the mysteries of faith"[51] over the products of human reason. Why? Because, as Richard Weaver reminds us, humans face a peculiar dilemma: "How frequently it is brought to our attention that nothing good can be done if the will is wrong! . . . If the disposition is wrong, reason increases maleficence."[52] The human problem is that our disposition is too often wrong. But faith — that is, a willingness to trust God and take him at his word   holds out the hope that this disposition can be turned. We can come to the text of

48. Bock, *Purpose-Directed Theology,* pp. 25-26.
49. Wolterstorff, *Divine Discourse,* p. 296.
50. Meneses, "No Other Foundation," p. 537.
51. *Fides et Ratio,* 53.
52. *Ideas Have Consequences* (Chicago: University of Chicago Press, 1984), p. 19.

Scripture and, if we are willing to join in the Church's historic project, find there the plumb line we require for understanding the world.

A Christian worldview stipulates, then, the priority of revealed knowledge precisely because this revealed perspective is the lens we require to reorient ourselves so as to understand aright our discovered knowledge. As David Naugle says, "All human beings see things aslant, Christians included. This is what having a worldview, biblical or otherwise, is all about. It has to do with viewing the cosmos and all things within it through a particular set of lenses or from a specific point of view."[53] For the Christian, the Christ-centered revelation of God's Word is that point of view. Without it, we lack not only revealed knowledge; we will not truly or fully understand the world of discovered knowledge either. But with it, "a whole new world and worldview is open to behold. Everything can now be seen and interpreted clearly in the light of God himself."[54]

An early American example of this classical approach to Christian thinking is Jonathan Edwards. Says historian Mark Noll,

> The intellectual accomplishment of Jonathan Edwards was his refusal to admit that [Enlightenment] assumptions were in fact the starting points of thought. His work was important for his own time and for later Christians precisely because it dealt constantly with world views at their most basic level. Edwards refused to acknowledge that matter or the human perception of the world was the foundation of intellectual activity. And his refusal rested self-consciously on explicitly Christian convictions. God was the source of reality; God was the source of truth; human intellect and the world itself were ever and always dependent on him. For Edwards, truth was . . . "the consistency and agreement of our ideas with the ideas of God."[55]

---

53. Naugle, *Worldview,* p. 106.

54. Naugle, *Worldview,* p. 286. For an excellent discussion of this point, see Naugle's chapter entitled, "Theological Reflections on 'Worldview,'" pp. 253-90.

55. "Christian World Views and Some Lessons of History," in *The Making of a Christian Mind: A Christian World View and the Academic Enterprise,* ed. Arthur Holmes (Downers Grove: InterVarsity Press, 1985), p. 44. Later Edwards says: "After all that has been said and done, the only adequate definition of truth is the agreement of our ideas with existence. To explain what this existence is, is another thing. . . . 'Tis impossible that we

Edwards believed that we can gain a great deal from the world of learning, including from unbelieving scholars. But, says Noll, for Edwards this knowledge is always secondary; "Only a heart changed by God's grace will understand itself, God, the world of nature and the proper potential of human existence."[56]

Noll considers Edwards to be in many ways a model for Christian thinkers today: "The challenge [Edwards] poses to later Christians lies partly in the actual conclusions which he reached. Even more, it lies in his effort to think about all the major dimensions of life distinctly as a Christian, from a Christian base, and with Christian principles."[57] All of his intellectual work demonstrated the same rigorous pattern: "The basis was always God's being and our understanding of God's actions through Scripture. Edwards was properly respectful of the human ability to understand nature, whether physical or human. But he also always denied that this natural knowledge was the highest or finest. That kind of understanding we receive through faith in Christ by God's grace."[58]

Science and Revelation

All of this raises again the vexed but fascinating question about the role of science for a Christian. Modern science by definition rigorously limits itself to the world of the seen. But it is worth noting that this was not always so, as James Turner argues in his story of the rise of unbelief in America. During the nineteenth century, Turner says, a sea change occurred in American thinking: "Where science had once pointed beyond nature to God, it now pointed only to nature, behind which lay, if anything, the Unknowable."[59] In effect, says Turner, "sci-

---

should explain and resolve a perfectly abstract and mere idea of existence; only we always find this, . . . that God and real existence are the same." "The Mind," in Jonathan Edwards, *Scientific and Philosophical Writings,* ed. Wallace E. Anderson (New Haven: Yale University Press, 1980), pp. 344-45.

56. Noll, "Christian World Views and Some Lessons of History," p. 44.

57. Noll, "Christian World Views and Some Lessons of History," p. 45.

58. Noll, "Christian World Views and Some Lessons of History," p. 45.

59. *Without God, Without Creed: The Origins of Unbelief in America* (Baltimore: Johns Hopkins University Press, 1985), p. 187.

ence by fiat redefined its meaning of 'natural' so as to preclude the traditional necessity of a supernatural on which nature depended. It did this de facto, not by denying the supernatural, but by refusing to consider as within the bounds of scientific knowledge anything but the physical. . . . As far as science went, knowledge had shrunk to physical knowledge."[60] As a result, science today limits its purview to the world of the seen, that which is humanly accessible. Science is in fact considered the supreme implement for exploring this world. Hence modern scientists, when speaking as scientists, rule out addressing anything that deals with what the Apostle Paul refers to as the world of the unseen. That, they will insist, is simply not what science is equipped to do.

But if this were the case, wouldn't that raise for the Christian a question mark over the study of science? When Paul instructs Christians to fix their eyes on the *unseen* rather than the *seen,* is this an indictment of, among other things, a modern understanding of the scientific method? Is Paul here warning us away from scientific investigation?

We should not conclude that he is. As we have already argued, there are strong reasons for studying the world of the seen. The Apostle nowhere argues that this world is worthless; nor yet, in some misguided Platonic or gnostic sense, that it is inherently evil. The Son demonstrated God's great love for the world of the seen by becoming part of it; that is, by taking upon himself *flesh* and dwelling here as Immanuel, "God with us." The Bible graphically stresses Jesus' oneness with the world of our physical senses by stipulating of him that, though he was "from the beginning," yet he could also be heard with human ears, seen with human eyes. "We have looked upon [him] and touched [him] with our hands," says John (1 John 1:1). The fact that much of the work of Satan and the work of sinful humanity also contribute to the world of the seen does not render it unworthy of our attention. God is the ultimate creator of the seen, and he is not through with it. He has set humans as stewards over it, and we honor him by giving it our full attention. Christians have a high stake in the contemporary world of science.

Yet the distinction Paul makes does suggest at least a few observations regarding a Christian's approach to science. First, the Christian

60. Turner, *Without God, Without Creed,* pp. 185-86.

will always argue for the appropriate boundaries of science. If science insists upon limiting itself to the world of the seen, as modern science certainly does, then non-scientists are justified in insisting in return that it refrain from making quasi-scientific pronouncements about the unseen. An atheist philosopher might argue without sacrificing her professional identity that the material world is all that exists, but no scientist, speaking *as a scientist,* could make such a pronouncement. To their credit, most contemporary scientists understand these strictures and are scrupulous in observing them.

The scientific method itself has always been a friend to the gospel. It seeks the truth about the created order and that truth is always of interest to the Christian, never a threat. Having been alerted by thinkers such as Michael Polanyi and Thomas Kuhn, we are, to be sure, more aware today than ever that the practice of science is not as objective as it might once have claimed. Yet neither is it as subjective as the more radical postmodern thinkers want to make it. Science is simply the most powerful instrument humans have ever devised for studying the created order. When maintained within those boundaries it is something Christians can and do revere. Not a few of history's greatest scientists have been Christians. There need be no warfare between Christianity and science.

But scientism is science gone awry. In his book, *The Ghost in the Machine,* Arthur Koestler spoke of the foolishness of the surveyor who supposes for the sake of his work that the earth is flat, and then winds up insisting that the earth is flat. This is what occurs when a scientist assumes for the sake of his work that the natural world is all he can study, and then allows this assumption to mutate into pronouncements that, therefore, the natural world is all that exists. It is the fool who has said in his heart, "There is no God" (Ps. 14:1). This is materialist philosophy masquerading as science. Science itself makes no such pronouncement, nor could it. The Christian thinker will always be at pains to resist the overreaching pretensions of such scientism.

Second, the Christian will always want to practice science in the end to learn more about the handiwork of God. Paganism is marked by its worship of the created order: the stars, the sun, the moon, the earth, a rock, a tree. But biblical religion has always insisted on more. To those who are willing to view it through the lens we discover in the Scriptures, the world of the seen can serve as a pointer to the world of the unseen. It is like the Master's finger pointing toward food. Christians will never settle for a merely dog-like sniffing of the finger; they desire what it's pointing to. This is the distinctive approach of the Christian to science. It views science as an opportunity for worship — indeed, as virtually an act of worship in itself, not of the creation but of the Creator. Christians will often therefore possess a passion for science — "Great are the works of the Lord, studied by all who have pleasure in them," says the psalmist (111:2) — but if their passion is to rise above a pagan fascination with the world of the seen it will always manifest itself, in the end, in a "Who then is this?" wonder at the God who created it all. More even than that, it will manifest a determination to use science as an opportunity to "declare his glory among the nations, his marvelous works among all the peoples" (Ps. 96:3).[61]

Third, science for the Christian will always turn out to be a Christ-centered endeavor. Jesus stands at the center of the created order studied by science. His is the magnificent story of the universe, of human history. It is the grand account of God's creating and redeeming work through his Son. If it is true that postmodern thinkers demonstrate, in the famous phrase of Jean François Lyotard, an incredulity toward meta-narratives, then we should not be surprised that they find Christianity troublesome. Christianity represents the ultimate meta-narrative, the all-encompassing report of what God is doing through his Son.

But of course, we will never see the Christ-centeredness of anything unless we are willing to follow the lead of the Apostle Paul. We must view the world of the seen through the prism of what God has told us about the unseen. By itself, all that can be discovered about the world of the seen will always be deficient, even in some ways misleading because of its insufficiency. It will be inadequate for answering life's most important questions. In fact it will even be inadequate for understanding the world of the seen. For that we require the plumb line of revelation, which is for us "a lamp unto our feet, and a light unto our path" (Ps. 119:105). Only in that light can we understand aright the world of the seen.

---

61. On evangelism within the scientific community, see *Evangelism within Academia: Two Symposia,* ed. Terry Morrison (Ipswich, Mass.: American Scientific Affiliation, 2002).

Conclusion

Christians serve a God who has spoken. If he had not spoken we would have no access to the unseen. We would be cut off, with no possibility of faith in the biblical sense — and so let us be done with any notion of "the integration of faith and learning." But because he *has* spoken, he calls us to take him at his word and to live by it. This means that our academic discourse must take place "within the ambit of revealed truths which are the guide, and are not the upshot, of the discussion."[62] For the Christian who seeks to integrate his faith and learning, such a stance is not an option. Jesus said, "It is written, 'Man shall not live by bread alone, but by every word that proceeds from the mouth of God'" (Matt. 4:4).

> Therefore everyone who hears these words of mine and acts on them, may be compared to a wise man who built his house on the rock. And the rain fell, and the floods came, and the winds blew and slammed against that house; and yet it did not fall, for it had been founded on the rock. Everyone who hears these words of mine and does not act on them, will be like a foolish man who built his house on the sand. The rain fell, and the floods came, and the winds blew and slammed against that house; and it fell — and great was its fall. (Matt. 7:24-27)

62. McInerny, *Characters in Search of Their Author,* p. 131.

10 The Voluntary Principle

CHALLENGE *To Reconcile Institutional Commitments with Individual Freedoms*

A few years back the *Atlantic Monthly* ran a long article entitled "The Opening of the Evangelical Mind." It was authored by Boston College social scientist Alan Wolfe, a scholar well known in academic circles for his thoughtful analyses of the contemporary scene. The article was designed to raise the question, if not to answer it, of whether evangelical Protestantism — which according to Wolfe ranks "dead last" in intellectual culture among America's religious traditions — might not be in the process of turning itself around. Wolfe visited Wheaton as part of his research, and the college featured prominently in what he wrote.

In the often illiberal times in which we live, where not a few secularists seem to think the terms "evangelical mind" and "evangelical scholar" are, to quote one of the article's responders, oxymora, Wolfe's piece served as a whiff of fresh air. Whatever arguments we may have with his analysis, for the most part both his affirmations of what evangelicals are doing well and his criticisms of what we are not doing so well will help make Christian colleges stronger.

The Loyalty Oath Problem

Professor Wolfe stressed one central criticism, however, that is worthy of response, if only because it serves our present purpose to do so. It is what Wolfe referred to as "The Loyalty-Oath Problem."[1] In essence Wolfe criticized institutions such as Wheaton because we are defined around a Statement of Faith, which is yearly affirmed not by any of our students but by all of our faculty.

To his splendid credit, in offering this criticism Wolfe acknowledged that analogous situations are, at the *de facto* level, common throughout the academic world: "There are political science departments at elite universities that will not hire anyone unwilling to subscribe to rational-choice theory, just as analytically trained philosophers do not like to hire Continental philosophers and vice versa. To be sure no formal statements of faith have to be signed, but there are all kinds of ways — from the jargon applicants use to the journals in which they publish — in which commitment to a particular orthodoxy can be established, and hiring committees will look with suspicion on any deviation from whatever happens to be prescribed."[2]

Wolfe is no doubt right in this assessment; in fact, his point could be argued with considerably more force and detail. And in this light one might argue that a Christian college's transparent commitments are demonstrably more honest and fair than the covert types Wolfe cites. Yet Wolfe did not hesitate to take us to task for our particular arrangement: We have a formal Statement of Faith, a feature he finds unpalatable on two levels.

First, Wolfe criticizes our particular confession because he considers it too narrow. For some of his readers this criticism may seem in-

1. Casting this discussion in terms of "loyalty" is indicative of the politicized categories within which some tend to view this issue. See Arval A. Morris, "Academic Freedom and Loyalty Oaths," in *Academic Freedom: The Scholar's Place in Modern Society,* ed. Hans W. Baade and Robinson O. Everett (New York: Oceana Publications, 1964), pp. 57-84. This framework is perhaps understandable since, as David Rabban notes, "Government investigations into the loyalty of professors during the McCarthy period of the 1950s prompted the cases in which the Supreme Court first recognized academic freedom as a distinctive First Amendment liberty" ("Academic Freedom, Individual or Institutional," *Academe* [November-December], p. 17). But it is less than useful to have these political categories imposed on the rather different issue of theological conviction. Our present discussion has little to do with issues of loyalty, unless the loyalty in question is loyalty to the Lordship of Jesus Christ.

2. See Wolfe's fuller treatment of this problem in "The Potential for Pluralism," in *Religion, Scholarship and Higher Education,* ed. Andrea Sterk (Notre Dame: University of Notre Dame Press, 2002), pp. 22-39.

congruous, coming as it does from one who elsewhere in his article argues that evangelicalism may be too "democratic" and not therefore sufficiently discerning. "Once sentenced to intellectual mediocrity because they kept too many ideas out," he says, "conservative Christian institutions face the prospect of returning to mediocrity because they let too many in." Yet however that may be, Wolfe takes our self-consciously evangelical identity as evidence of "defensiveness," by which he means an unwillingness to engage views other than our own. "As long as evangelical scholars insist on drawing up statements of faith that shut them off from genuine intellectual exchange," he says, "they will find it difficult to become the kind of intellectually exciting institutions they hope to be."

Wolfe seemed particularly incensed that Wheaton College has no Roman Catholic faculty. Because as an evangelical Protestant institution Wheaton is non-Catholic, Wolfe portrays us as anti-Catholic. This was not because he found any Catholic-bashing at Wheaton; quite the contrary. According to Wolfe, "Wheaton professors borrow from Catholicism to make up for the gaps in their own traditions. Wheaton's English department has a love affair with Catholic — and Anglo-Catholic — writers, including Flannery O'Connor and Walker Percy. Wheaton boasts of having important papers of C. S. Lewis, G. K. Chesterton, and Dorothy L. Sayers. Without a literature that is in one way or another a product of Catholicism, Wheaton could not aspire to a life of the mind. A college that would not allow on its faculty authors whose letters are welcome in its archives has a problem it needs to resolve."

There surely is a problem needing resolution here, but it is largely with the cogency of Wolfe's argument. Like other Christian colleges, our library and archives are filled with the works of people whose ideas we engage and learn from but with which we may not necessarily agree. Must any or all of these authors be eligible for our faculty simply because they show up in our library or archives? Wolfe's argument seems to be that if a scholar would not be invited to join our faculty, then we are inconsistent in valuing his or her work. But no one at Wheaton would endorse such an idea, representing as it does not much more than a caricature of what some think religious institutions *must* be like.[3] By putting it

---

3. For example, Alan Peshkin on fundamentalist Christian schools: "As true believers, it is contradictory for them to advance a concept like pluralism. They want to

forth Professor Wolfe may be signaling that he has not fully grasped what we mean when we affirm as bedrock the ideas entailed in the slogan we have already examined, namely, "All truth is God's truth."

I will return to Professor Wolfe's concern about the purported narrowness of our confessional stance in the next chapter, but for now let us settle for this observation. If we must acknowledge, as does David Bebbington, that evangelicalism has not over the years always avoided creating its own backwaters, by the same token, neither has it typically been a stagnant pool.[4] Does not Wolfe's own description of Wheaton work against the charge of defensiveness? In what sense can an institution so fully engaged with the best of the Catholic tradition that Wolfe can call it a love affair be portrayed as anti-Catholic? Wolfe refers derisively to gaps in the evangelical intellectual tradition: of course there are gaps. There are gaps in every tradition. Which is why we engage all ideas from whatever source, including Roman Catholicism, willingly, constantly, and with gratitude. That we do so from a discernable location on the intellectual landscape does not lessen that engagement. It energizes it.[5]

This is the point often missed by critics. For example, writing in *Academic Freedom and Tenure*, Fritz Matchlup argues,

> If teachers are bound by oath to adherence to, or rejection of, certain ideas, students will be deprived of the freedom to learn about

---

thrive, but they do not want a multitude of competing doctrines to thrive. How could they if their Truth is singular?" (*God's Choice: The Total World of a Fundamentalist Christian School* [Chicago and London: University of Chicago Press, 1986], p. 293); or Stanley Fish: "To put the matter baldly, a person of religious conviction should not want to enter the marketplace of ideas but to shut it down, at least insofar as it presumes to determine matters that he believes have been determined by God and faith. The religious person should not seek an accommodation with liberalism; he should seek to rout it from the field, to extirpate it, root and branch" ("Why We Can't All Just Get Along," *First Things*, February 1996, p. 21).

4. D. W. Bebbington, *Evangelicalism in Modern Britain: A History from the 1730s to the 1980s* (London: Unwin Hyman, 1989), p. 276.

5. Alasdair MacIntyre: "Commitment to some particular theoretical or doctrinal standpoint may be a prerequisite for — rather than a barrier to — an ability to characterize data in a way which will enable enquiry to proceed." *Three Rival Versions of Moral Enquiry: Encyclopaedia, Genealogy, and Tradition* (Notre Dame: University of Notre Dame Press, 1990), p. 17.

those controversial matters which teachers will avoid discussing. But worse than that, even if teachers are willing to enter the danger zone of controversial ideas prescribed or proscribed by their oath, their effectiveness will be sorely weakened. The better students will not have respect for the teacher's opinions on questions about or around the ideas controlled by the oath. These students have confidence only in what they consider the honest opinion of their teacher, and they will not believe that an opinion can be completely honest if it is prescribed or controlled by a compulsory oath.[6]

In my view, advocates for Christian colleges should honestly acknowledge that concerns such as Matchlup's pose potential challenges for confessional institutions,[7] challenges we do not always surmount. But we should also insist that these challenges are not ours alone. Matchlup's criticisms are based upon the expressed notion that the teacher must never give up her "complete impartiality"; she must always remain a "disinterested scholar." Any "loss of disinterestedness" is unacceptable. But Matchlup's vision is an illusion; as we have already argued, there is no such thing as an utterly disinterested scholar, or an academic environment that places no boundaries on what or how a scholar may teach.

After years of interviewing faculty candidates, Robert Sloan, President of Baylor University, described a phenomenon often observed in Christian institutions. "At Baylor," he says, "I have witnessed any number of occasions where faculty members who have taught in state institutions have come to our institution and have made the remarkable assertion that there is more freedom on our campus to ask questions, to have discussions with students, and to pursue certain research projects than they found at their state institutions. How is it possible — consider the absurdity of it for a moment — that we could ever have something called a university or school, whereby a child, a student, a teacher,

---

6. Fritz Matchlup, "On Some Misconceptions Concerning Academic Freedom," in *Academic Freedom and Tenure: A Handbook of the American Association of University Professors,* ed. Louis Joughin (Madison: University of Wisconsin Press, 1967), pp. 207-8.

7. I use the term "confessional institution" broadly in this book to refer not just to technically creedal institutions, but also to those non-creedal "systemic" institutions (see Chapter Two) that insist on drawing their faculty from among those who confess faith in Jesus Christ.

or any other honest inquirer could be told, 'I am sorry, we do not discuss that here'?"[8]

Let the record show that at Wheaton I have repeatedly observed exactly the same phenomenon, and heard precisely the same faculty comments. Professors at Christian institutions are free to explore the entire realm of human experience, while at secular institutions this is not always the case. Why? Because as University of North Carolina sociologist Christian Smith points out, the "persistent and deeply internalized mental schemes" of today's academic culture are not merely secular but anti-religious. This is not, Smith says, because secular academics are evil people, but because they have been inculturated into a secularized way of thinking that pervades the contemporary academic world. "None of the anti-religious faculty I know as individuals are nasty people out to make religious believers feel bad. They're smart, interesting, morally serious, and well-intentioned. . . . They're not *aiming* to be anti-religious, anti-Christian. They don't have to try. It just comes naturally to them, almost automatically, as if from a fundamental predisposition. . . . In their anti-religion, these faculty are expressing a deeply interiorized mental scheme that is more prereflective than conscious, more conventional than intentional — yet one that has an immense power to reproduce a pervasive institutional culture."[9] And that pervasive institutional culture often restricts what given professors can or cannot teach. Thus Sloan asks, "Between one institution that is not afraid to ask any questions, including religious questions, and another institution that says, 'We do not ask religious questions here,' which has a greater freedom? Where is there greater openness?"[10]

The notion of the utterly disinterested scholar has been widely debunked. There is no such thing as the so-called "view from nowhere"; every teacher teaches from somewhere. What is more, every academic environment holds the potential for circumscribing the academic work of its members in some way. Does the fact that a given professor teaches from her particular somewhere mean that some things in her

8. Robert B. Sloan, Jr., "Preserving Distinctively Christian Higher Education," in *The Future of Christian Higher Education,* ed. David S. Dockery and David P. Gushee (Nashville: Broadman & Holman, 1999), p. 31.

9. Christian Smith, "Force of Habit: Hostility and Condescension Toward Religion in the University," *Books and Culture,* September/October 2002, pp. 20-21.

10. Sloan, "Preserving Distinctively Christian Higher Education," p. 32.

classroom wind up distorted or left out of the discussion altogether? There is that danger, but this need not and most often is not the case. At any rate, it is by no means a danger unique to confessional institutions. Do restrictions of the academic setting, including those mentioned by Sloan, mean that students lose confidence that they are hearing the honest opinion of their teacher? It is always a possibility, in the secular as well as a confessional setting. But it is much less likely, at least in Christian colleges, if the teacher from his passionately held personal convictions genuinely embodies the confessional stance of the institution.

In such cases there are no grounds for supposing students will be more suspicious of a discernibly committed Christian professor in a Christian setting than they are of, say, a perceivably committed atheist professor in a secular setting. Either professor — not despite his convictions, but because of them — may turn out to be the best teacher the student encounters. Neither professor is or can be utterly impartial; nor should such an illusion constitute our model of the ideal teacher. Our ideal professor should be one who is anything but disinterested. Rather, he is passionate about his subject, reflective and honest about his own somewhere, and is profoundly committed to a pedagogy that maximizes the students' opportunity to grapple with the subject for themselves. And if this is our ideal, I would argue that such professors can be found as readily at places like Wheaton College and Baylor University as in the strongest secular institutions.

Academic Freedom

In the end, however, the purported narrowness of our confession was not Professor Wolfe's chief concern. At a deeper level he was scandalized by the "mere existence" of such a thing as a confession in an academic institution. A Statement of Faith at a place like Wheaton, he says, "is bound to make a modern liberal uncomfortable," and should "rightly be considered hostile to academic freedom."

This is a hoary old criticism those in Christian higher education have heard many times. But it remains an ironic one. As I have observed, Christian faculty who have taught in secular environments will often comment on the relief it is to come to a Christian college where they finally experience *true* academic freedom — that is, the freedom to write and say and teach exactly what they really think. The artificial strictures of the secular setting, which often extend well beyond any genuine church-state issues even in public institutions, much less private ones, force them to compartmentalize their intellectual lives in ways expected of no other scholars. They tell anecdotes of an almost unique hostility in such settings to orthodox Christianity. To be sure, many Christian professors learn to cope within such strictures and even thrive within them. But for others these restraints become painful and wearying, forcing them into what they experience as truncated lives. For such scholars the freedom they discover in a Christian college to think openly and freely as a Christian comes as a great relief. Hence the irony of secularists taking Christian colleges to task for some purported hostility to academic freedom.

Christian colleges obviously do not consider themselves hostile to anyone's academic freedom. And they are not alone. In offering his criticism Professor Wolfe is undoubtedly speaking for others within the secular academy, yet not all there would agree with him. The classic 1940 *Statement of Principles on Academic Freedom and Tenure,* which was issued jointly by the American Association of University Professors (AAUP) and the Association of American Colleges (AAC) and continues to this day to define academic freedom for the scholarly community, makes space for confessional institutions, provided only that they are clear about their identity at the outset with all who come their way.[11]

This practice of full disclosure is one Christian colleges not only

---

11. An institution's right to define itself has often been expressed in terms of "the four essential freedoms of a university," among them, the right "to determine for itself on academic grounds who may teach, what may be taught, how it shall be taught, and who may be admitted to study." See, for example, Justice Frankfurter, *Sweezy v. New Hampshire,* 354 U.S. 234 (1957). But for a discussion of the still controversial and tenuous nature of this right, see Committee A, "The 'Limitations' Clause in the 1940 Statement of Principles," *Academe,* September-October 1988, pp. 52-56. See also Walter P. Metzger, who bemoans the fact that the 1940 Statement is still capable of being construed so as to make room for confessional institutions, and that, as a result, "there remains to this day no dearth of administrators of religious colleges who take comfort in the 1940 Statement's presumed assurance that they can eat their academic freedom cake and have it too" ("The 1940 Statement of Principles on Academic Freedom and Tenure," in *Freedom and Tenure in the Academy,* ed. William W. Van Alstyne [Durham: Duke University Press, 1993], p. 38).

accept, it is one we insist upon. We realize that a forthright planting of the college's flag is important for all involved.[12] In fact it is nothing less than crucial for the Christian college's continued existence, due to the fact that such institutions face a peculiar dilemma. These institutions are "poised between the demands of free academic inquiry and of committed theological loyalty. Without the first, it is hard to see the Christian colleges preserving intellectual viability, but without the second they will not retain their Christian character."[13] How do Christian institutions manage these dual tensions? Only through what I have come to call the *Voluntary Principle*. Were this principle to be lost, Christian colleges could not exist.

The Voluntary Principle

Christian colleges are committed to both sides of the Voluntary Principle. On the one hand, the members of their academic community will insist as vehemently as the most ardent secular defender of academic freedom that coercing another's conscience, beliefs, speech, teaching, or intellectual work is intolerable. Their insistence will include all the standard arguments plus some Christian ones as well. Yet to retain its historic identity and mission the college requires faculty who live and work and teach from its expressed commitments, from a shared religious vision. How to reconcile these two demands? Only through the Voluntary Principle; that is, only by allowing the college to draw its staff from those whose personal convictions, developed of their own volition, align them with the college's publicly stated commitments. As long as both sides of this principle are faithfully observed, not only will individual academic freedoms not be violated, they will be guarded.

12. Transparency on this point protects both sides: "Problems sometimes arise through the failure of an institution to be explicit about its particular limitations at the time of appointing a teacher, or the failure of a teacher to observe limitations which he has accepted." Editor's note on the "limitations clause," in *Academic Freedom and Tenure,* ed. Louis Joughin (Madison: University of Wisconsin Press, 1967), p. 36, n. 5.

13. Mark A. Noll, "Christian Colleges, Christian Worldviews, and an Invitation to Research," in *The Christian College: A History of Protestant Higher Education in America,* ed. William C. Ringenberg (Grand Rapids: Eerdmans, 1984), p. 36.

In his defense of academic freedom against political loyalty oaths, Justice Hugo Black famously stressed this personal voluntary dimension: "I am certain that loyalty to the United States can never be secured by the endless proliferation of 'loyalty' oaths," he wrote. "Loyalty must arise spontaneously from the hearts of people who love their country and respect their government."[14] Such *a priori*, "from the heart" commitment is precisely analogous to the sort of personal religious conviction confessional institutions seek in selecting their faculty. No one would claim that a political loyalty oath — or an affirmation of an institution's statement of faith — *could not* be a heartfelt and genuine expression of an individual's personal convictions. In both instances, however, it is beyond question that the mere mouthing of the words will not "secure" that conviction. In the case of Christian colleges, the assumption is not that an individual's affirmation of the institution's statement of faith *produces* the conviction; in fact, it is critical for the institution's identity that this emphatically *not* be the case. The sincerely held conviction must predate the affirmation, with the affirmation serving merely as a vehicle of its heartfelt expression. This is the Voluntary Principle at work.

Sustaining Institutional Identity

Every Christian college embodies a specific identity. It is an identity that exists prior in time to each of its members. What is more, if the institution is to endure it must be designed so that this identity can be sustained. The institution must be able to outlive succeeding generations of its own members in such a way that after they have come and gone the institution remains intact, identifiably the same school.

How is that possible? The answer is that the institution must not be overly identified with the particular members who constitute it any given moment. Former Yale President Bartlett Giamatti once described the university as "a patient and persuasive hierarchy, designed to cherish a particular value-laden process and the individuals within it."[15]

14. *Speiser v. Randall*, 357 (1958).
15. *A Free and Ordered Space: The Real World of the University* (New York: W. W. Norton and Co., 1988), p. 48.

And so it is. Few academic institutions function as simple democracies, and this is especially the case with confessional institutions. Their identity must be conceived of as an independent thing, something that transcends their present members. It is something those members come to and participate in, but it is not something they own. Nor should they expect it to change to accommodate their inclinations.

"In ancient Athens, and, as Europe entered into a period of intellectual awakening, in places like Bologna, Oxford and Paris, universities began as voluntary and spontaneous assemblages or concourses"[16] to which students came to learn. Similarly, Christian colleges are voluntary communities of scholars, teachers, and learners. No one is ever coerced to join these communities; only those become members who proactively seek to do so, presumably because they believe in and support the institution's publicly stated identity. Those who do not value that identity — or perhaps some key aspect of it — do not join, or if already a member, do not remain. This is the only way a Christian college can retain its historic identity while violating no one's conscience. It is, as the Danforth Commission put it, "the indispensable means" by which Christian colleges remain Christian:

> Where the purposes of an institution require special faculty qualifications beyond the requirement of impartial scholarship, this should be made clear in advance to candidates for teaching positions and to prospective students. The religious commitments of institutions are a case in point. If, for example, a college intends to be a Christian community and to conduct its work within a Christian context, the appointment of faculty members who are sympathetic with this purpose and can make a contribution to such a community is an important factor in selection. From the point of view of academic integrity, it is essential to make the additional qualification explicit to every one concerned. The selection of personnel is, of course, the indispensable means by which an institution carries out its purposes. The [institution's] purpose and [the issue of] staffing are intimately associated in a well-administered institution.[17]

16. Justice Anthony Kennedy, *Rosenberger v. Rector and Visitors of the University of Virginia* (94-329), June 29, 1995.

17. *Church-Sponsored Higher Education in the United States: Report of the Danforth Com-*

We can see just how indispensable this principle is by pondering the alternative. Suppose we reversed the poles. Imagine that instead of a Christian college's theological identity determining its membership, the institution's membership determined its theological identity. The college would thus cease drawing its professors and administrators and governing board from that pool of people who of their own volition identify themselves and their work with the institution's historic, publicly stated stance. Instead, it would now become the task of its ever-changing membership to define the college's identity democratically as they see fit. How long would such an institution remain recognizably what it had been? With its identity no longer a fixed thing but now an evolving artifact of a perpetually changing membership, the institution perhaps generations have known and loved inevitably develops into something they no longer recognize. This scenario has unfolded so many times throughout the history of American higher education that its dynamics are scarcely a matter of speculation. The end result is nothing short of inevitable.

The fact is, the only way Christian colleges can retain their identity without compromising individual conscience is by upholding the Voluntary Principle. Those who come to such a college know this. For its part, the institution works hard to keep its fundamental identity clear, explicit, and public. Those who value this identity and find themselves in accord with it, in the sense that they recognize it as the very stance from which they already live and work, join the community. Those who do not find this identity to their liking do not join. This is the Voluntary Principle at work.

---

mission, ed. Manning M. Pattillo, Jr., and Donald M. Mackenzie (Washington: American Council on Education, 1966), p. 63. So important is this issue of the selection of personnel that Nathan Hatch argues that Christian institutions need to put a premium on "responsiveness or flexibility": "We have to be responsive to look for the best people and move quickly if they become available. If issues of character and belief and of faith and learning are important, it may well mean that disciplinary specialization may have to be compromised and that budgets may have to be stretched in a given year to accomplish a 'target of opportunity'" ("Christian Thinking in a Time of Academic Turmoil," in *Faithful Learning and the Christian Scholarly Vocation,* ed. Douglas V. Henry and Bob R. Agee [Grand Rapids: Eerdmans, 2003], p. 98).

The Issue of Integrity

During his visit to Wheaton I spoke with Alan Wolfe about this principle, citing it as crucial to the institution's existence. Professor Wolfe was apparently unimpressed. "When careers are at stake," he writes, "it is hard to take seriously Litfin's insistence that signing Wheaton's declaration is a purely voluntary act." But, it is fair to ask in return, why should that be so? Why should such a thing be hard to take seriously, at least for people of integrity? Can we allow this Voluntary Principle, indispensable as it is to the existence of Christian colleges, to be so airily dismissed?

The argument seems to be that "when careers are at stake" the Voluntary Principle is bound to fail. Perhaps when teaching jobs are scarce an eager young scholar will be tempted to profess a false accordance with a college's stated theological position. Or a veteran teacher whose views have changed will be tempted to hide his or her lack of accord to keep the job. And who could blame them? With such high stakes, Wolfe seems to argue, they may sign the institution's statement, but we are fooling ourselves if we think they are doing so voluntarily.

The problem with this analysis is that it misconstrues the key issue. It mistakenly sets the gaining or keeping of a job as the paramount concern, the center around which all other considerations must revolve. But for the Christian such a shift constitutes a serious error. The paramount issue for the Christian, the issue that must come before all others, is obedience to Christ. Thus, in facing such a dilemma, the central issue for a Christian professor would not be her job, but the issue of her integrity, not merely before others but before her Lord. If she gets the integrity piece right, the matter of her job will take care of itself.

Notice that for a Christian, saying the job will take care of itself is not merely a flip way of dismissing a difficult or even agonizing dilemma. It is instead an acknowledgment that when faced with a choice between obeying God and keeping one's job, the Christian must obey God. The question of one's job at that point becomes, more precisely, a question of one's willingness to trust God's providence and provision. The three young men facing death in a Babylonian furnace couched the matter in terms we can all understand: "Our God whom we serve is able to deliver us from the fiery furnace; and he will deliver us out of your hand, O King. But if not, be it known to you that we will not serve your gods or worship the golden image which you have set up" (Dan. 3:17-18). Do the right thing and God is able protect you from hard consequences; but even if he does not choose to do so in this situation, do the right thing anyway, and then cast yourself upon him for your future. This sort of faith is a radiant and lovely thing, a virtue to which all Christians must aspire.

I suppose I can speak from personal experience on this count, for the hypothetical situation of one's livelihood being at stake in a confessional institution applies as much to me as to anyone. Like everyone else at Wheaton I annually reaffirm my personal agreement with the college's theological stance, or else explain wherein my convictions have changed should I no longer be able to do so. And in this affirmation my "career" is as much at stake as anyone's. Yet as a Christian, the notion of dissembling about such a thing in order to keep my job is repugnant. I cannot imagine affirming Wheaton's statement as my own if I did not genuinely believe it, whatever the consequences.

It is in this sense that for the Christians of a Christian college community, voluntarily is the only way they *can* sign the institution's confession of faith; no other option lies open to them. They either affirm it voluntarily because they believe it, or they refuse to affirm it because they do not believe it, some or all. But as Christians they do not have the option of signing it fraudulently even if their "careers" are at stake. I do not suggest that this latter dilemma, were it to occur, would be an easy one. It certainly would not be easy for me. My point is merely that signing an institutional statement of faith fraudulently or under duress would not be one of our options for resolving it.

History rightly reveres a moral giant like Socrates for his unwillingness to dissemble to avoid his own execution. Thomas More is admired as a paragon of integrity for his refusal to affirm something he did not believe, even at the cost of his life. Daniel and his three friends provide the model for choosing what is right, even at great personal cost. We rightly admire such moral heroes and uphold them as models. Why then would anyone argue that "where careers are at stake" it is unrealistic to expect members of a Christian college community to exhibit a similar integrity?

The case of Thomas More is particularly instructive here. King Henry was insistent that his former Lord Chancellor, Master More, should affirm the Act of Succession by which Henry's marriage to

Catherine of Aragon was deemed "void and annulled" and the succession established through the children of Anne Boleyn. Parliament had passed the Act, the clergy of London had signed on, and now Thomas More was escorted to Lambeth Palace for his own signing. Along with others, including his daughter, More's wife had urged him to make the affirmation, despite the fact that she knew he believed otherwise. She argued that God regards the heart rather than the tongue, and that the meaning of the oath thereby "goeth upon that they thinke, and not upon that they say." But, says More's biographer, Peter Ackroyd, "More was not capable of such dissimulation."[18]

> *The Duke of Norfolk:* "By the Mass, Master More, it is perilous striving with princes. And therefore I would wish you somewhat to incline to the king's pleasure. For, by God's body, Master More, *Indignatio principis mors est.*" ("The wrath of the king means death.")
>
> *Thomas More:* "Is that all, my lord? Then in good faith there is no more difference between your grace and me, but that I shall die today and you tomorrow."[19]

Thomas More's integrity before God was worth more to him than even his life. He would die in the Tower before he would affirm something he did not believe.

Nor is it just the moral giants of history who must deal with challenges to their integrity. Ordinary Christians living ordinary lives face difficult ethical dilemmas every day. An acquaintance who runs a small business recounted this tale for me. His largest customer, he said, one whose business was crucial to the existence of his own small firm, approached him after the first of the year about changing the dates on some invoices. It seems that dating them in the new year, though the transaction had clearly taken place late in the previous year, would save the customer a sizable amount in taxes. But this would mean the small businessman would have to falsify the invoices, which would be both dishonest and illegal. So he explained to the customer that he was not able to comply.

18. *The Life of Thomas More* (New York: Anchor Books, 1998), p. 361.
19. *The Life of Thomas More,* p. 356.

The customer upped the ante. "Listen," he said, "if you want to keep our business you'll change these invoices. It'll cost you nothing but it will make a real difference for us. Our other venders would do it for us. If you won't accommodate us on this simple request we'll be taking our orders elsewhere in the future."

What was this small businessman to do? More importantly, what would we *expect* him to do? His "career" was most definitely at stake. Would we have him lie? After all, his livelihood was in jeopardy.

This businessman took the difficult path of conscience, as every Christian must. "Look," he said, "you are our most important customer. We prize your business. In fact we need it. But as a Christian I cannot do what you're asking. It's not a question of how hard it would be; if that were all that was at stake we would do it in a minute. But what you're asking would be a violation of my integrity and that of my company. And it would be illegal as well. I cannot postdate those invoices even if it means losing your business."

It was a difficult decision but it was clearly the right one, the only one a person of integrity could make. In this case, thankfully, the matter turned out well, because the Christian businessman went on to say to his customer: "But think of it this way. Someone who would lie *for* you may also lie *to* you. You are seeing here an example of how we operate. When we tell you something, you can count on it. In a world where you can easily be cheated by your vendors, isn't it worth something to work with people whom you've seen will be scrupulously honest with you?" The customer thought about it for a while, then replied, "You're right. I admire you, and you're exactly the kind of people we want to do business with. I apologize for asking you to change the dates on the invoices."

Refusing to violate one's integrity will not always turn out so happily, as the examples of Socrates and Thomas More demonstrate. But that is beside the point. For Christians the essence of their integrity is that they seek to determine their actions not by some preferred outcome, but by what is right, by what will please Christ. The Voluntary Principle at Christian colleges is utterly dependent upon this sort of integrity. The ability of these colleges to maintain their historic identity rests upon the assumption that no Christian would lie about his or her core convictions, even if his or her job should be at stake. If we admire this in the moral giants of history, and we expect it of ordinary Christians everywhere, why would we not expect if of ourselves?

Lately colleges and universities, including Christian ones, are experiencing a tidal wave of plagiarism. Alarmed professors are astonished at the ease with which students in a pinch will pluck research papers off the Internet, place their names on them, and hand them in as their own work. Increasingly teachers must begin their courses with presentations designed to impress upon students the realization that such behavior represents a fundamental breach of integrity. But Jesus said, "A student will not turn out better than his teacher; every one when he is fully taught will be like the one who taught him" (Luke 6:40). If we assume that professors will dissemble to squeeze themselves past a pressure point, why would we expect our students to be different? Or conversely, if we desire to turn out students of character, must we not be willing to model it for them?

Necessity of the Principle

But, someone may say, let us grant that everyone begins by sharing the institution's confessional stance voluntarily, or else they would not affirm it. Thus far no one's conscience has been coerced. But what if a person's sincerely held convictions change? That would require him to cease affirming the institution's stance and could lead to the loss of his position. What could possibly justify maintaining an arrangement that holds the potential for forcing people into such agonizing choices? No scholar should have to face such a dilemma. Why not eliminate the statement of faith and transform the institution into simply another good liberal arts college with a religious heritage?

Surely this question cuts to the heart of the matter. We in Christian higher education consider the potential of such conscience-testing choices to be the price we pay for the continued existence of places like Wheaton College, and we view it as a price well worth paying. After all, we who have voluntarily joined the institution are the only ones who may ever have to pay it, and each of us knows from the beginning that such a thing could occur. Yet we also know that the alternative is the extinction of Wheaton and similar institutions as we know them. Should we not be willing to pay this cost, were it to come due, in order to preserve these historic colleges?

There are certainly some who believe the answer must be No. We need only think of those within the AAUP who have argued that the 1940 *Statement of Principles on Academic Freedom and Tenure* should be revised so as "to drum offending institutions out of the universe of 'authentic seat[s] of higher learning.'"[20] Thankfully, such a step has been resisted by wiser and more moderate heads in the academy, but it is sobering to realize that some are so eager to see Christian colleges driven from the academic marketplace.

We believe that Christian colleges have long played a wonderfully fruitful role in the academy, and that the larger academic discourse would be significantly diminished were they to disappear. If the commitment of the academic community to genuine diversity is more than mere cant, the loss of such institutions must be considered grievous. This is the crux of the issue. Does the confessional nature of systemic institutions reduce their engagement with the fullest range of ideas, or compromise the academic freedom of any of their members? To the extent that both the institution and its members are observing the Voluntary Principle, it does neither. But it does enable them to enjoy the synergy of working together with others of like mind to strengthen their contribution to the intellectual arena, which we believe is in everyone's best interests. We do not wish to see this come to an end.

Deliberate Naiveté

All of the above is vulnerable, I suppose, to the criticism that such a vision of integrity is today hopelessly naive. In fact it should not surprise us if Professor Wolfe were to find it so. One need only read his book, *Moral Freedom: The Search for Virtue in a World of Choice,*[21] which its publisher describes as an exploration of "the advantages and painful difficulties of living in a society where rather than simply accepting strict

20. Michael McConnell, "Academic Freedom in Religious Colleges and Universities," in Van Alstyne, ed., *Freedom and Tenure in the Academy*, p. 317. Cf. Eugene H. Bramhall and Ronald Z. Ahrens, "Academic Freedom and the Status of the Religiously Affiliated University," in *The Future of Religious Colleges*, ed. Paul J. Dovre (Grand Rapids: Eerdmans, 2002), pp. 318-19. For an early expression of this view within the AAUP, see "Report of Committee A for 1920," *AAUP Bulletin* 9 (1921).

21. *Moral Freedom: The Search for Virtue in a World of Choice* (New York: W. W. Norton, 2002).

conventions, each individual struggles to forge a moral life. . . . On the heels of political and economic freedom, Wolfe concludes, an exhilarating and unnerving new era of moral freedom has indeed arrived." The book in fact is more than this blurb might suggest; it is a sobering and useful survey of contemporary American moral thinking and practice. Yet it also reveals Professor Wolfe as one whose assumptions about moral freedom might not render him sympathetic to the above notions of integrity.

Closer to home, however, there may be others who deem the above analysis inadequate in other ways. They might ask, for example, isn't there such a thing as degrees of belief? Are there not some convictions we hold with greater degrees of confidence than others? Aren't there some things we would die for, and others we still hold but more tentatively?

The appropriate answer to each of these questions would seem to be Yes. Beliefs are not like light switches, either on or off. We should probably think of our belief system as spread across something like a target of concentric circles. Some core beliefs are so central that they reside in the bull's eye. Others range out toward the periphery. This is the reality of any belief system.

But this reality in no way undercuts the above analysis. It is the individual who must deal with these ambiguities, not the institution. Christian colleges do not go about policing the thoughts of their members; they are utterly dependent on the integrity of the individuals involved. When a member of the community, having honestly examined her own convictions, affirms that the confessional stance of the institution expresses her personal convictions as well — that is, that she stands where the institution stands — the college must take that at face value. The assumption is that with each item of the statement the individual has weighed the intensity of her conviction and before God come to the conclusion that, whatever the variations, she can nevertheless affirm, "Yes, I do believe this; these are part of the convictions from which I, of my own volition, live and teach." If her degree of uncertainty were at any point such that it failed to reach the threshold her Christian integrity requires to enable her to make such an affirmation, she would refrain from doing so. This is the institution's core assumption. But notice that it is the individual who is doing the soul-searching, not the institution.

But this observation may only lead to a further charge of naiveté. Surely, the skeptic may say, you are assuming too much. Not everyone who signs the institution's statement will do so with such an idealized notion of integrity. Not everyone is as honest as you assume. There are any number of ways people may equivocate so as to rationalize signing affirmations they do not truly believe.

How should one reply to such skepticism? On the one hand, Christians are called to treat one another with love, which, among other things, requires one to "believe all things, hope all things" (1 Cor. 13:7). We are not to assume the worst of people; we are to presume the best until forced to conclude otherwise. Christian colleges must assume that their members are people of integrity and treat them accordingly. This means that when professors say they believe something, the college must take them at their word.

On the other hand, we should also acknowledge there is something to the skeptic's concerns. Ours is a time and place that has lost its moral compass. When the culture around us has lowered or eliminated its standards, we can easily find ourselves seduced into following along. In such an environment equivocation in signing a doctrinal statement becomes all too easy. Does this happen at Christian colleges? Let us be clear about it: the human heart being what it is, of course it does. In some cases people may simply sign the statement falsely. To put a fine point on it, their affirmations are a lie. They do not believe what they are claiming to believe, but they want to gain or keep a job. So they prevaricate.

More often, however, the deception, perhaps of themselves as well as others, may take more subtle forms. For instance, some may keep themselves in a state of willing denial about what they are doing. The act of signing the statement is reduced to a physical act of their hand, an annual ritual carried out perhaps in conjunction with signing their new contract. The act is intentionally kept neutral and without meaning, lest they be forced to confront the fact that they really cannot sign the statement honestly.

Another version may occur when one affirms the statement but holds mental reservations about some of its provisions. In this case the individual has thought about the issues and knows that on this or that provision he is probably not in agreement with the institutional stance. But on the other items he does agree, perhaps enthusiastically. So he signs, saying to himself that he will do so but only with these honest reservations. The problem is, kept to oneself, such reservations are anything but honest. Yet the deceit inherent in saying one thing to himself while affirming something different before others is conveniently ignored.

And there are even more subtle forms of dissimulation. Professors may sign the statement knowing they have significant reservations about some of its provisions. Yet they intentionally keep themselves ignorant about the issues for fear of where they might come out if they studied it through. They do not want to have to confront the difficult moral choice that might present itself were they to search out the issues and find themselves outside the confessional boundaries of the institution. So they sign the statement while keeping themselves culpably ignorant, fulfilling the letter of the law if not the spirit.

In other cases persons may affirm the institutional faith statement but consider the act to be nothing more than an affirmation of what the institution holds, not what they believe. I recall hearing a renowned Oxford cleric and theologian, famous for his denials of historic Christian doctrines, offer just this sort of equivocation. He was asked whether he recites the Apostles' Creed on Sunday mornings, and if so, how he could make such affirmations when he was on record as believing no such thing. He answered that when he recites the Creed he is merely affirming what the historic Church has believed, not what he believes. Never mind that the Creed begins, "I believe," or that signing a statement of faith is essentially a statement about one's own convictions, not the institution's. If one is looking for a way of seeming to affirm something one does not really believe, such duplicity may do.

For their part, confessional institutions may be tempted to wink at this stratagem. But if so, they should not give in to the temptation. The institution's distinctives will not long endure if they are affirmed only in such a halfhearted, secondhand way. As soon as there exists a critical mass of people who do not personally hold these distinctives, the pressure will mount to change them. But worse, in the meantime the institution's confessional stance serves as a straightjacket on those who affirm it. Instead of providing an outlet for the expression of their own freely held commitments, the institution's position becomes a stricture on what they might otherwise say or teach. The Voluntary Principle is being breached, with a price to be paid on both sides. It is a sad arrangement, and is the very thing critics will cite to argue that confessional institutions are illegitimate.

Perhaps the most likely stratagem, however, is a hermeneutical one. This involves a reinterpretation of the institution's theological stance to fit the individual. This approach considers the signing of the statement to be an act of interpretation wherein the individual first decides how he or she will construe the statement, and then signs it accordingly.

A faculty member I know once said to her president, "Here's what I mean when I sign the statement." At that the president politely stopped her and said, "When you sign the college's statement you are not being asked what it *means*. If you need clarification of its meaning, please ask and I'll get you whatever you require. But it's not up to you to decide what the institution's doctrinal statement *means;* establishing its meaning and keeping that meaning clear is the institution's responsibility. What you're being asked when you sign the statement is not, What does it *mean?*, but, Do you *agree* with it?"

This faculty member had misunderstood the act of signing the institution's statement of faith. The point of having such a statement is to create a community of people who, whatever other differences they will inevitably manifest, at least on these core issues speak with one accord. It is the platform on which they have come to stand and from which each lives and works and attempts to engage the world. But if a statement of faith is to serve this unifying and centralizing purpose it is crucial that the statement actually be allowed to *function* as a point of unity, a point of agreement. This requires the institution to keep its meaning clear, explicit, and public. Conversely, it also means that no individual is free to decide for himself or herself what the statement means. To have everyone affirming the statement only after construing it to mean what they prefer it to mean is to negate the unifying function of the statement altogether.

This is an important point, but unfortunately one that is sometimes lost. To affirm "I agree with you" presupposes that I have first understood what *you* mean; it is an affirmation that I consider my understanding of things to coincide with yours. When members of a confessional community affirm the institution's statement of faith they are saying, "I stand where the institution stands." They are giving testimony that they comprehend how the institution understands itself and that this understanding expresses not just the institution's commitments, but their own freely held personal convictions as well. Beyond these limited specified issues, the differences between and among the institution's members will be many and varied. But on the issues specified in the institution's self-definition, the signer is affirming, "We stand together. We are a community of the like-minded. We represent a 'school of thought.' On these theological convictions I willingly stand in solidarity with the other members of the college's community. I stand where the institution stands."

Conclusion

It is sad to have to acknowledge that some in the world of Christian colleges may use evasions to sign a doctrinal statement they do not truly believe in whole or, more likely, in part. I am not in the least naive about this reality. How much is there of this sort of thing? Only God knows.

But this much *is* clear: if we are to deal with one another in love, we must not allow ourselves to become cynical about the matter. We must operate on the assumption that the Christians we are dealing with are people of integrity who would not resort to such dishonest tactics. When they affirm that they stand as one with the theological position of the institution, they mean exactly what they say, in the straightforward spirit of James's admonition to "let your yes be yes and your no be no, that you may not fall under condemnation" (5:12). Embracing this assumption does not require the institution to bury its head in the sand. If something emerges in the lives or the teaching or the writing of its members that indicates they do not believe what they have affirmed, it is the obligation of the college to inquire about the inconsistency. But short of that, the institution must take its members at their word, under the presumption that they are people of integrity who will not equivocate. The Voluntary Principle, so essential to the existence of confessional institutions, depends entirely upon this lovely assumption.

11 Institutional Breadth

CHALLENGE *To Appreciate Our*
Institutional Uniqueness

I n the previous chapter we explored the importance of the Voluntary
Principle to the functioning of Christian colleges. There I argued
that, poised as such institutions are, in Mark Noll's words, "between
the demands of free academic inquiry and of committed theological
loyalty," this principle is simply indispensable for their continued existence. Now I want to return to Alan Wolfe's earlier objection to the purported narrowness of such institutions.

Even if, as I have argued, an academic institution can maintain itself around a confession of faith without compromising its members'
academic freedom; and if, as I will argue later, such institutions play a
valid and important role in a society's marketplace of ideas; the question must still be asked, how broadly or narrowly should this confessional identity be stated? And more basic still, who decides?

The answers to both of these questions will vary from institution
to institution. Some Christian colleges will define themselves more
broadly, others more narrowly. At one end of the spectrum some may
be fully creedal; at the opposite end, others may require nothing more
than a profession of faith in Jesus Christ from their faculty. In most instances institutional identities will reach back to the school's founders
and founding documents; they will likely be anchored in the school's
history and heritage, its ecclesiastical affiliations, and its mission statement. Moreover, while alumni, students, faculty, staff, and administration all play important roles in maintaining this identity, the ultimate
responsibility for its continuity typically rests with the school's govern-

ing board, which in a very literal sense holds the institution in trust. But one thing all such schools hold in common: each must work hard to keep its identity clear, explicit, and public. Whatever the arrangement, if either the Christian identity of the college or the responsibility for maintaining (or amending) it is not clear, the college is likely already to be in the process of evolving away from it.

Why should that be? The history of Christian higher education offers countless instances of this sort of evolution. These examples are so well known and often cited that I will refrain from rehearsing them here. For details one need only turn to books with titles such as *The Christian College: A History of Protestant Higher Education in America* (1984), *The Secularization of the Academy* (1992), *The Soul of the American University: From Protestant Establishment to Established Nonbelief* (1994), *Faith and Knowledge: Mainline Protestantism and American Higher Education* (1994), *Contending with Modernity: Catholic Higher Education in the Twentieth Century* (1995), or *The Dying of the Light: The Disengagement of Colleges and Universities from Their Christian Churches* (1998).[1] In these pages the reader will find ample testimony to what Gregory Alan Thornbury calls "the slow and often imperceptible choices"[2] that loosened various institutions from their theological moorings.

What I will cite, however, is the intriguing pattern that emerges in the evolving identities of many of these institutions. It is their journey across a familiar continuum: from the specific, to the less specific, to

---

1. William Ringenberg, *The Christian College: A History of Protestant Higher Education in America* (Grand Rapids: Christian University Press and Eerdmans, 1984); *The Secularization of the Academy,* ed. George M. Marsden and Bradley J. Longfield (New York: Oxford University Press, 1992); George M. Marsden, *The Soul of the American University: From Protestant Establishment to Established Nonbelief* (New York: Oxford University Press, 1994); Douglas Sloan, *Faith and Knowledge: Mainline Protestantism and American Higher Education* (Louisville: Westminster/John Knox Press, 1994); Philip Gleason, *Contending with Modernity: Catholic Higher Education in the Twentieth Century* (New York: Oxford University Press, 1995); James T. Burtchaell, *The Dying of the Light: The Disengagement of Colleges and Universities from Their Christian Churches* (Grand Rapids: Eerdmans, 1998). But for an exploration of some institutions which have resisted this trend, see Robert Benne, *Quality with Soul: How Six Premier Colleges and Universities Keep Faith with Their Religious Traditions* (Grand Rapids: Eerdmans, 2001).

2. "The Lessons of History," in *Shaping a Christian Worldview: The Foundations of Christian Higher Education,* ed. David S. Dockery and Gregory Alan Thornbury (Nashville: Broadman and Holman, 2002), p. 42.

the generic, to minimally Christian, to Christian in name only, to Christian in history only, and finally, to the secular, a point of rest often marked by a certain nervous embarrassment over, or even outright repudiation of, the religious roots of the institution.[3]

Nowhere to my knowledge do the above authors attempt such an analysis,[4] but it seems to me it would be possible to trace the journey of many of the examples they cite across some version of this continuum. Not all began their journey at the same location on the continuum, but the direction of their drift was the same. It was a process of abandoning particularity, a move from the more specific to the less. If Christian institutions move at all, this is almost the only direction they can take. Why? Because of the Voluntary Principle.

A confessional institution can jettison some aspect of its identity — that is, move toward the less specific — without inherently compromising the consciences of its members. But it cannot do the reverse. It cannot in fairness add something to its confessional identity, thereby becoming more specific, and then expect its members merely to sign on. That would violate the Voluntary Principle and the front-end aspect of the covenant that exists between the institution and its members. The movement across the continuum can only flow in one direction, from the more specific to the less.

This tendency is compounded by the fact that virtually all the pressure for change lies in the same direction. Externally Christian colleges find themselves out of step with and often misunderstood by a secular academic establishment. As T. S. Eliot remarked, "When the Christian faith is not only felt, but thought, it has practical results which may be inconvenient."[5] Criticisms such as those of Alan Wolfe sting; no one wants to be viewed as intolerant and defensive. So the promise is enticing: jettison your specifics and we will respect you.[6] In-

---

3. Cf. Benne's "topology of church-related colleges," which begins to capture a sense of this continuum (*Quality with Soul,* pp. 48-53).

4. But George Marsden comes close: see "What Can Catholic Universities Learn from Protestant Examples?" in *The Challenge and Promise of a Catholic University,* ed. Theodore M. Hesburgh (Notre Dame: University of Notre Dame Press, 1994), pp. 187-98.

5. *The Idea of a Christian Society* (London: Faber and Faber, 1939), p. 8.

6. S. M. Hutchins states the matter baldly as he spells out what he takes to have been "an article of faith for more than a half century" in the academic world: "No confessedly Evangelical (indeed, one must say, any Christian) institution, no matter how

ternally some of the college's own members may long for just this sort of respect. Faculty, for example, may want to be accepted by the guilds within which they have been trained and to which they belong, and they may see some of the specifics of the institution's Christian identity as unnecessary embarrassments. Alumni, administrators, and boards are eager to see their school ranked ever higher in the eyes of an educational establishment that has little sympathy for the institution's Christian identity. Couldn't we minimize the offense by dispensing with some of these particulars? they ask themselves. Others think the institution would be a finer place were it located further along the continuum. To them, certain institutional specifics appear to be troublesome choke points in the recruitment of, say, the strongest possible faculty. Eliminating these choke points would certainly make things easier by expanding the pool of qualified faculty from which the institution might draw. And to all of this we may add insistent financial and enrollment pressures: Wouldn't shucking off some troublesome specifics enable the institution to appeal to a broader constituency?

All such pressures, internal and external, typically mount themselves against the specific, almost never toward it.[7] And over time they take their toll. A certain weariness sets in. As Joel Carpenter observes, "The more an intellectual vision gains acceptance and adherents, the more it tends to become diluted and stale. Such visions experience trouble especially in the passing and rising of generations. Rather than being the wellspring of fresh insight for younger scholars, a school of thought can come to be seen as a body of clichés that have been worn out by one's intellectual parents."[8] This explains why instances of institutional movement away from a Christian identity abound, while cases of the reverse are hard to find. The story seems always to be one of colleges losing their Christian identity, not regaining it.

Notice that none of the above motives are villainous. Some may

---

loose it sits to its professed beliefs, will have the respect of the intellectual establishment until institutional Christianity becomes a part of a history overcome" (*Touchstone,* November 2003, p. 4).

7. Cf. Marsden, "What Can Catholic Universities Learn from Protestant Examples?" p. 192.

8. "The Perils of Prosperity: Neo-Calvinism and the Future of Religious Colleges," in *The Future of Religious Colleges,* ed. Paul J. Dovre (Grand Rapids: Eerdmans, 2002), p. 201.

be more elevated than others, but even the criticisms of an outsider like Alan Wolfe are well intentioned. Seldom will it be suggested that the institution should jettison its Christian identity immediately and altogether. The appeal is always for just the next move across the continuum. This generation thinks such-and-such can be eliminated with impunity, but the institution should go no further; the next feels the same about some aspect of what remains. Thus in time does the institution drift inexorably but without design, increment by increment, across a continuum from the more specific to the less. And as the record will show, the ultimate destination is entirely predictable: the institution will wind up just another formerly religious school, basically secular in reality if not in name.

Pressure and openness, both in the same direction. No reversal available. It's a prescription for movement, and all, over time, in a predictable direction. I vividly recall a nerve-wracking quarter hour one afternoon caught in the multi-lane traffic circling the *Arc de Triomphe du Carrousel* in Paris. Was it only fifteen minutes? It seemed like an hour. In France, traffic merging from the right owns the right of way. So under the pressure of giving way to this traffic we drifted to the left, toward the center. That way seemed almost magically open to us because, after all, we had the right of way; we too were merging from the right. Pressure and openness, both in the same direction. In no time we found ourselves in the inner ring of this multi-lane roundabout. But now we had to get out again against the crush of traffic, all of which was to our right and all of which held the right of way. It was as if we had traveled through an anti-siphon valve in a water system; under pressure the water flows easily in the one direction, but no reversal is permitted. We must have circled that roundabout thirty times, and certainly irritated not a few French drivers, before we could extricate ourselves from that merry-go-round of automobiles.

Pressure and openness in the same direction. As I say, it's a prescription for movement, in an entirely predictable direction. This represents nothing new or unique, of course; Christians have always and in every place been in danger of being co-opted by their cultural moment. As David Lyon says, "While secularization does present peculiar threats, and while the modern situation does magnify the challenge in several ways simultaneously, we are really experiencing new twists for age-old problems. The whole sociological paraphernalia of 'accommodating' or 'resistance' is clearly anticipated in the New Testament injunction to be 'in but not of the world.'"[9] Yet there is also little doubt that our contemporary situation is particularly acute, and that, as Lyon also argues, today's "secularization should both be taken seriously, and be seriously criticized."[10] Its sheer pervasiveness suggests that Christian colleges must be highly intentional about retaining their identity if they are to endure. Nathan Hatch has bemoaned not only "the pervasive secularization of higher education in the twentieth century, but also the feeble efforts of church-related institutions to retain a distinctive Christian character."[11] Unless feebleness is replaced with determined efforts, that trend will continue.

In a sense, these institutions are like the proverbial salmon swimming upstream: the task requires effort and attention, without which there is only one way to go. Says David O'Connell in his piece on "Staying the Course":

> Once the distinctive identity of the religious college is established, the future of the institution depends upon the way in which that identity influences or impacts the academic enterprise and life beyond it. What unique contribution does the particular college as a religious institution make to and within higher education or society as a whole? What does it *mean* that such an institution is religious? Here is [one] key to the future: mission. Identity must be coupled with a mission that reinforces the identity, or the identity falls flat. Mission must be derived and flow from a distinctive identity in visible, tangible ways.[12]

To make all this work, O'Connell says, "There must be an *institutional* imperative that the college remain religious. In other words, those responsible for the college and its future must see an advantage, make that determination, adhere to it, and provide for the necessary in-

9. *The Steeple's Shadow: On the Myths and Realities of Secularization* (Grand Rapids: Eerdmans, 1985), p. 134.

10. Lyon, *The Steeple's Shadow*, p. 115.

11. "Christian Thinking in a Time of Academic Turmoil," in *Faithful Learning and the Christian Scholarly Vocation*, ed. Douglas V. Henry and Bob R. Agee (Grand Rapids: Eerdmans, 2003), p. 90.

12. "Staying the Course: Imperative and Influence Within the Religious College," in Dovre, ed., *The Future of Religious Colleges*, pp. 69-70.

stitutional and external support, financial and otherwise." In addition, "the religious character or identity of the religious college must be evident through the operations and activities of the institution that guarantee its continued existence."[13] Intentionality on the part of all, but especially the leadership, is the key. Which is why I say that those responsible must work hard to keep both the institution's identity and the established means of maintaining it clear, explicit, and public.

An Ideal Location

But we are still left with a question something like this: Might not there be, so to speak, an *ideal* location along this continuum, a point where the demands of a truly Christian education and the pressures prevailing across the continuum find the best compromise?

The answer, predictably, is almost certainly Yes, but also and with equal certainty, No. No, in the sense that there is no single ideal point for all Christian institutions. But yes, in the sense that there may be an ideal point for each individual institution.

Let us consider Wheaton College as a case study, since for me its defining features are close at hand. Here is one president's assessment of one well-known Christian college's understanding of itself. I offer it not even as a final word on the subject for Wheaton, much less as a pattern for others. It is merely one case study in the sorts of things one must consider in evaluating the merits of a school's institutional markers.

Alan Wolfe criticized Wheaton for its specificity: it is an evangelical Protestant institution. Therefore it does not, for instance, hire Catholics for its faculty. Wheaton would apparently be more to Wolfe's liking if it were to abandon this piece of its historic identity, thereby moving it along the continuum toward the more generic. What should we make of this criticism?

The question of where a college such as Wheaton has located, or should locate, itself on our continuum is in my estimation a prudential one, not a theological one. The question boils down to this: Where best should lie the boundaries of this particular college? And to this ques-

13. O'Connell, "Staying the Course," p. 72.

tion there is nothing, as the saying goes, written in stone and handed down from the mountain. One's answer inevitably constitutes a judgment call, and we must recognize it as such. Different organizations — a college, a mission agency, a church, a publishing house, a denomination, an evangelistic campaign, a seminary, a different college — may require different configurations. Each organization must make its own decisions, in the full light of its unique history, constituency, affiliations, and purpose, about where its boundaries must lie.

As for Wheaton College, its identity can only be understood as the product of a particular historical and theological heritage. From its inception in 1860, Wheaton has been explicitly committed, as the preface to the first doctrinal statement (1926) put it, to "the historic faith of Protestantism." In 1978 that preface was revised to make the point more explicit still: "The statement accordingly reaffirms salient features of the historic creeds, thereby identifying the College not only with the Scriptures but also with the Reformers and the evangelical movement of more recent years." This statement, the preface goes on to say, "defines the biblical perspective which informs a Wheaton education." These are the sentiments that represent, as the current preface puts it, both "the historic theological commitments of the College" and our present stance. Indeed, the published explanation attending the 1992 revision of Wheaton's Statement of Faith specifically stated that one of the primary goals of the new statement was to keep the college's theological stance "continuous with Wheaton's past distinctives." In other words, thus it has always been at Wheaton College and thus it remains today.

This is why Alan Wolfe found no Catholics teaching on Wheaton's faculty. The fact is, the Catholic tradition would never produce a Statement of Faith such as Wheaton's, both because the saliency of this particular list of items (not to mention the absence of others) reflects a distinctively Protestant emphasis, and because the Catholic tradition would not typically have generated a doctrinal statement for an institution such as Wheaton in the first place. Shorn of their theological and historical context, the twelve points of Wheaton's doctrinal statement might conceivably be affirmed by a Catholic believer, but no one has any business doing that kind of shearing. To be faithfully understood and appreciated, the points in this statement must not be severed from their context. A Reformation heritage can no more be disentangled from Wheaton's identity than a Roman Catholic heritage can be disentangled from Notre Dame's.

Wheaton College is inevitably the historical and theological product of American evangelical Protestantism, and its constituency is almost entirely Protestant. This identity is no accident of history; it is a matter of conviction. In virtually every one of the Reformation/Catholic differences, Wheaton by conviction will be found standing on the Reformation side. Wheaton need not be — and indeed is not — anti-Catholic. But nor is it willing to say that the differences do not matter. Wheaton's Reformation distinctives are the product of deeply thought out and long held convictions. The college is committed to maintaining an irenic spirit toward all, acknowledging and celebrating all that we hold in common with others, and in remaining teachable and open to instruction from every quarter. But in the end it must be said that Wheaton College is not a neutral party in the matter. Like everyone else, we are "situated." There has not been a day of its history that Wheaton has not stood with the Reformation on the critical issues. It is not, nor has it ever been, anything other than an evangelical Protestant institution with an evangelical Protestant theological stance.

Wheaton's Statement of Faith requires this sort of historical and theological context in order to be understood. Were it forced to stand alone it would fall between two stools. On the one hand, it contains too much to function as a minimalist, Apostles' Creed sort of standard for Wheaton's community. And this is by design. Wheaton has always seen itself as something more specific than a "mere Christianity" institution. On the other hand, by itself Wheaton's Statement of Faith is too brief to function as the great confessions of the church have served others. It has not enough weight and texture. But this too is by design. Wheaton's statement was always viewed as a pointer to something larger, which in turn is why this statement must not be forced to stand alone. Like the bulk of an iceberg that, though it lies out of sight, nevertheless supplies the necessary support and ballast to the tip we see, Wheaton's broad Reformational heritage provides the crucial weight and depth and perspective needed by an otherwise thin doctrinal stance.

It is for this reason that Wheaton does not have Catholics teaching on its faculty. It appears obvious that one cannot understand Wheaton's evangelical Protestant theological stance and meaningfully affirm it while also affirming a genuinely Catholic stance. While there is much overlap between these two theological worlds, as many recent efforts toward dialogue between evangelicals and Catholics have shown, there also remain significant differences. And until such time as those differences are resolved — a noble endeavor in which I have been personally involved — they should not be merely ignored.

Our changing cultural environment has made increasingly clear a point I have insisted on for years: divisions among Christians are often luxuries we afford ourselves when we hold cultural hegemony. Never mind that the Body of Christ should never indulge itself such divisions in the first place; today the secularization of our culture is forcing upon us an awareness of who our friends truly are. Inevitably this will deepen within many a willingness to look past former stereotypes and see how much we hold in common, we "evangelicals and Catholics together," and this in turn may enable us to work together more effectively in areas of common cause. But none of this should prompt us to paper over serious theological differences merely because they are inconvenient. Many of these issues have shown themselves over the centuries to be of profound theological importance, and both sides will gloss over them only at their peril.

The "EOCU"

But, some may still ask, if despite their differences, Catholic, Orthodox, and Protestant Christians still hold so much in common, why couldn't a Christian college position itself far enough along the continuum that it becomes generic enough to encompass all three categories? Why indeed?

I think a good case can be made for what some have called an "ecumenically orthodox Christian university" (EOCU),[14] which is to say, an institution of higher learning with its "mere Christianity" boundaries drawn broadly enough to encompass all, including those with Reformational commitments, Catholics, Orthodox, and a range of others — any-

14. See David M. Ciocchi, "Orthodoxy and Pluralism in the Christian University," *Faculty Dialogue* 21 (Spring-Summer 1994): 31-62. For a description of a Baptist version of an EOCU (i.e., "an ecumenically Christian university in the Baptist tradition"), see Michael D. Beaty, "Baptist Models: Past, Present, and Future," in Dovre, ed., *The Future of Religious Colleges*, pp. 138ff.

one, say, who could affirm the Apostles' Creed. I for one would enjoy such an environment and thrive in it. Far from compromising something in me, such a post would constitute in some ways a release.

Yet in saying this I am speaking in principle. Let us again use Wheaton College as an example. Given my position at this particular institution there is a more specific question I must ask: Should *we* aspire to become this kind of institution? That way along the continuum lies open, and the pressure to move there is substantial. Should Wheaton do so?

In answering such a question, a Christian college president should not be unduly worried about either public relations implications or how he or she will be remembered by history. Both concerns are valid, but neither should drive one's answer to a question of such moment. Much wiser, it seems, is a determination to do the right thing as best one sees it, and then let the proverbial chips fall where they may. As I have said, I judge this to be a prudential issue, not a theological one. So the question is, where best should lie the confessional boundaries of Wheaton College? Given Wheaton's governance structure, this is in the end a question only our governing board could answer. But at least during my tenure as president, in what direction should I bend whatever influence I may have?

I am not set in concrete on this question, but my current inclination is to think that Wheaton should not move toward an EOCU model, for two reasons. First, I am not convinced that an EOCU model can remain a stable one for an institution over the long run. Here's my question: In Christian schools which lack denominational ties, such as Wheaton College, can such a minimalist/inclusivist definition by itself hold the institution? By this I mean, can it hold it through the generations as Wheaton has been held? My suspicion is that it cannot. It may well be an institution's distinctives that serve as tent pegs when the winds are blowing. Without such pegs, the tent itself becomes vulnerable to collapse.

I think a serious concern along these lines represents something more than paranoia. As Mark Noll observes, "The slippery slope, if it is not the only possibility, is certainly still one of the possibilities."[15]

---

15. "The Future of the Religious College: Looking Ahead by Looking Back," in Dovre, ed., *The Future of Religious Colleges*, p. 90.

There are sound reasons for careful vigilance, and with the publication of the studies cited above these reasons are not merely anecdotal. From the specific, to the generic, to the Christian in name only, to the secular — one school after another has taken this trek, reminding us that not all slippery slope arguments are specious.

A "mere Christianity" location along the continuum may prove to be a difficult place to stop. In fact I cannot think of a single independent institution of Wheaton's vintage that has managed to move to "mere Christianity" and then halt there. Some can be documented to have passed through this stage, but always on their way to somewhere else. They aspired to maintaining themselves as an EOCU, perhaps, but they were unable to fulfill their aspirations. But then, what does that tell us? It is just this disparity between aspiration and fulfillment that prompts me to question whether the EOCU model is a stable one. As a distinctive institution Wheaton has sustained its theological identity over many generations; would, or could, that continue were Wheaton to move to "mere Christianity"? Or is the EOCU a will-o'-the-wisp? There may be no more striking evidence that the law of unintended consequences remains unrepealed than this history of the secularizing of formerly Christian institutions. Academic dilettantes can afford to trivialize or ridicule this concern, but those who will give an account cannot.

Given these realities, it appears to me that Wheaton is thriving as what it is; why would its leadership experiment so dangerously with an institution that has worked so well for so long? Thinking in terms of a risk/reward ratio, what promise of greater glory could justify embarking on such a perilous course? "If it ain't broke, don't fix it," says the homely aphorism, and there is wisdom here, especially for 150-year-old Christian colleges. The farmer who killed his golden-egg-laying goose under the illusion that he had a better idea proved to be profoundly mistaken, and so could we. I fail to see the justification for introducing what could be such a hazardous and disorienting change to a place like Wheaton.

Second, there are numerous other, often ecclesiastically-related institutions whose understanding of themselves more or less approximates the EOCU model; in other words, that market is being served, both for those who want to teach in such an environment and for students who want to study there. Why then should a place like Wheaton give up its distinctiveness, leaving much of its constituency behind, to attempt something so fraught with institutional danger, only to become just another member of the crowd? Why wouldn't such a move both diminish Wheaton's uniqueness and impoverish the universe of discourse to which Wheaton contributes its distinctive voice?

Truth be told, I am not a neutral observer here. Unlike some who appear annoyed by a heritage such as Wheaton's, I rather admire it for what it has been and for what it is. Some, like Professor Wolfe, think we are too narrow or specific; others consider us too generic, "watered down."[16] I for one think that the institution is essentially on the right track, or at least, the right track for us. I appreciate Wheaton's past, I enjoy its present, and I see great promise for its future. The college is surely flawed, but so is every other human institution and tradition. I would find an EOCU type institution a stimulating place to be; but then, in its own way, Wheaton too is a wonderfully stimulating place to be. So why not value Wheaton for what it is, value denominational institutions for what they are, and value EOCU institutions for what they are?

If someone wants an EOCU, they can fairly easily find one. Likewise, if someone wants what Wheaton has to offer (and as our strong faculty and bulging applicant pool seem to indicate, a great many do), they come to Wheaton, or to other schools like us. Why must the one type of institution be pressed to become the other? Because there are barbarians at the gate, and we Christians must join forces in order to endure? My reply is that this is a worthy, indeed a necessary, goal, but

16. For example, here is the verdict of a faculty reading group at a denominational university upon studying Robert Benne's account of Wheaton College in his *Quality with Soul:* "The reading group did note that Wheaton College is an example where faculty members representing diverse denominations reside side by side in harmony and an overall evangelical Christian orthodoxy is maintained; however, Wheaton has never had a single sponsoring tradition and cannot be construed as a template for a move by [this university] into some form of broad evangelicalism. One could also argue that this denominational diversity at Wheaton is one of its few weaknesses. In order to achieve unity, divergent theologies at Wheaton come together under a general banner of evangelicalism by assenting to a shared, watered-down view of Christian faith. One infers from Benne that Wheaton doesn't have the same degree of focus and some of the intellectual vigor of a Calvin College. Calvin enjoys a clear view of what its Reform[ed] theology is, requires a uniform church membership of faculty, and inculcates the Reformed theology in students and faculty. There is no need or pressure to 'water down.'"

achieving it need not demand a dramatic reconfiguration of institutional identity. There are innumerable ways schools like Wheaton can and do team up with a variety of others without forfeiting their historic distinctives. We need only be willing to work from common ground wherever we can and agree to disagree (agreeably) about the rest. And this Wheaton is fully willing to do. Where, then, is the impetus for Wheaton becoming an EOCU?

As Alan Wolfe himself observed, Wheaton College is already fully engaged with the best of Catholic thinkers and writers. But might it not be possible to bring aboard, let us say, some Catholic faculty without compromising the clarity or firmness of our Reformational convictions? The vision attracts me, but then I think of the reality. In principle it might make an animating contribution to the campus, but in practice would it not lead to a gradual sacrificing of Wheaton's distinctives? Could the college's Reformational distinctives genuinely be espoused, for example, in such an unbalanced arrangement without giving the impression of ganging up on Catholic professors? But if we establish a situation where we are unable or unwilling to champion our own distinctives, where does that road lead?

In the end, my own inclination is to think that Wheaton's historic identity is the right one for Wheaton. If other schools wish to define themselves more narrowly, and many do, I wish them well. If still other schools prefer to draw their boundaries more broadly, I wish them well too. But until Wheaton as a whole is ready to amend its definition of itself, this is the one I am quite happy to live with and will work to maintain.

Entropy Intercepted

And what of others? Not external critics now, but voices within the community who would like to see the identity of a Christian college perhaps broaden out? Picture me, for example, as a member of a hypothetical Christian college community, perhaps a trustee, an administrator, or a faculty member. I presumably joined this college because I was more or less enthusiastic about its identity; indeed, being a true believer, I wanted to be a part of furthering it. But with time I began to lose heart for its distinctives. I haven't left the college because I can still say I personally in some sense hold these distinctives, but I do so without enthusiasm. I no longer think these distinctives are important, much less am I willing to celebrate them. Instead they increasingly embarrass me, so I stop talking about them altogether in hopes that through inattention they'll atrophy and drop away. Eventually I move beyond indifference to outright opposition to using these distinctives to define the institution. In short, I want my college to become something, say, more akin to an EOCU.

This is not a happy scenario for either me or my college. I continue to affirm its statement of faith every year, but I do so holding my nose, so to speak. Not because I believe some of its provisions to be in themselves wrong — then I would not be able to sign it — but because I think those provisions ought not be part of the college's definition of itself. I love my college and enjoy serving there, but I believe those in charge are mistaken in trying to retain its historic identity. So because I have never anywhere promised always to agree that the college is positioned in just the right way, I begin using whatever influence I have to press the college into broadening. The question then would be, what is the president of my college, whose task it is, among many other things, to preserve the identity of the college, to do with me? On this count at least I am working directly against her intentional leadership. What should we expect of her?

I do not have a definitive answer to this question. In his book, *Leadership Is an Art*, Max DePree observes that one of the responsibilities of an organization's leaders is "the interception of entropy."[17] Entropy is the process of degradation, a running down, a trending toward disorder. Every human organization is susceptible to it, DePree notes, and if the organization is to thrive, every leader must be willing to intercept it and thwart its effects.

To some, the drift of a Christian college across the continuum from the specific to the generic to the secular gives the appearance of an extended organizational entropy, a tragic decline from an ordered Christian identity to a nebulous secular one. But of course that is not how those who favor the move construe it. For them the less defined condition represents not entropy but a necessary improvement, a strengthening of the institution. Which is it to be?

17. *Leadership Is an Art* (New York: Doubleday, 1989), p. 98.

My own view is that changes in an institution's identity that are the product of careful thought and decision-making by those within the institution who carry the appropriate responsibility[18] need not constitute organizational entropy. They are no more than the judgments we have said lie at the heart of every institution's definition of itself. They may be wise decisions or foolish ones, but institutions are never static; they are living things and require a constant choosing, even if only a choosing not to change.

On the other hand, a member's loss of commitment to the institution's distinctives is not a sign of health. As we have already observed, if an institution's confessional identity is to endure over time, the institution must be designed in such a way that it maintains the capacity to sustain that identity. A college must be able to outlive succeeding generations of its own members, so that after they have passed off the scene, the institution remains recognizably the same institution for succeeding generations. Its identity is thus something that must transcend any particular member or group of members; it is something to which they come and in which they participate, but it is not something they own. Nor can they expect to modify it to suit their personal preferences.

Longstanding members of a college community can lose sight of this. Because they are valued participants in the college's life, they can over time come to think of themselves as its proprietors. As such they view themselves as having every right, even the obligation, to alter the institution's identity as they see fit. Perhaps they have tried unsuccessfully to influence those whose specific commission it is to define the institution. So now, having failed, they will simply circumvent them in whatever way possible. Such a development probably does represent a kind of organizational entropy leaders must intercept. In a Christian community, how they intercept it is all-important, but if they are not to fail in their stewardship, intercept it they must.

Far better in such situations was the approach taken by a faculty colleague at a different institution. He increasingly found himself out of step with the institution he and I served. Finally he decided he

18. The subject is too subtle and complex to plunge into here, but it is worth noting that such institutional structures and responsibilities, if we take a longer view, are not as static as they may sound. See John Milbank's discussion of the "self-canceling hierarchy" and "a democracy of time" in "The Politics of Time: Community, Gift, and Liturgy," *Telos* 113 (Fall 1998): 63-64.

needed to leave its faculty. One afternoon, grateful for his friendship and not wanting to lose him, I tried to talk him into staying. I argued that he should remain and work from within to change the school. But my friend was wiser (and more godly), and he took a different view, one with a good deal more integrity. To my argument that he should try to maneuver the institution from within, he replied: "No, that would be wrong. It's me who has changed, not the institution. I love this school and value deeply how God has used it in the lives of many generations of students. I have no business trying to pour it into my mold. I need to let it be what it is, and leave any changing it needs up to the Lord. As for me, I just need to go somewhere where there's a more natural fit."

That was twenty-five years ago, but I have never forgotten my colleague's wisdom. He was right, and I was wrong. His response was a model of Christian maturity, a paradigm of how these things should work. The institution does not belong to us. It predates us, and it will likely, at least in this world, outlast us. Our task is to serve its mission faithfully as long as the institution's publicly stated identity matches our own. When that is no longer the case, we should leave the institution intact for those who follow. This was Anthony Diekema's counsel to the faculty of Christian colleges, but it applies to trustees and administrators as well:

> Be confident upon initial appointment that your own view of the world (worldview) is consistent with the mission of the college. . . . Do a "reality check" every two or three years to determine that your worldview and the college mission are still compatible and mutually supportive. . . . Be open and honest about any perceived differences in your worldview and the mission of the college. . . . If they seem irresolvable, look for other opportunities. Don't remain at a college where the nexus of your worldview and the college mission becomes (or is already) dysfunctional or fundamentally incompatible or inconsistent. . . . Your task is not to change or transform the college and its mission, but rather to join as a full partner in an educational enterprise with common ends.[19]

---

19. Anthony J. Diekema, *Academic Freedom and Christian Scholarship* (Grand Rapids: Eerdmans, 2000), pp. 133-34.

12 Our Place in the Academy

CHALLENGE *To Engender a More Congenial*
Academic Environment

Let us begin this concluding chapter with a final reference to Alan Wolfe's *Atlantic Monthly* article, "The Opening of the Evangelical Mind." Professor Wolfe's title was a gloss on two books which near the end of the twentieth century received a wide reading: *The Closing of the American Mind* (1987) by Allan Bloom, and *The Scandal of the Evangelical Mind* (1994) by Mark Noll. As we have noted, Wolfe's article treated evangelicalism more sympathetically than one might have expected, so much so that he was afterwards taken to task by some of his fellow secularists for doing so. But Wolfe had done his homework. Many evangelicals found both his affirmations and criticisms useful.

Where Wolfe's analysis was less helpful was in his failure to engage one of the distinctives of the evangelical intellectual tradition: academic institutions structured after what I have called the Systemic model. Wolfe simply assumes this model away, dismissing it at several points without examination or argument. Along with some others in the contemporary academy, Wolfe appears to leave no place in the constellation of American higher education for such institutions.

This is not, we should observe, because Professor Wolfe disdains religion itself. Though he describes himself as "a nonbeliever when it comes to faith,"[1] he appears to appreciate what religion — or some facsimile thereof, such as a natural law tradition — can offer the academic

---

1. "The Intellectual Advantages of a Roman Catholic Education," *The Chronicle of Higher Education*, May 31, 2002, p. B7.

community. After all, he teaches at Boston College, a Roman Catholic institution founded in 1863 by the Society of Jesus. Today Boston College is headed by a Jesuit who is eager to see its religious heritage not disappear. "Boston College is committed to maintaining and strengthening the Jesuit, Catholic mission of the University," says the university literature, "especially its commitment to integrating intellectual, personal, ethical, and religious formation." If Alan Wolfe chooses to teach at such an institution, it is plain he is not simply anti-religious. In fact, the opposite is true; though a professed unbeliever, he often demonstrates genuine religious insight[2] and has become something of an advocate for a version of academic plurality that includes religion.[3]

What Wolfe opposes, it appears, is something more specific. It is the Systemic model for religious schools. He surely understands and even values the pluralism of the Umbrella model, as found, for example, at Boston College. There, under a Catholic canopy, genuinely Christian thinking will presumably not be ruled out of order simply because it is religious. Boston College's teachers are not all Catholic, but we may assume that those who are know the freedom to work and teach from their religious worldview. Such a pluralistic arrangement Professor Wolfe appears to understand and value. What he leaves little room for are those institutions that seek to draw all of their faculty from a pool of scholar/teachers who embody a common religious commitment. Such institutions appear to Wolfe to be *by definition* intolerant and violative of their members' academic freedom. He portrays such institutions as closed, defensive, and intolerant.

Wolfe does not, of course, stand alone in this criticism. Not a few within the secular academy may echo his concerns. Listen, for example, to the former executive secretary of the Phi Beta Kappa Society argue that the only good Systemic institution is a former one, even as he documents the use of Phi Beta Kappa's clout to pressure institutions in this direction: "Not too long ago, we received a chapter application from a fine institution [not Wheaton] that insists that every member of its faculty be a Christian. While I could say much that was commend-

2. For example, see "What Would Jesus Do at Baylor?" *The Chronicle of Higher Education,* October 3, 2003, p. B20.

3. See Wolfe, "Intellectual Advantages"; cf. also Wolfe, "The Potential for Pluralism," in *Religion, Scholarship and Higher Education,* ed. Andrea Sterk (Notre Dame: University of Notre Dame Press, 2002), pp. 22-39.

able about the institution, I had to point out to its president that this restriction was inconsistent with Phi Beta Kappa's commitment to freedom of inquiry. He was most unhappy, and following our meeting, Phi Beta Kappa received many angry letters from the institution's alumni and friends. Recently, I learned that the restriction would be lifted and that Phi Beta Kappa had been instrumental in the change."[4]

A Matter of Definition

What are we to make of such critics? Is there something to be said in reply? Many who serve in Christian colleges believe there is.

Perhaps the operative words in the above observations are "by definition." If one begins by defining such concepts as tolerance, pluralism, and academic freedom in such a way as to rule out Systemic model institutions from the start, the discussion grinds to a halt. But are such definitions inevitable? Are they fair? Or are they ideologically driven definitions gerrymandered in effect to evict from the conversation at the outset competing presuppositions and worldviews?

Consider the notion of academic freedom itself. During the twentieth century the idea became — popularly, though not legally or constitutionally[5] — radically privatized. In earlier generations the intellectual rights of individuals were protected, but few thought this required eliminating confessional institutions or requiring absolute institutional neutrality. As long as each participant understood the arrangement from the outset and so joined the community with eyes open, such institutions were deemed to have a legitimate role in the academic community. On this point both the American Association of

4. Douglas Foard, "A Key Collaboration: Phi Beta Kappa, the AAUP, and the Future of the Academy," *Academe*, November-December 2001, p. 48.

5. See David M. Rabban, "Academic Freedom, Individual or Institutional?" *Academe*, November-December 2001, pp. 16-20; cf. Rabban, "A Functional Analysis of 'Individual' and 'Institutional' Academic Freedom Under the First Amendment," *Law and Contemporary Problems* 53, no. 3 (1990): 227-301. As Gary Pavela puts it, "Many faculty members think that constitutionally protected academic freedom is a special prerogative of professors. Most judges, however, don't agree with this perspective" ("A Balancing Act: Competing Claims for Academic Freedom," in *Law and Contemporary Problems* 53, no. 3 [1990]: 21).

University Professors and Association of American Colleges were agreed as late as 1940.[6]

As the twentieth century progressed, however, this agreement appeared to deteriorate. The idea of academic freedom came increasingly to be defined in purely individual terms — so rigidly, in fact, that the idea's corporate implications were eclipsed.[7] The right of the individual scholar to work and teach from whatever perspective he or she saw fit was to be held inviolate; the right of voluntary communities of like-minded scholars to do the same was somehow delegitimized. In fact the two were often set as mutually exclusive, as if in some zero-sum game. At the individual level academic freedom was considered crucial to the vitality of the intellectual conversation, but at the institutional level homogeneity was to be encouraged. Institutions were to be designed after a single model, with every institution, at least on this count, looking just like every other. The full heterogeneity of the academy as a whole was to be required of each institution; what was true of the macrocosm was to be replicated in each of its parts. If not, no matter how intellectually engaged the institution might be, it would be deemed insular, defensive, and proprietary. Its members, no matter how voluntary their gathering, would be deemed, by the sheer fact of their membership in a confessional community, to lack full academic freedom. By the mere shifting of a popular definition was the legitimacy of an entire category of colleges, many of which had long been valued contributors to the nation's academic dialogue, thus called into question.

Every high school debater knows that if you can dictate the terms of the debate, the outcome will be yours. And as things stand, the

---

6. But see the argument of Walter P. Metzger to the effect that the AAUP backed into this accommodation in the 1940 *Statement* without fully realizing or intending it, in "The 1940 Statement of Principles on Academic Freedom and Tenure," in *Freedom and Tenure in the Academy*, ed. William W. Van Alstyne (Durham: Duke University Press, 1993), pp. 12-38.

7. See Frederick J. Crosson, "Two Faces of Academic Freedom," in *The Challenge and Promise of a Catholic University*, ed. Theodore M. Hesburgh (Notre Dame: University of Notre Dame Press, 1994), pp. 46-47. But again, we should note Walter Metzger's counterintuitive argument that the notion of "institutional neutrality" was stronger, at least within the AAUP, at the beginning of the twentieth century than at the end (Metzger, "The 1940 Statement").

above terms appear very unfriendly to institutions following the Systemic model. But Christian colleges need not and must not acquiesce to such a skewed reading of the academic setting. They must offer a winsome alternative, one that will appeal, if not to the ideologues, at least to the fair-minded everywhere. It must be an alternative that does not depend upon special pleading, as if Christian colleges require a unique dispensation. Instead it must be grounded in the historic democratic traditions common to us all. Such an alternative would have to look beyond the academy to the larger cultural picture, setting the academy's intellectual forum, as the U.S. Constitution does, in the context of our society's broader marketplace of ideas. While making its own case, the argument would have to offer a critique of some currently reigning paradigms, teasing out hidden premises and bringing them to the surface where they can be examined.[8] This in turn could lead to newer — though in reality, older — and more workable ways of defining what we mean by tolerance, pluralism, and academic freedom. To be of any use, such an alternative would have to confront controversial issues head on; thus it would need to be couched in clear, straightforward, and unapologetic terms. But equally so, it would also need to be balanced and carefully worded, attempting "to speak the truth in love."

Is such an alternative possible? If so, what form might it take? Perhaps it might take the form of a manifesto, maybe even something along the lines of what follows. I offer it not as a finished product or final word, but the opposite: a proposal, open to discussion, critique and, no doubt, revision into something far stronger and better.

8. Cf. Alvin Plantinga's call for what he calls "consciousness raising" and "cultural criticism" on the part of Christian scholars ("On Christian Scholarship," in Hesburgh, ed., *The Challenge and Promise of a Catholic University*, p. 291); or George Marsden's appeal for a Christian agenda "directed toward building for our community as solid a place in the pluralistic intellectual life of our civilization as is consistent with our principles" ("The State of Evangelical Christian Scholarship," *Christian Scholar's Review* 17, no. 4 [1988]: 356). Says Marsden, "Helping to establish the intellectual viability of our worldview and pointing out the shortcomings of alternatives can be an important service to our community and an important dimension of our witness to the world."

Christian Colleges and the Marketplace of Ideas

We in the Christian college movement are committed to a classical understanding of the marketplace of ideas. We do not advocate the establishment of some sort of enforced Christian society at large. That way we believe lies tyranny at worst and a corrupting of the Church's mission at best. Christian colleges thrive best within a social environment where every idea may be entertained in the public sphere and none is ruled out by definition; where discourse is open and free and the listener is under no compulsion to embrace any particular line of thought. In short, Christian colleges remain committed to the classic concept of pluralism.

The principles that undergird such democratic notions as the marketplace of ideas and pluralism reach back at least to the ancient Greeks, but more to figures such as Isocrates than, say, to Plato. Plato was skeptical of democratic ideals because he distrusted the *dēmos,* the free citizenry. He viewed the people as not much more than rabble. Plato held that only philosophers possessed the dialectical skills of inquiry by which truth could be discovered. In his view the contributors to the public dialog were usually misguided and tendentious. He therefore disdained their efforts, believing they could lead few to the truth since they had not yet discovered it for themselves.

Isocrates, who was Plato's contemporary and prime competitor for the allegiance of Athens's youth, took a broader perspective. He viewed the voices in the public arena as contributors to a larger macro-dialectic by which a people searched out their way. Thus he set as parallel to one another the public voices contending "on matters which are open to dispute," and the informed individual seeking light for himself "on things which are unknown."[9] Both, Isocrates argued, use the same faculties for the same purpose: the search for wisdom.

Isocrates acknowledged that competing claims might well be in themselves partial, fashioned to drive home the best possible case for some particular point of view. But he also saw the inadequacy of this limited perspective. He insisted on viewing each claimant against the backdrop of other competing voices in a society that valued free speech. Provided the listeners retain their freedom of choice, the competing

9. *Nicocles* 8.

claims come to be seen as having genuine social value. According to Isocrates, hearing the voices in the public arena make their cases for or against this idea or that was akin to listening to an intelligent and informed person reasoning through a difficult issue aloud. The marketplace of ideas was simply society thinking out loud.

Just as in a court of law truth and justice have a stake in encouraging advocacy, with the strongest possible cases being presented to the jury both for and against conviction, so Isocrates taught that truth holds a stake in encouraging discourse and prompting the claimants to their best efforts. After all, he asks, "How can men wisely pass judgment on the past or take counsel for the future unless they examine and compare the arguments of opposing speakers, themselves giving an unbiased hearing to both sides?"[10] The social function of truth claims within society is larger than the limited aims of any given speaker. At the macro level their purpose is to provide counsel to the people, to help them make informed decisions, both individually and corporately.

Fortunately, it was Isocrates' brighter democratic vision of discourse, where all sides can be heard and listeners are free to choose, which won the day, particularly in the realm of education. As the distinguished French historian of education, H. I. Marrou, says, "On the level of history Plato had been defeated; posterity had not accepted his educational ideals. The victor, generally speaking, was Isocrates, and Isocrates became the educator first of Greece and then of the whole ancient world."[11] Though with time Plato would become more famous, it was the ideals espoused by thinkers like Isocrates that eventually shaped our concepts of what an educated person looks like and how a society of free people should conduct itself.

It is important to note, of course, that this classical ideal of the marketplace of ideas was not interpreted in overly individualistic terms. At its best and freest the open arena of discourse always made

10. *On the Peace* 11.

11. *A History of Education in Antiquity,* trans. G. Lamb (London: Sheed and Ward, 1956), p. 194. Says Marrou, "On the whole it was Isocrates, not Plato, who educated fourth-century Greece and subsequently the Hellenistic and Roman worlds; it was from Isocrates that, 'as from a Trojan horse,' there emerged all those teachers and men of culture, noble idealists, simple moralists, lovers of fine phrases, all those fluent, voluble speakers, to whom classical antiquity owed both the qualities and the defects of its main cultural tradition" (p. 79). Marrou's Trojan horse reference is to Cicero, *De Or.* 2.94.

room for schools of thought. Whether we call to mind the ancient schools — the Peripatetics, the Stoics, or Plato's own Academy — or the countless other formal and informal groupings of thinkers who have voluntarily banded together through the centuries, such schools of thought have strengthened the cultural dialog by allowing a synergism of the like-minded to make stronger contributions than individuals working alone could muster. Since the intellectual marketplace holds an interest in encouraging the strongest possible contributions, far from inhibiting the richness of the discourse, the presence of voluntary schools of thought has immeasurably enhanced it. Such schools have therefore traditionally been viewed as valuable contributors to the marketplace of ideas.

We in Christian higher education concur with this classical conception and therefore believe that a healthy academic marketplace of ideas will view academic freedom as the right not only of individuals but also of voluntary groups or communities of individuals. We celebrate the fact that the academic world remains honeycombed with such schools of thought and we support the combined AAUP/AAC *Statement on Academic Freedom and Tenure,* which explicitly makes room for them. We value the contribution of voluntary communities of thinkers who join with one another to add their concerted voices to the marketplace of ideas, and we resist those overly individualized understandings of academic freedom that would seek to invalidate their role.

The classical ideal of the free marketplace of ideas is, of course, just that: an ideal. But that is not to say it is merely a fiction. In free societies individuals and groups do not seek to force their ideas upon one another; they depend on the availability of an open forum where they can attempt to persuade one another through argument. Healthy democracies can afford nothing less.

Dogmatic Religion

While we in Christian higher education are committed to the classical democratic concepts of pluralism and the free marketplace of ideas, history has shown that these ideals have been difficult to achieve, and still more difficult to maintain. Open forums for the free interchange of ideas have always proven vulnerable to the imposition of dogma by the powerful. And honesty requires us to acknowledge that too often over the centuries that power has been wielded by religionists, and the dogma imposed has been religious dogma.

One might have hoped that over the millennia Christians, for example, would have become consistent advocates for the democratic ideals of the marketplace of ideas. But history will show that, given the right conditions, belief in revealed truth has sometimes led in the opposite direction. Well-meaning religionists who, like Plato, distrusted the judgment of the people, or who glossed over the principle that human choices must be free if they are to be choices at all, or who were simply seduced by power, have imposed religious dogma upon peoples who were not free and then prohibited discourse that did not comport with their dogma. Though this sort of tyranny exists today primarily in non-Christian parts of the world, we recognize that in too many times and places such coercion has been carried out in the name of Christianity.

Furthermore, we in Christian higher education grasp the underlying temptation. We recognize that truth claims based on alleged revelation may be particularly susceptible to the coercive impulse. After all, who could disagree with Simmias when he speaks to Socrates in the *Phaedo* of the superiority of revealed knowledge?

> I think, Socrates, as perhaps you do yourself, that it is either impossible or very difficult to acquire clear knowledge about these [ultimate] matters in this life. And yet he is a weakling who does not test in every way what is said about them and persevere until he is worn out by studying them on every side. For he must do one of two things; either he must learn or discover the truth about these matters, or if that is impossible, he must take whatever human doctrine is best and hardest to disprove and, embarking upon it as upon a raft, sail upon it through life in the midst of dangers, unless he can sail upon some stronger vessel, some divine revelation, and make his voyage more safely and securely.[12]

Were it available, we must concur with Simmias, divine revelation would surely be a superior way of knowing. Thus it should not be surprising to discover that those who believe they have found it are partic-

---

12. *Phaedo* 85c-d (Loeb); or, "if he cannot find some word of God which will more surely and safely carry him" (Jowett).

ularly liable to coercive tactics. Overestimating what they think they know from revelation and losing sight of the imperative of free decision-making on the part of all, claimants who stake their positions on what they take to be revealed truth may be unduly inclined to force their views on others. We acknowledge these potential dangers.

But we also insist that these dangers are only potential; they are neither intrinsic nor inevitable. Coerciveness may be a Siren's snare for the unwary religionist, but coercive behavior is by no means entailed in a religious stance. In fact, in the case of Christians who seek to ground their behavior in Scripture, the opposite is true: It is precisely that which Christians consider divine revelation that insists upon the dignity of the other and the integrity of the other's choice-making. Thus it is this very revelation which itself forbids coercion. To the extent that Christians engage in coercive tactics, to that extent they are functioning in a manner that is explicitly non-Christian. Conversely, to the extent that Christians ground their behavior in what they consider divine revelation, to that extent they renounce coercion.

We in Christian higher education repudiate all forms of restricted or coerced ideas as unworthy and unchristian. However subtle or overt the means, attempting to force or restrict a person's thinking or beliefs violates the fundamental Christian principle of the dignity and worth of individual human beings. It also undermines the free interplay of ideas and decision-making that is so vital to healthy democratic societies, as argued, for example, by John Locke in his famous "Letter on Toleration." We embrace instead the classical ideas of pluralism and the marketplace of ideas. We consider these ideas to be in full concert with our Christian understanding of the obligations humans owe one another, and we seek no more than a place in that arena. We are convinced that in a free society's open forum, where truth claims of whatever sort may be freely set forth and freely entertained or rejected, our ideas will more than hold their own.

Dogmatic Rationalism

But there are dogmas other than religious that hold the potential to stifle the marketplace of ideas, particularly in the academy. One of these is the dogma of autonomous human reason.

We in Christian higher education hold no quarrel with the exercise of human reason. We celebrate reason as one of God's gifts to humanity, even one of the ways in which human beings image God himself. Our difficulty arises only when we encounter that radical dogma that insists unaided human reason is the only legitimate avenue to knowledge, and therefore that only those ideas discoverable through reason will be allowed into the academic marketplace. This dogma, with its stifling of genuine pluralism, we oppose.

We educators who are Christian concur that when, for example, a powerful Church censured Galileo for denying a geocentric universe, the Church was in the wrong. But it is crucial to see in what ways it was wrong. The Church was mistaken not only in its cosmology or its interpretation of Scripture; just as important, it was mistaken in its use of power to impose its own ideas and close off dissent.

Regardless of what the Church at the time thought could be known through divine revelation, from a Christian standpoint human reason must be deemed a legitimate way of knowing. Truth has nothing to fear from itself, whatever the source. Thus the Church's most grievous error in the instance of Galileo was attempting to limit the field of discourse to those who would begin from the correct starting point. Ideas that were in fact Aristotelian were taken to be biblical and were thus viewed as divinely revealed. Moreover, because the Church held the upper hand it declared these ideas to be the reigning dogma; contending voices would be prohibited. Revelation was decreed by an act of power to be in effect the only legitimate way of knowing, and ideas that gave weight to scientific ways of knowing were dismissed and disenfranchised. Thus religious dogma effectively stifled the marketplace of ideas.

In modern times, however, the shoe has often been on the other foot. In a secular world dominated by philosophical naturalism, autonomous human reason has gained the upper hand. Science as science quite properly limits its purview to the naturalistic world, since this is what the scientific method is designed to explore. But scientific naturalism, sometimes called scientism, takes the additional step of insisting that nothing exists or can be known beyond what can be addressed by the scientific method, which is to say, the material world. According to this view, autonomous human reason constitutes the only legitimate way of knowing, and the only evidence that deserves to be called evidence is scientific evidence.

Naturalism in its various forms is widely held in the academy today, and we believe it is entitled to its voice in this arena of discourse. But a dogmatic naturalism becomes dangerous when, like the dogmatists of old, it declares its way of knowing to be the only legitimate one and then seeks to disenfranchise other voices. Genuine science, much of it grounded in a Christian worldview and conducted through the centuries by committed Christians, is a wonderfully powerful engine of learning, and we in Christian higher education are committed to its furtherance. But being a good scientist does not require a commitment to a comprehensive naturalism. Thus we reject the more radical attempts of philosophical naturalism to dictate the rules of the academy in such a way that its way of knowing becomes the only one permitted in that marketplace, all others being precluded by definition.

It has sometimes been argued that religionists must abandon their claims to a place in the academy. As one commentator put it, "We had the Enlightenment and religion lost." According to this argument, truth claims based on alleged revelation and/or tradition had created so much intolerance and suffering for so long that the Enlightenment was forced to banish them from the academy.[13] Only those objective, publicly verifiable ideas discoverable by human reason would be allowed in this forum.

This argument is not much more than a truism so long as we are talking about issues that are genuinely scientific. It amounts to saying that when we are discussing things scientific, we should discuss what is scientific. We in Christian higher education concur. But what are we to make of academic authorities who as an expression of their philosophical naturalism declare, for example, that the material universe is all

---

13. In an article in *The New York Times Magazine* following the bombing of the World Trade Center ("This *Is* a Religious War," October 7, 2001), Andrew Sullivan compared Christian fundamentalists to Muslim terrorists because both hold to exclusivist beliefs. But this comparison badly misconstrues the real danger. The threat, *contra* Sullivan, is not strongly held, even exclusivist beliefs; such beliefs, whether secular or religious, when coupled with a commitment to discourse, are no more dangerous than any others. The danger, whether under religious auspices (the Inquisition, the Taliban) or secular (Nazism, Stalinism), stems from the totalitarian recourse to coercion. In this light, for Sullivan to equate the fundamentalism of a Jerry Falwell to that of Osama Bin Laden is both unfair and misguided.

that exists, all that ever has existed, all that ever can exist?[14] Here are claims that, while masquerading as scientific, launch out into realms well beyond the purview of science. How other than by sheer coercive power — not by a powerful Church this time, but by a different dogma that now holds the upper hand — could religious ideas be ruled out of such a discussion?

The fact is, the world of higher learning is riddled with issues human reason in general and the scientific method in particular cannot claim as their sole preserve. If the marketplace of ideas is to be truly free and open, other voices must be allowed equal access. If the objection is raised that religion had the upper hand for many centuries and was found too dangerous, it must be replied that the danger was in its holding the upper hand, not in its ideas being religious. History will show that the upper hand is a dangerous thing for any ideas to hold. Witness the fact that during the past century far more perished at the hands of totalitarian regimes committed to philosophical naturalism than ever suffered under religious inquisitors. Tyranny is tyranny, whoever's dogma is stifling dissent.

The point of an open arena of free discourse is that no set of ideas will be allowed the upper hand. No one worldview will be permitted to dictate the terms of the debate. Beyond a bedrock commitment to honesty and integrity, there must be only one stipulation for entry into the discussion, and it is this: each participant must be willing to ante up a commitment to discourse, and a corresponding disavowal of restriction or coercion.[15] After that, all ideas from whatever worldview must be entertainable and all must compete on their own merits. We in Christian higher education are committed to this classical democratic

---

14. As for example in Michael Shermer's citation of Richard Dawkins's claim — a claim Shermer approvingly labels "one of the most existentially penetrating statements ever made by a scientist" — that the universe appears "at bottom" to evidence "no design, no purpose, no evil and no good, noting but blind, pitiless indifference" ("The Gradual Illumination of the Mind," *Scientific American,* February 2002, p. 35).

15. "To a university, even more than to other institutions in a free society, the right of free speech, the free exchange of ideas, the presentation of unpopular points of view . . . are vital. Discussion, argument, and persuasion are the devices appropriate to the life of the mind, not suppression, obstruction, and intimidation" (Donald Kagan, "What Is a Liberal Education?" *The McDermott Papers* [Dallas: University of Dallas, 2002], p. 5).

ideal and therefore oppose the tendency to allow naturalistic presuppositions to serve as the only valid starting point for discussion within the academy.

Dogmatic Relativism

In this critique of the Enlightenment's efforts to absolutize its own way of knowing we in Christian higher education do not stand alone. Today the chorus that is postmodernism echoes this critique, revealing modernity's claims of exclusivity to be a pretense. But now postmodernism threatens to impose a dogma of its own.

As its name implies, postmodernism is essentially a reactionary movement. Less a single view than a type of view with many instances, postmodernism represents a complex set of reactions against modernist philosophy and its foundationalist presuppositions. Or this is, at least, how we will use the term here.

Foundationalism holds that while much of what we can know is known inferentially, this body of inferential knowledge can all be traced back in one way or another to bedrock truths we know directly or non-inferentially. Hence human knowledge rests upon a solid "foundation" of reliable truths. The rationalism whose dogma increasingly dominated the academy in modern times is essentially foundationalist. It is built upon certain fundamental assumptions about human reason and its ability to apprehend reality. These foundational assumptions have made possible the development of vast bodies of what rationalists have taken to be neutral, objective knowledge about the world. This in turn has prompted the widespread confidence in the possibilities of technology and the inevitability of human progress that serve as hallmarks of modern thought.

Postmodernity, by contrast, is profoundly anti-foundationalist. As old as the ancient Sophists but given impetus in modern times through the work of thinkers such as Immanuel Kant and Albrecht Ritschl, anti-foundationalism boasts a long pedigree. One such anti-foundationalist describes its contemporary version as follows:

> Anti-foundationalism teaches that questions of fact, truth, correctness, validity, and clarity can neither be posed nor answered in ref-

erence to some extracontextual, ahistorical, nonsituational reality, or rule, or law, or value; rather, anti-foundationalism asserts, all of these matters are intelligible and debatable only within the precincts of the contexts or situations or paradigms or communities that give them their local and changeable shape. It is not just that anti-foundationalism replaces the components of the foundationalist world-picture with other components; instead, it denies to those components the stability and independence and even the identity that is so necessary if they are to be thought of as grounds or anchors. . . . In short, the very essentials that are in foundationalist discourse opposed to the local, the historical, the contingent, the variable, and the rhetorical, turn out to be irreducibly dependent on, and indeed to be functions of, the local, the historical, the contingent, the variable, and the rhetorical. Foundationalist theory fails, lies in ruins, because it is from the very first implicated in everything it claims to transcend.[16]

Due to its anti-foundationalism, postmodernism rejects the notion of knowledge as an accurate or objective account of reality or of truth as correspondence to that reality. For postmodernists there can be no such thing as a description of the world "as it really is." There are only perspectives, all of which are marked by their utter situatedness. Thus postmodern thought tends to be relativistic. To the postmodernist, no absolute principles, laws, values, or truths are normative or binding for all times, places, and people. Human ideas are from first to last theory-laden, paradigm-based, and socially constructed.

As a result, postmodernism vigorously opposes all viewpoints that make claims to transcendence and condemns any worldview that attempts to portray a unified picture of reality. Such "totalizing metanarratives," postmodernism insists, are worse than false; they are dangerous creeds designed to marginalize and oppress the weak. Truth claims turn out to be mere opinions tricked up as truth in order to legitimize power. Hence those who make truth claims must be viewed as authoritarian zealots.

Insofar as postmodernism has shown that modernity's rational-

16. Stanley Fish, "Anti-Foundationalism, Theory Hope, and the Teaching of Composition," in *Doing What Comes Naturally: Change, Rhetoric, and the Practice of Theory in Literary and Legal Studies* (Durham: Duke University Press, 1989), pp. 344-45.

ism could not achieve the exalted heights the Enlightenment's children set for themselves, we in Christian higher education concur. Christians have long been skeptical of the rationalistic hubris that asserted that human reason could rise to such heights on its own. Modernity's naive realism, uncritical confidence in progress, and undue fascination with technology were ripe for criticism.

Yet we also urge that modernity's rationalism not be deposed as the academy's reigning dogma only to be replaced by postmodernity's still more dangerous relativism. In the end, postmodernism may turn out to be not much more than a form of hyper-modernism; it may represent only modernism's destined encounter with its inevitable brick wall, the bankruptcy of modernism made manifest. But whatever postmodernism turns out to be, its dogma must not be allowed merely to supplant an older one.

At first blush this might seem an unlikely threat. After all, postmodernism claims to represent the overthrow of dogma, the denunciation of all totalizing meta-narratives that would exclude others from the marketplace. Thus on the surface postmodernism might appear a friend of the open forum. But is this in fact the case?

If postmodernism's sweeping repudiation of foundations were sound, it would follow that its proponents could be committed to a genuine marketplace of ideas. But it is testimony to the need for some footing for thought that postmodernism's radical anti-foundationalism itself represents, in postmodernism's own terms, only another totalizing meta-narrative designed to instruct us about the world "as it really is." Listen again to the above proponent:

> Foundationalist methodology is based on *a false picture of the human situation*. Since *it is not the case*, as foundationalists assume, that the "scene" of communication includes a free and independent self facing a similarly independent world to which it can be linked by the rules of a universal language, a methodology based on these assumptions will necessarily fail of its goal. And conversely, if *the true picture of the human situation* is as anti-foundationalism gives it — a picture of men and women whose acts are socially constituted and who are embedded in a world no more stable than the historical and conventional forms of thought that bring it into being — if this is *the correct picture of the human situation* then surely we can ex-

trapolate from this picture a better set of methods for operating in the world we are constantly making and remaking.[17]

If as this proponent of anti-foundationalism has already argued, "Foundationalist theory fails . . . because it is from the very first implicated in everything it claims to transcend," it is equally true that radical anti-foundationalism fails because it turns out to be an instance of the very thing it condemns. According to anti-foundationalism, all ideas are radically situated, being nothing other than social constructions "intelligible and debatable only within the precincts of the contexts or situations or paradigms or communities that give them their local and changeable shape." But then this must apply to anti-foundationalist ideas as well. Yet here is an ardent anti-foundationalist arguing for what is or is not "the case" concerning "the human situation," contending against the "false" foundationalist picture and for a "true" or "correct" anti-foundationalist picture of the fundamental nature of things.

In the end, what we have here are dueling epistemological systems, foundationalism and anti-foundationalism. The one is realist, holding to something akin to a correspondence theory of truth; the other is anti-realist and denies that there can be such a thing as truth. But what the two hold in common is that they are both worldviews, each contending in the arena for their understanding of things. This is as true for the anti-worldview postmodern stance as it is for its alternatives.

Yet just here lies the threat. Postmodernism appears unwilling to view itself as simply another contender in the marketplace of ideas. Modernity considered its own to be the superior worldview, but it at least acknowledged itself as a worldview. Postmodernism, by contrast, tends to view its anti-foundationalism as the demise or deconstruction of all worldviews. "It is not just that anti-foundationalism replaces the components of the foundationalist world-picture with other components," claims the anti-foundationalist; "instead, it denies to those components the stability and independence and even the identity that is so necessary if they are to be thought of as grounds or anchors." Denies these things, that is, except to itself. Apparently anti-foundationalism alone is to be

17. Fish, "Anti-Foundationalism," p. 346 (italics added).

granted the stability and independence it requires to function as "the true picture of the human situation."

Pointing out such self-contradiction cannot, in and of itself, be considered a refutation of postmodern constructivism. From within its own system these kinds of internal inconsistencies may not pose a difficulty; hence merely highlighting them does not constitute a refutation. But our point here is not that such presuppositions are wrong. We are concerned only that these presuppositions be recognized for what they are: the premises of a particular worldview. Thus, if the marketplace of ideas is to remain open and free, such views must not be established as the *a priori* premises one must share to join the debate. Instead, and despite their wide currency today, these ideas must themselves remain open to examination and challenge by those who stand outside them.

It is here, however, that postmodernism may constitute a threat to that marketplace. Posing as an open system, radical anti-foundationalism — due to its inability from within to recognize itself as merely another contender in the marketplace of ideas,[18] combined with its absolutizing of the perspectival and the consequent tendency to reduce everything to matters of power — in fact demonstrates a bent toward restriction and coercion. In the footsteps of its dogmatic predecessors, postmodern relativism appears to want to declare the presuppositional battle won and establish its own constructivist views of knowledge as the reigning dogma of the academy. With such a victory in hand it can then take a stance of openness — but only toward those who have embraced its creed. Voices in the marketplace who refuse to adopt its constructivist presuppositions are demonized as oppressors who claim their opinions as true only in order to impose them violently on others. For not acceding to constructivist premises these contenders sometimes find themselves classed with "sexists," "fascists," "racists," even the "insane." Ironically, radical anti-foundationalists can justify such violent tactics only by enforcing their constructivist dogma as the "right" one. Apparently they do not see that in doing so they are engaging in the very totalizing behavior they claim to deplore in others.[19]

---

18. See David K. Naugle, *Worldview: The History of a Concept* (Grand Rapids: Eerdmans, 2002), p. 174.

19. As Christian Smith observes, "Sometimes it is the biggest proponents of self-

Such blindness is a danger to an open marketplace of ideas. Classical pluralism does not fear truth claims; it welcomes them. It permits anyone to think he or she is right and willingly offers to all their turn at the microphone to make their best case in the open forum. But dogmatic relativism demands the reverse. Because there is no intolerance more intolerant than the one invoked in the name of defending tolerance, under a relativist regime no one can be permitted to think that he or she is right, since such a stance implies premises that undermine the regime itself. Thus are contending voices silenced in the marketplace.

This is dogmatic relativism at work, not pluralism, and the two must not be confused. One of the functions of an open marketplace of ideas is to preserve diversity by providing a sanctuary where currently unfashionable ideas can be kept alive. This was John Stuart Mill's argument when he said, "The peculiar evil of silencing the expression of an opinion, is that it is robbing the human race, posterity as well as the existing generation; those who dissent from the opinion, still more than those who hold it. If the opinion is right, they are deprived of the opportunity of exchanging error for truth: if wrong, they lose, what is almost as great a benefit, the clearer perception and livelier impression of truth, produced by its collision with error."[20]

Were constructivist dogma established as the starting point for debate in the academy, non-relativist worldviews would be delegitimized and banished from the discussion, and the open arena for discourse would be compromised. We in Christian higher education believe that such a demand for ideological conformity is today a significant threat, and we urge that it be identified and resisted.

---

reflexivity who seem least aware of their own incongruities" ("Force of Habit: Hostility and Condescension Toward Religion in the University," *Books and Culture,* September/October 2003, p. 21). In this regard it is instructive to recall Leo Strauss's comments half a century ago regarding the then-regnant logical positivism. He spoke of positivism as "constitutionally unable to conceive of itself as a problem. Positivism may be said to be more dogmatic than any other position of which we have records. Positivism can achieve this triumph because it is able to present itself as very sceptical; it is that manifestation of dogmatism based on scepticism in which the scepticism completely conceals the dogmatism from its adherents" ("The Liberalism of Classical Political Philosophy," *Review of Metaphysics* 12 [September 1958-June 1959]: 390).

20. *On Liberty,* ed. Alburey Castell (New York: Appleton-Century-Crofts, 1947), p. 16 (40).

Conclusion

Christian colleges stand committed to genuine pluralism in the academy: a pluralism of ideas, of epistemological stances, of academic models, of academic communities. We endorse those classical democratic concepts that reach back to the ancient ideal of an arena of discourse where free individuals and schools of thought may conduct an open conversation, debating without hindrance their diverse perspectives. It is an arena where all ideas are required to compete on their own merit, coercion is disallowed, and no reigning dogma imposed. Serving often as a refuge against the suppression of currently unpopular ideas,[21] this marketplace must remain an environment of civility, where a people educated for freedom render their best judgments as to where they think the truth may lie.

If democratic societies are to remain open and healthy they must hold this ideal high and guard it from all who would attempt to diminish it. Moreover, they must develop within their citizens the habits of civility and the skills to listen respectfully, evaluate critically, and respond usefully that make the marketplace possible. These are the habits and skills we in Christian higher education seek to instill within our students. We do this, to be sure, for our own uniquely Christian reasons, but we do it also because we believe these are the skills and habits that will enable our students to develop into responsible participants in a democratic, pluralistic society.

---

21. "Scholars and teachers of religious commitment may well function within the academy, as it were, counter-cyclically, keeping alive certain types of questions, topics, interests that the prevailingly dominant academic norms may have had the effect of delegitimating, sidelining, or, at least, extruding into the academic shadows." Francis Oakley, "Concluding Reflections on the Lilly Seminar," in *Religion, Scholarship and Higher Education,* ed. Andrea Sterk (Notre Dame: University of Notre Dame Press, 2002), p. 240.

Index

AAUP/AAC 1940 *Statement on Academic Freedom and Tenure,* 31-33, 221-22, 221n., 231, 256-57, 261

Academic freedom, 214-36; defined in individual terms, 257-58; defining/clarifying notion of, 256-58; early notions of, 256-57; and full disclosure of institutional identity, 221-22; as greater in Christian colleges than secular, 217-21; and healthy marketplace of ideas, 261; and "limitations clause," 32-33; and the loyalty oath problem, 214-20; and 1940 *Statement,* 31-33, 221-22, 231, 256-57, 261; and students' respect, 217-18, 219-20; and Systemic model institutions, 257; and Wheaton College faculty, 216-17, 243, 244-46; and Wolfe's criticisms of evangelical scholarship, 214-20, 226-27, 231-32, 237, 239, 241, 249, 250, 254-56. *See also* Academic freedom and the voluntary principle

Academic freedom and the voluntary principle, 222-36; "careers at stake" criticism, 226-27; and Christian personal integrity, 226-29, 232-35; criticisms of, 226-27, 231-36; as deliber-

ate naiveté, 231-36; and institutional identity, 223-25, 235-36; and the institution's trust, 236; integrity issues, 226-30, 231-35; lying/equivocating in statements, 226-27, 233-35; necessity of, 230-31; and plagiarism, 230; and prior individual affirmations of faith, 222-23; signing statements in hermeneutic stance, 235; signing statements while in denial, 233; signing statements with mental reservations, 233-34; Wolfe's criticisms, 226-27, 231-32

Academic Freedom and Tenure (Matchlup), 217-18

Academic models, 11-33; academic freedom and the "limitations clause," 31-33; and Benne's categories, 14; Carlin and, 15-16, 27; CCCU schools, 19; and the continuum of Christian institutions, 24-30; and Danforth Commission categories, 13-14; defining "religious colleges," 13; and faculty/personnel decisions, 15, 18-19; framework for evaluating, 20-30; and Kerr's continuum, 24-27; and Kerr's portrait of the multiversity, 20-26; and respecting institu-